Dynamic Policy Interactions in a Monetary Union

Michael Carlberg

Dynamic Policy Interactions in a Monetary Union

Springer

Prof. Dr. Michael Carlberg
Department of Economics
Helmut Schmidt University
Holstenhofweg 85
22043 Hamburg
Germany
carlberg@hsu-hh.de

ISBN 978-3-642-18227-3 e-ISBN 978-3-642-18228-0
DOI 10.1007/978-3-642-18228-0
Springer Heidelberg Dordrecht London New York

Library of Congress Control Number: 2011920823

Cover design: eStudio Calamar

Printed on acid-free paper

Springer is part of Springer Science+Business Media (www.springer.com)

Preface

This book studies the dynamics of monetary and fiscal interactions in the Euro Area. The policy makers are the European Central Bank and national governments. The primary target of the ECB is low inflation. And the primary target of a national government is low unemployment. However, there is a short-run trade-off between low inflation and low unemployment. Here the main focus is on sequential policy decisions. Another focus is on simultaneous and independent policy decisions. And a third focus is on policy cooperation. There are demand shocks, supply shocks, and mixed shocks. There are country-specific shocks and common shocks. The key question is: Given a shock, what are the dynamic characteristics of the resulting process?

The present book is part of a larger research project on European Monetary Union, see the references given at the back of the book. Some parts of this project were presented at the World Congress of the International Economic Association, at the International Conference on Macroeconomic Analysis, at the International Institute of Public Finance, and at the International Atlantic Economic Conference. Other parts were presented at the Macro Study Group of the German Economic Association, at the Annual Meeting of the Austrian Economic Association, at the Göttingen Workshop on International Economics, at the Halle Workshop on Monetary Economics, at the Research Seminar on Macroeconomics in Freiburg, at the Research Seminar on Economics in Kassel, and at the Passau Workshop on International Economics.

Over the years, in working on this project, I have benefited from comments by Iain Begg, Michael Bräuninger, Volker Clausen, Valeria de Bonis, Peter Flaschel, Helmut Frisch, Wilfried Fuhrmann, Franz X. Hof, Florence Huart, Oliver Landmann, Jay H. Levin, Alfred Maußner, Jochen Michaelis, Reinhard Neck, Manfred J. M. Neumann, Klaus Neusser, Franco Reither, Armin Rohde,

Sergio Rossi, Gerhard Rübel, Michael Schmid, Gerhard Schwödiauer, Dennis Snower, Egbert Sturm, Patrizio Tirelli, Harald Uhlig, Bas van Aarle, Uwe Vollmer, Jürgen von Hagen and Helmut Wagner. In addition, Arne Hansen and Christian Gäckle carefully discussed with me all parts of the manuscript. Last but not least, Christine Bergner did the secretarial work as excellently as ever. I would like to thank all of them.

Michael Carlberg

Executive Summary

1) Sequential policy decisions. First the central bank decides, then the governments decide. Step 1 refers to a specific shock. Step 2 refers to the time lag. Step 3 refers to monetary policy in Europe. The European central bank sets European money supply so as to achieve zero inflation in Europe. Step 4 refers to the time lag. Step 5 refers to fiscal policies in Germany and France. The German government sets its purchases of German goods so as to achieve zero unemployment in Germany. And the French government sets its purchases of French goods so as to achieve zero unemployment in France. Step 6 refers to the time lag. Step 7 refers to monetary policy in Europe. The European central bank sets European money supply so as to achieve zero inflation in Europe. Step 8 refers to the time lag. Step 9 refers to fiscal policies in Germany and France. The German government sets its purchases of German goods so as to achieve zero unemployment in Germany. And the French government sets its purchases of French goods so as to achieve zero unemployment in France. Step 10 refers to the time lag. And so on.

Given a demand shock in Germany, sequential policy decisions produce zero unemployment and zero inflation in each of the member countries. There is an increase in European money supply, an increase in German government purchases, a reduction in French government purchases, and no change in European government purchases as a whole. Given a supply shock in Germany, sequential policy decisions cause uniform oscillations in unemployment and inflation. And what is more, there is an explosion of government purchases and an implosion of money supply.

2) Simultaneous and independent policy decisions. Step 1 refers to a specific shock. Step 2 refers to the time lag. In step 3, the central bank and the governments decide simultaneously and independently. The European central bank sets European money supply so as to achieve zero inflation in Europe. The German government sets its purchases of German goods so as to achieve zero unemployment in Germany. And the French government sets its purchases of French goods so as to achieve zero unemployment in France. Step 4 refers to the

time lag. In step 5, the central bank and the governments decide simultaneously and independently. The European central bank sets European money supply so as to achieve zero inflation in Europe. The German government sets its purchases of German goods so as to achieve zero unemployment in Germany. And the French government sets its purchases of French goods so as to achieve zero unemployment in France. Step 6 refers to the time lag. And so on.

Given a demand shock in Germany, simultaneous and independent policy decisions cause uniform oscillations in unemployment and inflation. In addition, there are uniform oscillations in money supply and government purchases. Given a supply shock in Germany, simultaneous and independent policy decisions lower German unemployment and raise German inflation. On the other hand, they raise French unemployment and lower French inflation. And what is more, there is an explosion of government purchases and an implosion of money supply.

3) Policy cooperation. Given a demand shock in Germany, policy cooperation achieves zero unemployment and zero inflation in each of the member countries. Given a supply shock in Germany, policy cooperation is ineffective. There is no change in money supply and government purchases. Correspondingly, there is no change in unemployment and inflation. Judging from this point of view, policy cooperation seems to be superior to policy interaction.

Contents in Brief

Contents

Introduction

1. Subject and Approach

This book studies the dynamic policy interactions in a monetary union. The monetary union consists of two countries, say Germany and France. The policy makers are the European central bank, the German government, and the French government. Here the focus is on sequential and simultaneous policy decisions. We assume that the European central bank is independent. There is a short-run trade-off between unemployment and inflation. In other words, there is a short-run Phillips curve.

1) The policy model. An increase in European money supply lowers unemployment in Germany and France. On the other hand, it raises inflation there. An increase in German government purchases lowers unemployment in Germany. On the other hand, it raises inflation there. Correspondingly, an increase in French government purchases lowers unemployment in France. On the other hand, it raises inflation there.

The primary target of the European central bank is zero inflation in Europe, and the secondary target is zero unemployment there. The instrument of the European central bank is European money supply. There are two targets but only one instrument, so what is needed is a loss function. We assume that the European central bank has a quadratic loss function. The amount of loss depends on inflation and unemployment in Europe. The European central bank sets European money supply so as to minimize its loss. The first-order condition for a minimum loss gives the reaction function of the European central bank. Suppose the German government raises its purchases of German goods. Then, as a response, the European central bank lowers its money supply.

The primary target of the German government is zero unemployment in Germany, and the secondary target is zero inflation there. The instrument of the German government is its purchases of German goods. There are two targets but only one instrument, so what is needed is a loss function. We assume that the

M. Carlberg, *Dynamic Policy Interactions in a Monetary Union*,
DOI 10.1007/978-3-642-18228-0_1, © Springer-Verlag Berlin Heidelberg 2011

German government has a quadratic loss function. The amount of loss depends on unemployment and inflation in Germany. The German government sets its purchases of German goods so as to minimize its loss. The first-order condition for a minimum loss gives the reaction function of the German government. Suppose the European central bank lowers its money supply. Then, as a response, the German government raises its purchases of German goods.

The primary target of the French government is zero unemployment in France, and the secondary target is zero inflation there. The instrument of the French government is its purchases of French goods. There are two targets but only one instrument, so what is needed is a loss function. We assume that the French government has a quadratic loss function. The amount of loss depends on unemployment and inflation in France. The French government sets its purchases of French goods so as to minimize its loss. The first-order condition for a minimum loss gives the reaction function of the French government. Suppose the European central bank lowers its money supply. Then, as a response, the French government raises its purchases of French goods.

The Nash equilibrium is determined by the reaction functions of the European central bank, the German government, and the French government. As a result there is no Nash equilibrium.

2) Sequential policy decisions. We assume that the central bank and the governments decide sequentially. First the central bank decides, then the governments decide. Step 1 refers to a specific shock. Step 2 refers to the time lag. Step 3 refers to monetary policy in Europe. Step 4 refers to the time lag. Step 5 refers to fiscal policies in Germany and France. Step 6 refers to the time lag. Step 7 refers to monetary policy in Europe. Step 8 refers to the time lag. Step 9 refers to fiscal policies in Germany and France. Step 10 refers to the time lag. And so on. The key questions are: Given a specific shock, can the process of sequential policy decisions reduce the existing loss? And to what extent can it do so? To illustrate this process there are some numerical examples.

3) Simultaneous and independent policy decisions. We assume that the central bank and the governments decide simultaneously and independently. Step 1 refers to a specific shock. Step 2 refers to the time lag. Step 3 refers to monetary and fiscal policies. Step 4 refers to the time lag. Step 5 refers to

monetary and fiscal policies. Step 6 refers to the time lag. And so on. The key question is: Given a specific shock, can the process of simultaneous and independent policy decisions reduce the existing loss?

4) This book consists of four major parts:

- first the central bank decides, then the governments decide
- first the governments decide, then the central bank decides
- central bank and governments decide simultaneously and independently
- central bank and governments cooperate.

Now the approach will be presented in greater detail.

2. Some Basic Models

1) The static model. This section deals with a closed economy. An increase in money supply lowers unemployment. On the other hand, it raises inflation. Correspondingly, an increase in government purchases lowers unemployment. On the other hand, it raises inflation. The target of the central bank is zero inflation. The instrument of the central bank is money supply. From this follows the reaction function of the central bank. Suppose the government raises its purchases. Then, as a response, the central bank lowers its money supply. Similarly, the target of the government is zero unemployment. The instrument of the government is its purchases. From this follows the reaction function of the government. Suppose the central bank lowers its money supply. Then, as a response, the government raises its purchases. The Nash equilibrium is determined by the reaction functions of the central bank and the government. As a result there is no Nash equilibrium.

2) Sequential policy decisions. We assume that the central bank and the government decide sequentially. First the central bank decides, then the government decides. Step 1 refers to a specific shock. Step 2 refers to the time lag. Step 3 refers to monetary policy. Step 4 refers to the time lag. Step 5 refers

to fiscal policy. Step 6 refers to the time lag. Step 7 refers to monetary policy. Step 8 refers to the time lag. Step 9 refers to fiscal policy. Step 10 refers to the time lag. And so on.

Now have a closer look at the process of sequential policy decisions. Step 1 refers to a specific shock. This could be a demand shock, a supply shock, or a mixed shock. Step 2 refers to the time lag. This includes both the inside lag and the outside lag. Step 3 refers to monetary policy. The central bank sets its money supply so as to achieve zero inflation. Step 4 refers to the time lag. Step 5 refers to fiscal policy. The government sets its purchases so as to achieve zero unemployment. Step 6 refers to the time lag.

Step 7 refers to monetary policy. The central bank sets its money supply so as to achieve zero inflation. Step 8 refers to the time lag. Step 9 refers to fiscal policy. The government sets its purchases so as to achieve zero unemployment. Step 10 refers to the time lag. And so on. The key questions are: Given a specific shock, can the process of sequential policy decisions reduce the existing loss? And what are the dynamic characteristics of this process?

3) Inverse sequential policy decisions. We assume that the government and the central bank decide sequentially. First the government decides, then the central bank decides. Step 1 refers to a specific shock. Step 2 refers to the time lag. Step 3 refers to fiscal policy. Step 4 refers to the time lag. Step 5 refers to monetary policy. Step 6 refers to the time lag. Step 7 refers to fiscal policy. Step 8 refers to the time lag. Step 9 refers to monetary policy. Step 10 refers to the time lag. And so on.

Now take a closer look at the process of inverse sequential policy decisions. Step 1 refers to a specific shock. Step 2 refers to the time lag. Step 3 refers to fiscal policy. The government sets its purchases so as to achieve zero unemployment. Step 4 refers to the time lag. Step 5 refers to monetary policy. The central bank sets its money supply so as to achieve zero inflation. Step 6 refers to the time lag. Step 7 refers to fiscal policy. The government sets its purchases so as to achieve zero unemployment. Step 8 refers to the time lag. Step 9 refers to monetary policy. The central bank sets its money supply so as to achieve zero inflation. Step 10 refers to the time lag. And so on. The key question is: Given a specific shock, can the process of inverse sequential policy decisions reduce the existing loss?

4) Simultaneous and independent policy decisions. We assume that the central bank and the government decide simultaneously and independently. Step 1 refers to a specific shock. Step 2 refers to the time lag. Step 3 refers to monetary and fiscal policies. Step 4 refers to the time lag. Step 5 refers to monetary and fiscal policies. Step 6 refers to the time lag. And so on.

Now have a closer look at the process of simultaneous and independent policy decisions. Step 1 refers to a specific shock. Step 2 refers to the time lag. In step 3 the central bank and the government decide simultaneously and independently. The central bank sets its money supply so as to achieve zero inflation. And the government sets its purchases so as to achieve zero unemployment. Step 4 refers to the time lag. In step 5 the central bank and the government decide simultaneously and independently. The central bank sets its money supply so as to achieve zero inflation. And the government sets its purchases so as to achieve zero unemployment. Step 6 refers to the time lag. And so on. The key question is: Given a specific shock, can the process of simultaneous and independent policy decisions reduce the existing loss?

5) Policy cooperation. We assume that the central bank and the government cooperate. The targets of policy cooperation are zero inflation and zero unemployment. The instruments of policy cooperation are money supply and government purchases. We assume that the policy makers agree on a common loss function. The amount of loss depends on inflation and unemployment. The policy makers set money supply and government purchases so as to minimize the common loss. The cooperative equilibrium is determined by the first-order conditions for a minimum loss. It yields the optimum combinations of money supply and government purchases. The key questions are: Given a specific shock, can policy cooperation reduce the existing loss? Is policy cooperation superior to sequential policy decisions? And is policy cooperation superior to simultaneous and independent policy decisions?

3. The Monetary Union of Two Countries

1) The static model. An increase in European money supply lowers unemployment in Germany and France. On the other hand, it raises inflation there. An increase in German government purchases lowers unemployment in Germany. On the other hand, it raises inflation there. Correspondingly, an increase in French government purchases lowers unemployment in France. On the other hand, it raises inflation there.

The targets of the European central bank are zero inflation in Germany and France. The instrument of the European central bank is European money supply. There are two targets but only one instrument, so what is needed is a loss function. We assume that the European central bank has a quadratic loss function. The amount of loss depends on inflation in Germany and France. The European central bank sets European money supply so as to minimize its loss. The first-order condition for a minimum loss gives the reaction function of the European central bank. Suppose the German government raises its purchases of German goods. Then, as a response, the European central bank lowers its money supply.

The target of the German government is zero unemployment in Germany. The instrument of the German government is its purchases of German goods. From this follows the reaction function of the German government. Suppose the European central bank lowers its money supply. Then, as a response, the German government raises its purchases of German goods. Correspondingly, the target of the French government is zero unemployment in France. The instrument of the French government is its purchases of French goods. From this follows the reaction function of the French government. Suppose the European central bank lowers its money supply. Then, as a response, the French government raises its purchases of French goods.

The Nash equilibrium is determined by the reaction functions of the European central bank, the German government, and the French government. As a result there is no Nash equilibrium.

2) Sequential policy decisions. We assume that the central bank and the governments decide sequentially. First the central bank decides, then the governments decide. Step 1 refers to a specific shock. Step 2 refers to the time lag. Step 3 refers to monetary policy in Europe. Step 4 refers to the time lag. Step 5 refers to fiscal policies in Germany and France. Step 6 refers to the time lag. Step 7 refers to monetary policy in Europe. Step 8 refers to the time lag. Step 9 refers to fiscal policies in Germany and France. Step 10 refers to the time lag. And so on.

Now have a closer look at the process of sequential policy decisions. Step 1 refers to a specific shock. This could be a demand shock, a supply shock or a mixed shock, in Germany or France. Step 2 refers to the time lag. This includes both the inside lag and the outside lag. Step 3 refers to monetary policy in Europe. The European central bank sets European money supply so as to achieve zero inflation in Europe. Step 4 refers to the time lag. Step 5 refers to fiscal policies in Germany and France. The German government sets its purchases of German goods so as to achieve zero unemployment in Germany. And the French government sets its purchases of French goods so as to achieve zero unemployment in France. Step 6 refers to the time lag.

Step 7 refers to monetary policy in Europe. The European central bank sets European money supply so as to achieve zero inflation in Europe. Step 8 refers to the time lag. Step 9 refers to fiscal policies in Germany and France. The German government sets its purchases of German goods so as to achieve zero unemployment in Germany. And the French government sets its purchases of French goods so as to achieve zero unemployment in France. Step 10 refers to the time lag. And so on. The key questions are: Given a specific shock, can the process of sequential policy decisions reduce the existing loss? And what are the dynamic characteristics of this process?

3) Inverse sequential policy decisions. We assume that the governments and the central bank decide sequentially. First the governments decide, then the central bank decides. Step 1 refers to a specific shock. Step 2 refers to the time lag. Step 3 refers to fiscal policies in Germany and France. Step 4 refers to the time lag. Step 5 refers to monetary policy in Europe. Step 6 refers to the time lag. Step 7 refers to fiscal policies in Germany and France. Step 8 refers to the time

lag. Step 9 refers to monetary policy in Europe. Step 10 refers to the time lag. And so on.

Now take a closer look at the process of inverse sequential policy decisions. Step 1 refers to a specific shock. Step 2 refers to the time lag. Step 3 refers to fiscal policies in Germany and France. The German government sets its purchases of German goods so as to achieve zero unemployment in Germany. And the French government sets its purchases of French goods so as to achieve zero unemployment in France. Step 4 refers to the time lag. Step 5 refers to monetary policy in Europe. The European central bank sets European money supply so as to achieve zero inflation in Europe. Step 6 refers to the time lag.

Step 7 refers to fiscal policies in Germany and France. The German government sets its purchases of German goods so as to achieve zero unemployment in Germany. And the French government sets its purchases of French goods so as to achieve zero unemployment in France. Step 8 refers to the time lag. Step 9 refers to monetary policy in Europe. The European central bank sets European money supply so as to achieve zero inflation in Europe. Step 10 refers to the time lag. And so on. The key question is: Given a specific shock, can the process of inverse sequential policy decisions reduce the existing loss?

4) Simultaneous and independent policy decisions. We assume that the central bank and the governments decide simultaneously and independently. Step 1 refers to a specific shock. Step 2 refers to the time lag. Step 3 refers to monetary and fiscal policies. Step 4 refers to the time lag. Step 5 refers to monetary and fiscal policies. Step 6 refers to the time lag. And so on.

Now have a closer look at the process of simultaneous and independent policy decisions. Step 1 refers to a specific shock. Step 2 refers to the time lag. In step 3, the central bank and the governments decide simultaneously and independently. The European central bank sets European money supply so as to achieve zero inflation in Europe. The German government sets its purchases of German goods so as to achieve zero unemployment in Germany. And the French government sets its purchases of French goods so as to achieve zero unemployment in France. Step 4 refers to the time lag.

In step 5, the central bank and the governments decide simultaneously and independently. The European central bank sets European money supply so as to achieve zero inflation in Europe. The German government sets its purchases of German goods so as to achieve zero unemployment in Germany. And the French government sets its purchases of French goods so as to achieve zero unemployment in France. Step 6 refers to the time lag. And so on. The key question is: Given a specific shock, can the process of simultaneous and independent policy decisions reduce the existing loss?

5) Policy cooperation. We assume that the central bank and the governments cooperate. The targets of policy cooperation are zero inflation and zero unemployment in each of the member countries. The instruments of policy cooperation are European money supply, German government purchases, and French government purchases. There are four targets but only three instruments, so what is needed is a loss function. We assume that the European central bank, the German government, and the French government agree on a common loss function. The amount of loss depends on inflation and unemployment in each of the member countries. The policy makers set European money supply, German government purchases, and French government purchases so as to minimize the common loss.

The cooperative equilibrium is determined by the first-order conditions for a minimum loss. It yields the optimum combinations of European money supply, German government purchases, and French government purchases. The key questions are: Given a specific shock, can policy cooperation reduce the existing loss? Is policy cooperation superior to sequential policy decisions? And is policy cooperation superior to simultaneous and independent policy decisions?

Part One

Some Basic Models

Chapter 1
First the Central Bank Decides, then the Government Decides

1. Target System A

1.1. The Model

1) The static model. This part deals with a closed economy. The target of the central bank is zero inflation. By contrast, the target of the government is zero unemployment. An increase in money supply lowers unemployment. On the other hand, it raises inflation. Correspondingly, an increase in government purchases lowers unemployment. On the other hand, it raises inflation.

The model of unemployment and inflation can be represented by a system of two equations:

$$u = A - M - G \tag{1}$$

$$\pi = B + M + G \tag{2}$$

Of course this is a reduced form. Here u denotes the rate of unemployment, π is the rate of inflation, M is money supply, G is government purchases, A is some other factors bearing on the rate of unemployment, and B is some other factors bearing on the rate of inflation. The endogenous variables are the rate of unemployment and the rate of inflation.

According to equation (1), the rate of unemployment is a positive function of A, a negative function of money supply, and a negative function of government purchases. According to equation (2), the rate of inflation is a positive function of B, a positive function of money supply, and a positive function of government purchases. A unit increase in A raises the rate of unemployment by 1 percentage point. A unit increase in B raises the rate of inflation by 1 percentage point. A unit increase in money supply lowers the rate of unemployment by 1 percentage

M. Carlberg, *Dynamic Policy Interactions in a Monetary Union*,
DOI 10.1007/978-3-642-18228-0_2, © Springer-Verlag Berlin Heidelberg 2011

point. On the other hand, it raises the rate of inflation by 1 percentage point. A unit increase in government purchases lowers the rate of unemployment by 1 percentage point. On the other hand, it raises the rate of inflation by 1 percentage point.

The target of the central bank is zero inflation. The instrument of the central bank is money supply. By equation (2), the reaction function of the central bank is:

$$M = -B - G \tag{3}$$

An increase in B requires a cut in money supply. And an increase in government purchases requires a cut in money supply too.

The target of the government is zero unemployment. The instrument of the government is its purchases. By equation (1), the reaction function of the government is:

$$G = A - M \tag{4}$$

An increase in A requires an increase in government purchases. And a cut in money supply requires an increase in government purchases as well.

The Nash equilibrium is determined by the reaction functions of the central bank and the government. From the reaction function of the central bank follows:

$$\frac{dM}{dG} = -1 \tag{5}$$

And from the reaction function of the government follows:

$$\frac{dG}{dM} = -1 \tag{6}$$

That is to say, the reaction curves do not intersect. As a result, there is no Nash equilibrium.

2) The dynamic model. We assume that the central bank and the government decide sequentially. First the central bank decides, then the government decides. Step 1 refers to a specific shock. Step 2 refers to the time lag. Step 3 refers to monetary policy. Step 4 refers to the time lag. Step 5 refers to fiscal policy. Step 6 refers to the time lag. Step 7 refers to monetary policy. Step 8 refers to the time lag. Step 9 refers to fiscal policy. Step 10 refers to the time lag. And so on.

Now have a closer look at the dynamic model. Step 1 refers to a specific shock. This could be a demand shock, a supply shock, or a mixed shock. Step 2 refers to the time lag. This includes both the inside lag and the outside lag. Step 3 refers to monetary policy. The central bank sets its money supply so as to achieve zero inflation. The reaction function of the central bank is:

$$M = - B - G \tag{7}$$

Step 4 refers to the time lag. Step 5 refers to fiscal policy. The government sets its purchases so as to achieve zero unemployment. The reaction function of the government is:

$$G = A - M \tag{8}$$

Step 6 refers to the time lag. Step 7 refers to monetary policy. The central bank sets its money supply so as to achieve zero inflation. The reaction function of the central bank is:

$$M = - B - G \tag{9}$$

Step 8 refers to the time lag. Step 9 refers to fiscal policy. The government sets its purchases so as to achieve zero unemployment. The reaction function of the government is:

$$G = A - M \tag{10}$$

Step 10 refers to the time lag. And so on. Then what are the dynamic characteristics of this process?

1.2. Some Numerical Examples

It proves useful to study four distinct cases:

- a demand shock
- a supply shock
- a mixed shock
- another mixed shock.

The target of the central bank is zero inflation. By contrast, the target of the government is zero unemployment.

1) A demand shock. Let initial unemployment be zero, and let initial inflation be zero as well. Step one refers to a decline in aggregate demand. In terms of the model there is an increase in A of 2 units and a decline in B of equally 2 units. Step two refers to the time lag. Unemployment goes from zero to 2 percent. And inflation goes from zero to – 2 percent.

Step three refers to monetary policy. Current inflation is – 2 percent, and target inflation is zero percent. So what is needed is an increase in money supply of 2 units. Step four refers to the time lag. Unemployment goes from 2 to zero percent. And inflation goes from – 2 to zero percent. Step five refers to fiscal policy. Current unemployment is zero percent, and target unemployment is the same. So what is needed is no change in government purchases. Step six refers to the time lag. Unemployment stays at zero percent, as does inflation. Table 1.1 presents a synopsis.

As a result, given a demand shock, sequential policy decisions produce zero unemployment and zero inflation. There is an increase in money supply but no change in government purchases. The loss functions of the central bank and the government are respectively:

$$L_1 = \pi^2 \quad (1)$$

$$L_2 = u^2 \quad (2)$$

The initial loss of the central bank is zero, as is the initial loss of the government.

The demand shock causes a loss to the central bank of 4 units and a loss to the government of equally 4 units. Then sequential policy decisions bring the loss of the central bank and the government down to zero each.

Table 1.1
Sequential Policy Decisions
A Demand Shock

Unemployment	2	Inflation	– 2
Change in Money Supply	2		
Unemployment	0	Inflation	0
Change in Govt Purchases	0		
Unemployment	0	Inflation	0

2) A supply shock. Let initial unemployment and inflation be zero each. Step one refers to the supply shock. In terms of the model there is an increase in B of 2 units and an increase in A of equally 2 units. Step two refers to the time lag. Inflation goes from zero to 2 percent. And unemployment goes from zero to 2 percent as well.

Step three refers to monetary policy. Current inflation is 2 percent, and target inflation is zero percent. So what is needed is a reduction in money supply of 2 units. Step four refers to the time lag. Unemployment goes from 2 to 4 percent. And inflation goes from 2 to zero percent. Step five refers to fiscal policy. Current unemployment is 4 percent, and target unemployment is zero percent. So what is needed is an increase in government purchases of 4 units. Step six refers to the time lag. Unemployment goes from 4 to zero percent. And inflation goes from zero to 4 percent.

Step seven refers to monetary policy. Current inflation is 4 percent, and target inflation is zero percent. So what is needed is a reduction in money supply of 4 units. Step eight refers to the time lag. Unemployment goes from zero to 4 percent. And inflation goes from 4 to zero percent. Step nine refers to fiscal policy. Current unemployment is 4 percent, and target unemployment is zero percent. So what is needed is an increase in government purchases of 4 units. Step ten refers to the time lag. Unemployment goes from 4 to zero percent. And inflation goes from zero to 4 percent. And so on. Table 1.2 gives an overview.

As a result, given a supply shock, sequential policy decisions cause uniform oscillations in unemployment and inflation. And what is more, there is an explosion of government purchases and an implosion of money supply. The economy oscillates between unemployment and full employment. Correspondingly, the economy oscillates between price stability and inflation. In the short run, according to the supply shock, unemployment and inflation are 2 percent each. In the long run, according to sequential policy decisions, average unemployment and average inflation are 2 percent each.

Table 1.2
Sequential Policy Decisions
A Supply Shock

Unemployment	2	Inflation	2
Change in Money Supply	– 2		
Unemployment	4	Inflation	0
Change in Govt Purchases	4		
Unemployment	0	Inflation	4
Change in Money Supply	– 4		
Unemployment	4	Inflation	0
Change in Govt Purchases	4		
Unemployment	0	Inflation	4
and so on			

3) A mixed shock. Let initial unemployment and inflation be zero each. Step one refers to the mixed shock. In terms of the model there is an increase in B of 4 units. Step two refers to the time lag. Inflation goes from zero to 4 percent. And unemployment stays at zero percent.

Step three refers to monetary policy. Current inflation is 4 percent, and target inflation is zero percent. So what is needed is a reduction in money supply of 4 units. Step four refers to the time lag. Unemployment goes from zero to 4 percent. And inflation goes from 4 to zero percent. Step five refers to fiscal policy. Current unemployment is 4 percent, and target unemployment is zero percent. So what is needed is an increase in government purchases of 4 units. Step six refers to the time lag. Unemployment goes from 4 to zero percent. And inflation goes from zero to 4 percent. And so on. For a synopsis see Table 1.3.

Table 1.3
Sequential Policy Decisions
A Mixed Shock

Unemployment	0	Inflation	4
Change in Money Supply	– 4		
Unemployment	4	Inflation	0
Change in Govt Purchases	4		
Unemployment	0	Inflation	4
and so on			

As a result, given a mixed shock, sequential policy decisions cause uniform oscillations in unemployment and inflation. And what is more, there is an explosion of government purchases and an implosion of money supply. The economy oscillates between unemployment and full employment. Correspondingly, the economy oscillates between price stability and inflation. In the short run, according to the mixed shock, unemployment is zero percent, and inflation is 4 percent. In the long run, according to sequential policy decisions, average unemployment and average inflation are 2 percent each.

4) Another type of a mixed shock. Let initial unemployment and inflation be zero each. Step one refers to the mixed shock. In terms of the model there is an increase in A of 4 units. Step two refers to the time lag. Unemployment goes from zero to 4 percent. And inflation stays at zero percent.

Step three refers to monetary policy. Current inflation is zero percent, and target inflation is the same. So what is needed is no change in money supply. Step four refers to the time lag. Unemployment stays at 4 percent, and inflation stays at zero percent. Step five refers to fiscal policy. Current unemployment is 4 percent, and target unemployment is zero percent. So what is needed is an increase in government purchases of 4 units. Step six refers to the time lag. Unemployment goes from 4 to zero percent. And inflation goes from zero to 4 percent.

Step seven refers to monetary policy. Current inflation is 4 percent, and target inflation is zero percent. So what is needed is a reduction in money supply of 4 units. Step eight refers to the time lag. Unemployment goes from zero to 4 percent. And inflation goes from 4 to zero percent. Step nine refers to fiscal policy. Current unemployment is 4 percent, and target unemployment is zero percent. So what is needed is an increase in government purchases of 4 units. Step ten refers to the time lag. Unemployment goes from 4 to zero percent. And inflation goes from zero to 4 percent. And so on. For an overview see Table 1.4.

As a result, given another type of a mixed shock, sequential policy decisions cause uniform oscillations in unemployment and inflation. And what is more, there is an explosion of government purchases and an implosion of money supply. The economy oscillates between unemployment and full employment. Correspondingly, the economy oscillates between price stability and inflation. In the short run, according to the mixed shock, unemployment is 4 percent, and inflation is zero percent. In the long run, according to sequential policy decisions, average unemployment and average inflation are 2 percent each.

5) Summary. Given a demand shock, sequential policy decisions produce zero unemployment and zero inflation. There is an increase in money supply and

no change in government purchases. Given a supply shock, sequential policy decisions cause uniform oscillations in unemployment and inflation. And what is more, there is an explosion of government purchases and an implosion of money supply. And much the same applies to mixed shocks.

Table 1.4
Sequential Policy Decisions
Another Mixed Shock

Unemployment	4	Inflation	0
Change in Money Supply	0		
Unemployment	4	Inflation	0
Change in Govt Purchases	4		
Unemployment	0	Inflation	4
Change in Money Supply	– 4		
Unemployment	4	Inflation	0
Change in Govt Purchases	4		
Unemployment	0	Inflation	4
and so on			

2. Target System B

2.1. The Model

1) The static model. The central bank has two targets, that is zero inflation and zero unemployment. By contrast, the government has a single target, that is zero unemployment. The model of unemployment and inflation can be characterized by a system of two equations:

$$u = A - M - G \tag{1}$$

$$\pi = B + M + G \tag{2}$$

An increase in money supply lowers unemployment. On the other hand, it raises inflation. Correspondingly, an increase in government purchases lowers unemployment. On the other hand, it raises inflation.

The targets of the central bank are zero inflation and zero unemployment. The instrument of the central bank is money supply. There are two targets but only one instrument, so what is needed is a loss function. We assume that the central bank has a quadratic loss function:

$$L_1 = \pi^2 + u^2 \tag{3}$$

L_1 is the loss to the central bank caused by inflation and unemployment. For ease of exposition we assume equal weights in the loss function. The specific target of the central bank is to minimize the loss, given the inflation function and the unemployment function. Taking account of equations (1) and (2), the loss function of the central bank can be written as follows:

$$L_1 = (B + M + G)^2 + (A - M - G)^2 \tag{4}$$

Then the first-order condition for a minimum loss gives the reaction function of the central bank:

$$2M = A - B - 2G \tag{5}$$

An increase in A requires an increase in money supply. An increase in B requires a cut in money supply. And an increase in government purchases requires a cut in money supply too.

The target of the government is zero unemployment. The instrument of the government is its purchases. By equation (1), the reaction function of the government is:

$$G = A - M \tag{6}$$

An increase in A requires an increase in government purchases. An increase in B requires no change in government purchases. And a cut in money supply requires an increase in government purchases.

The Nash equilibrium is determined by the reaction functions of the central bank and the government. From the reaction function of the central bank follows:

$$\frac{dM}{dG} = -1 \tag{7}$$

And from the reaction function of the government follows:

$$\frac{dG}{dM} = -1 \tag{8}$$

That is to say, the reaction curves do not intersect. As a result there is no Nash equilibrium.

2) The dynamic model. We assume that the central bank and the government decide sequentially. First the central bank decides, then the government decides. Step 1 refers to a specific shock. Step 2 refers to the time lag. Step 3 refers to monetary policy. Step 4 refers to the time lag. Step 5 refers to fiscal policy. Step 6 refers to the time lag. Step 7 refers to monetary policy. Step 8 refers to the time lag. Step 9 refers to fiscal policy. Step 10 refers to the time lag. And so on.

Now take a closer look at the dynamic model. Step 1 refers to a specific shock. Step 2 refers to the time lag. Step 3 refers to monetary policy. The central bank sets its money supply so as to reduce its loss. The reaction function of the central bank is:

$$2M = A - B - 2G \tag{9}$$

Step 4 refers to the time lag. Step 5 refers to fiscal policy. The government sets its purchases so as to achieve zero unemployment. The reaction function of the government is:

$$G = A - M \tag{10}$$

Step 6 refers to the time lag. Step 7 refers to monetary policy. The central bank sets its money supply so as to reduce its loss. The reaction function of the central bank is:

$$2M = A - B - 2G \tag{11}$$

Step 8 refers to the time lag. Step 9 refers to fiscal policy. The government sets its purchases so as to achieve zero unemployment. The reaction function of the government is:

$$G = A - M \tag{12}$$

Step 10 refers to the time lag. And so on. Then what are the dynamic characteristics of this process?

2.2. Some Numerical Examples

Here are four distinct cases:

- a demand shock
- a supply shock
- a mixed shock
- another mixed shock.

The central bank has two targets, that is zero inflation and zero unemployment. By contrast, the government has a single target, that is zero unemployment.

1) A demand shock. Let initial unemployment be zero, and let initial inflation be zero as well. Step one refers to a decline in aggregate demand. In terms of the model there is an increase in A of 2 units and a decline in B of equally 2 units. Step two refers to the time lag. Unemployment goes from zero to 2 percent. And inflation goes from zero to – 2 percent.

Step three refers to monetary policy. Current unemployment is 2 percent, and current inflation is – 2 percent. Accordingly, target unemployment and target inflation are zero percent each. So what is needed is an increase in money supply of 2 units. Step four refers to the time lag. Unemployment goes from 2 to zero percent. And inflation goes from – 2 to zero percent. Step five refers to fiscal policy. Current unemployment and target unemployment are zero percent each. So what is needed is no change in government purchases. Step six refers to the time lag. Unemployment stays at zero percent, as does inflation. Table 1.5 presents a synopsis.

As a result, given a demand shock, sequential policy decisions produce zero unemployment and zero inflation. There is an increase in money supply but no change in government purchases. The loss functions of the central bank and the government are respectively:

$$L_1 = \pi^2 + u^2 \quad (1)$$

$$L_2 = u^2 \quad (2)$$

The initial loss of the central bank is zero, as is the initial loss of the government. The demand shock causes a loss to the central bank of 8 units and a loss to the government of 4 units. Then sequential policy decisions bring the loss of the central bank and the government down to zero each.

Table 1.5
Sequential Policy Decisions
A Demand Shock

Unemployment	2	Inflation	– 2
Change in Money Supply	2		
Unemployment	0	Inflation	0
Change in Govt Purchases	0		
Unemployment	0	Inflation	0

2) A supply shock. Let initial unemployment and inflation be zero each. Step one refers to the supply shock. In terms of the model there is an increase in B of 2 units and an increase in A of equally 2 units. Step two refers to the time lag. Inflation goes from zero to 2 percent. And unemployment goes from zero to 2 percent as well.

Step three refers to monetary policy. Current unemployment and current inflation are 2 percent each. Accordingly, target unemployment and target inflation are 2 percent each. So what is needed is no change in money supply. Step four refers to the time lag. Unemployment stays at 2 percent, as does inflation. Step five refers to fiscal policy. Current unemployment is 2 percent, and target unemployment is zero percent. So what is needed is an increase in government purchases of 2 units. Step six refers to the time lag. Unemployment goes from 2 to zero percent. And inflation goes from 2 to 4 percent.

Step seven refers to monetary policy. Current unemployment is zero percent, and current inflation is 4 percent. Accordingly, target unemployment and target inflation are 2 percent each. So what is needed is a reduction in money supply of 2 units. Step eight refers to the time lag. Unemployment goes from zero to 2 percent. And inflation goes from 4 to 2 percent. Step nine refers to fiscal policy. Current unemployment is 2 percent, and target unemployment is zero percent. So what is needed is an increase in government purchases of 2 units. Step ten refers to the time lag. Unemployment goes from 2 to zero percent. And inflation goes from 2 to 4 percent. And so on. Table 1.6 gives an overview.

As a result, given a supply shock, sequential policy decisions cause uniform oscillations in unemployment and inflation. And what is more, there is an explosion of government purchases and an implosion of money supply. The economy oscillates between unemployment and full employment. Correspondingly, the economy oscillates between low and high inflation. In the short run, according to the supply shock, unemployment and inflation are 2 percent each. In the long run, according to sequential policy decisions, average unemployment is 1 percent, and average inflation is 3 percent.

Table 1.6
Sequential Policy Decisions
A Supply Shock

Unemployment	2	Inflation	2
Change in Money Supply	0		
Unemployment	2	Inflation	2
Change in Govt Purchases	2		
Unemployment	0	Inflation	4
Change in Money Supply	– 2		
Unemployment	2	Inflation	2
Change in Govt Purchases	2		
Unemployment	0	Inflation	4
and so on			

3) A mixed shock. Let initial unemployment and inflation be zero each. Step one refers to the mixed shock. In terms of the model there is an increase in B of 4 units. Step two refers to the time lag. Inflation goes from zero to 4 percent. And unemployment stays at zero percent.

Step three refers to monetary policy. Current unemployment is zero percent, and current inflation is 4 percent. Accordingly, target unemployment and target inflation are 2 percent each. So what is needed is a reduction in money supply of 2 units. Step four refers to the time lag. Unemployment goes from zero to 2 percent. And inflation goes from 4 to 2 percent. Step five refers to fiscal policy. Current unemployment is 2 percent, and target unemployment is zero percent. So what is needed is an increase in government purchases of 2 units. Step six refers to the time lag. Unemployment goes from 2 to zero percent. And inflation goes from 2 to 4 percent. And so on. For a synopsis see Table 1.7.

Table 1.7
Sequential Policy Decisions
A Mixed Shock

Unemployment	0	Inflation	4
Change in Money Supply	– 2		
Unemployment	2	Inflation	2
Change in Govt Purchases	2		
Unemployment	0	Inflation	4
and so on			

As a result, given a mixed shock, sequential policy decisions cause uniform oscillations in unemployment and inflation. And what is more, there is an explosion of government purchases and an implosion of money supply. The economy oscillates between unemployment and full employment. Correspondingly, the economy oscillates between low and high inflation. In the short run, according to the mixed shock, unemployment is zero percent, and inflation is 4 percent. In the long run, according to sequential policy decisions, average unemployment is 1 percent, and average inflation is 3 percent.

4) Another type of a mixed shock. Let initial unemployment and inflation be zero each. Step one refers to the mixed shock. In terms of the model there is an increase in A of 4 units. Step two refers to the time lag. Unemployment goes from zero to 4 percent. And inflation stays at zero percent.

Step three refers to monetary policy. Current unemployment is 4 percent, and current inflation is zero percent. Accordingly, target unemployment and target inflation are 2 percent each. So what is needed is an increase in money supply of 2 units. Step four refers to the time lag. Unemployment goes from 4 to 2 percent. And inflation goes from zero to 2 percent. Step five refers to fiscal policy. Current unemployment is 2 percent, and target unemployment is zero percent. So what is needed is an increase in government purchases of 2 units. Step six refers to the time lag. Unemployment goes from 2 to zero percent. And inflation goes from 2 to 4 percent.

Step seven refers to monetary policy. Current unemployment is zero percent, and current inflation is 4 percent. Accordingly, target unemployment and target inflation are 2 percent each. So what is needed is a reduction in money supply of 2 units. Step eight refers to the time lag. Unemployment goes from zero to 2 percent. And inflation goes from 4 to 2 percent. Step nine refers to fiscal policy. Current unemployment is 2 percent, and target unemployment is zero percent. So what is needed is an increase in government purchases of 2 units. Step ten refers to the time lag. Unemployment goes from 2 to zero percent. And inflation goes from 2 to 4 percent. And so on. For an overview see Table 1.8.

As a result, given another type of a mixed shock, sequential policy decisions cause uniform oscillations in unemployment and inflation. And what is more, there is an explosion of government purchases and an implosion of money supply. The economy oscillates between unemployment and full employment. Correspondingly, the economy oscillates between low and high inflation. In the short run, according to the mixed shock, unemployment is 4 percent, and inflation is zero percent. In the long run, according to sequential policy decisions, average unemployment is 1 percent, and average inflation is 3 percent.

5) Summary. Given a demand shock, sequential policy decisions produce zero unemployment and zero inflation. There is an increase in money supply but no change in government purchases. Given a supply shock, sequential policy decisions cause uniform oscillations in unemployment and inflation. And what is more, there is an explosion of government purchases and an implosion of money supply. And much the same applies to mixed shocks.

Table 1.8
Sequential Policy Decisions
Another Mixed Shock

Unemployment	4	Inflation	0
Change in Money Supply	2		
Unemployment	2	Inflation	2
Change in Govt Purchases	2		
Unemployment	0	Inflation	4
Change in Money Supply	– 2		
Unemployment	2	Inflation	2
Change in Govt Purchases	2		
Unemployment	0	Inflation	4
and so on			

3. Target System C

3.1. The Model

1) The static model. The targets of the central bank are zero inflation and zero unemployment. And the targets of the government are the same. The model of unemployment and inflation can be represented by a system of two equations:

$$u = A - M - G \tag{1}$$

$$\pi = B + M + G \tag{2}$$

An increase in money supply lowers unemployment. On the other hand, it raises inflation. Correspondingly, an increase in government purchases lowers unemployment. On the other hand, it raises inflation.

The targets of the central bank are zero inflation and zero unemployment. The instrument of the central bank is money supply. There are two targets but only one instrument, so what is needed is a loss function. We assume that the central bank has a quadratic loss function:

$$L_1 = \pi^2 + u^2 \tag{3}$$

L_1 is the loss to the central bank caused by inflation and unemployment. We assume equal weights in the loss function. The specific target of the central bank is to minimize the loss, given the inflation function and the unemployment function. Taking account of equations (1) and (2), the loss function of the central bank can be written as follows:

$$L_1 = (B + M + G)^2 + (A - M - G)^2 \tag{4}$$

Then the first-order condition for a minimum loss gives the reaction function of the central bank:

$$2M = A - B - 2G \tag{5}$$

An increase in A requires an increase in money supply. An increase in B requires a cut in money supply. And an increase in government purchases requires a cut in money supply too.

The targets of the government are zero unemployment and zero inflation. The instrument of the government is its purchases. There are two targets but only one instrument, so what is needed is a loss function. We assume that the government has a quadratic loss function:

$$L_2 = u^2 + \pi^2 \tag{6}$$

L_2 is the loss to the government caused by unemployment and inflation. We assume equal weights in the loss function. The specific target of the government is to minimize the loss, given the unemployment function and the inflation function. Taking account of equations (1) and (2), the loss function of the government can be written as follows:

$$L_2 = (A - M - G)^2 + (B + M + G)^2 \tag{7}$$

Then the first-order condition for a minimum loss gives the reaction function of the government:

$$2G = A - B - 2M \tag{8}$$

An increase in A requires an increase in government purchases. An increase in B requires a cut in government purchases. And a cut in money supply requires an increase in government purchases.

The Nash equilibrium is determined by the reaction functions of the central bank and the government. Obviously, equations (5) and (8) are identical. There are two endogenous variables, money supply and government purchases. On the other hand, there is only one independent equation. As a result there are multiple Nash equilibria.

2) The dynamic model. We assume that the central bank and the government decide sequentially. First the central bank decides, then the government decides.

Step 1 refers to a specific shock. Step 2 refers to the time lag. Step 3 refers to monetary policy. Step 4 refers to the time lag. Step 5 refers to fiscal policy. Step 6 refers to the time lag. Step 7 refers to monetary policy. Step 8 refers to the time lag. Step 9 refers to fiscal policy. Step 10 refers to the time lag. And so on.

Now have a closer look at the dynamic model. Step 1 refers to a specific shock. Step 2 refers to the time lag. Step 3 refers to monetary policy. The central bank sets its money supply so as to reduce its loss. The reaction function of the central bank is:

$$2M = A - B - 2G \tag{9}$$

Step 4 refers to the time lag. Step 5 refers to fiscal policy. The government sets its purchases so as to reduce its loss. The reaction function of the government is:

$$2G = A - B - 2M \tag{10}$$

Step 6 refers to the time lag. Step 7 refers to monetary policy. The central bank sets its money supply so as to reduce its loss. The reaction function of the central bank is:

$$2M = A - B - 2G \tag{11}$$

Step 8 refers to the time lag. Step 9 refers to fiscal policy. The government sets its purchases so as to reduce its loss. The reaction function of the government is:

$$2G = A - B - 2M \tag{12}$$

Step 10 refers to the time lag. And so on. Then what are the dynamic characteristics of this process?

3.2. Some Numerical Examples

Here are four distinct cases:

- a demand shock
- a supply shock
- a mixed shock
- another mixed shock.

The targets of the central bank are zero inflation and zero unemployment. And the targets of the government are the same.

1) A demand shock. Let initial unemployment be zero, and let initial inflation be zero as well. Step one refers to a decline in aggregate demand. In terms of the model there is an increase in A of 2 units and a decline in B of equally 2 units. Step two refers to the time lag. Unemployment goes from zero to 2 percent. And inflation goes from zero to – 2 percent.

Step three refers to monetary policy. Current unemployment is 2 percent, and current inflation is – 2 percent. Accordingly, target unemployment and target inflation are zero percent each. So what is needed is an increase in money supply of 2 units. Step four refers to the time lag. Unemployment goes from 2 to zero percent. And inflation goes from – 2 to zero percent. Step five refers to fiscal policy. Current unemployment and current inflation are zero percent each. Accordingly, target unemployment and target inflation are zero percent each. So what is needed is no change in government purchases. Step six refers to the time lag. Unemployment stays at zero percent, as does inflation. Table 1.9 presents a synopsis.

As a result, given a demand shock, sequential policy decisions produce zero unemployment and zero inflation. There is an increase in money supply but no change in government purchases. The loss functions of the central bank and the government are respectively:

$$L_1 = \pi^2 + u^2 \tag{1}$$

$$L_2 = \pi^2 + u^2 \tag{2}$$

The initial loss of the central bank is zero, as is the initial loss of the government. The demand shock causes a loss to the central bank of 8 units and a loss to the government of equally 8 units. Then sequential policy decisions bring the loss of the central bank and the government down to zero each.

Table 1.9
Sequential Policy Decisions
A Demand Shock

Unemployment	2	Inflation	– 2
Change in Money Supply	2		
Unemployment	0	Inflation	0
Change in Govt Purchases	0		
Unemployment	0	Inflation	0

2) A supply shock. Let initial unemployment and inflation be zero each. Step one refers to the supply shock. In terms of the model there is an increase in B of 2 units and an increase in A of equally 2 units. Step two refers to the time lag. Inflation goes from zero to 2 percent. And unemployment goes from zero to 2 percent as well.

Step three refers to monetary policy. Current unemployment and current inflation are 2 percent each. Accordingly, target unemployment and target inflation are 2 percent each. So what is needed is no change in money supply. Step four refers to the time lag. Unemployment stays at 2 percent, as does inflation. Step five refers to fiscal policy. Current unemployment and current inflation are 2 percent each. Accordingly, target unemployment and target inflation are 2 percent each. So what is needed is no change in government purchases. Step six refers to the time lag. Unemployment stays at 2 percent, as does inflation. Table 1.10 gives an overview.

As a result, given a supply shock, sequential policy decisions are ineffective. There is no change in money supply or government purchases. Correspondingly, there is no change in unemployment or inflation. The initial loss of the central bank is zero, as is the initial loss of the government. The supply shock causes a loss to the central bank of 8 units and a loss to the government of equally 8 units. Then sequential policy decisions keep the loss of the central bank and the government at 8 units each.

Table 1.10
Sequential Policy Decisions
A Supply Shock

Unemployment	2	Inflation	2
Change in Money Supply	0		
Unemployment	2	Inflation	2
Change in Govt Purchases	0		
Unemployment	2	Inflation	2

3) A mixed shock. Let initial unemployment and inflation be zero each. Step one refers to the mixed shock. In terms of the model there is an increase in B of 4 units. Step two refers to the time lag. Inflation goes from zero to 4 percent. And unemployment stays at zero percent.

Step three refers to monetary policy. Current unemployment is zero percent, and current inflation is 4 percent. Accordingly, target unemployment and target inflation are 2 percent each. So what is needed is a reduction in money supply of 2 units. Step four refers to the time lag. Unemployment goes from zero to 2 percent. And inflation goes from 4 to 2 percent. Step five refers to fiscal policy. Current unemployment and current inflation are 2 percent each. Accordingly, target unemployment and target inflation are 2 percent each. So what is needed is no change in government purchases. Step six refers to the time lag.

Unemployment stays at 2 percent, as does inflation. For a synopsis see Table 1.11.

As a result, given a mixed shock, sequential policy decisions lower inflation. On the other hand, they raise unemployment. There is a reduction in money supply but no change in government purchases. The initial loss of the central bank is zero, as is the initial loss of the government. The mixed shock causes a loss to the central bank of 16 units and a loss to the government of equally 16 units. Then sequential policy decisions bring the loss of the central bank and the government down to 8 units each.

Table 1.11
Sequential Policy Decisions
A Mixed Shock

Unemployment	0	Inflation	4
Change in Money Supply	– 2		
Unemployment	2	Inflation	2
Change in Govt Purchases	0		
Unemployment	2	Inflation	2

4) Another type of a mixed shock. Let initial unemployment and inflation be zero each. Step one refers to the mixed shock. In terms of the model there is an increase in A of 4 units. Step two refers to the time lag. Unemployment goes from zero to 4 percent. And inflation stays at zero percent.

Step three refers to monetary policy. Current unemployment is 4 percent, and current inflation is zero percent. Accordingly, target unemployment and target inflation are 2 percent each. So what is needed is an increase in money supply of 2 units. Step four refers to the time lag. Unemployment goes from 4 to 2 percent. And inflation goes from zero to 2 percent. Step five refers to fiscal policy. Current unemployment and current inflation are 2 percent each. Accordingly, target unemployment and target inflation are 2 percent each. So what is needed is no change in government purchases. Step six refers to the time lag. Unemployment stays at 2 percent, as does inflation. For an overview see Table 1.12.

As a result, given another type of a mixed shock, sequential policy decisions lower unemployment. On the other hand, they raise inflation. There is an increase in money supply but no change in government purchases. The initial loss of the central bank is zero, as is the initial loss of the government. The mixed shock causes a loss to the central bank of 16 units and a loss to the government of equally 16 units. Then sequential policy decisions bring the loss of the central bank and the government down to 8 units each.

Table 1.12
Sequential Policy Decisions
Another Mixed Shock

Unemployment	4	Inflation	0
Change in Money Supply	2		
Unemployment	2	Inflation	2
Change in Govt Purchases	0		
Unemployment	2	Inflation	2

5) Summary. Given a demand shock, sequential policy decisions produce zero unemployment and zero inflation. There is an increase in money supply but no change in government purchases. Given a supply shock, sequential policy decisions are ineffective. There is no change in money supply or government purchases. Correspondingly, there is no change in unemployment or inflation. Given a mixed shock, sequential policy decisions lower inflation. On the other hand, they raise unemployment. There is a reduction in money supply but no change in government purchases. Given another type of a mixed shock, sequential policy decisions lower unemployment. On the other hand, they raise

inflation. There is an increase in money supply but no change in government purchases.

Chapter 2
First the Government Decides, then the Central Bank Decides

1. Target System A

1.1. The Model

1) The static model. The target of the central bank is zero inflation. By contrast, the target of the government is zero unemployment. The model of unemployment and inflation can be represented by a system of two equations:

$$u = A - M - G \tag{1}$$

$$\pi = B + M + G \tag{2}$$

An increase in money supply lowers unemployment. On the other hand, it raises inflation. Correspondingly, an increase in government purchases lowers unemployment. On the other hand, it raises inflation.

The target of the central bank is zero inflation. The instrument of the central bank is money supply. By equation (2), the reaction function of the central bank is:

$$M = -B - G \tag{3}$$

An increase in B requires a cut in money supply. And an increase in government purchases requires a cut in money supply too.

The target of the government is zero unemployment. The instrument of the government is its purchases. By equation (1), the reaction function of the government is:

$$G = A - M \tag{4}$$

M. Carlberg, *Dynamic Policy Interactions in a Monetary Union*,
DOI 10.1007/978-3-642-18228-0_3, © Springer-Verlag Berlin Heidelberg 2011

An increase in A requires an increase in government purchases. And a cut in money supply requires an increase in government purchases as well.

The Nash equilibrium is determined by the reaction functions of the central bank and the government. From the reaction function of the central bank follows:

$$\frac{dM}{dG} = -1 \tag{5}$$

And from the reaction function of the government follows:

$$\frac{dG}{dM} = -1 \tag{6}$$

That is to say, the reaction curves do not intersect. As a result there is no Nash equilibrium.

2) The dynamic model. We assume that the government and the central bank decide sequentially. First the government decides, then the central bank decides. Step 1 refers to a specific shock. Step 2 refers to the time lag. Step 3 refers to fiscal policy. Step 4 refers to the time lag. Step 5 refers to monetary policy. Step 6 refers to the time lag. Step 7 refers to fiscal policy. Step 8 refers to the time lag. Step 9 refers to monetary policy. Step 10 refers to the time lag. And so on.

Now have a closer look at the dynamic model. Step 1 refers to a specific shock. This could be a demand shock, a supply shock or a mixed shock. Step 2 refers to the time lag. This includes both the inside lag and the outside lag. Step 3 refers to fiscal policy. The government sets its purchases so as to achieve zero unemployment. The reaction function of the government is:

$$G = A - M \tag{7}$$

Step 4 refers to the time lag. Step 5 refers to monetary policy. The central bank sets its money supply so as to achieve zero inflation. The reaction function of the central bank is:

$$M = -B - G \tag{8}$$

Step 6 refers to the time lag. Step 7 refers to fiscal policy. The government sets its purchases so as to achieve zero unemployment. The reaction function of the government is:

$$G = A - M \tag{9}$$

Step 8 refers to the time lag. Step 9 refers to monetary policy. The central bank sets its money supply so as to achieve zero inflation. The reaction function of the central bank is:

$$M = -B - G \tag{10}$$

Step 10 refers to the time lag. And so on. Then what are the dynamic characteristics of this process?

1.2. Some Numerical Examples

It proves useful to study four distinct cases:

- a demand shock
- a supply shock
- a mixed shock
- another mixed shock.

The target of the government is zero unemployment. By contrast, the target of the central bank is zero inflation.

1) A demand shock. Let initial unemployment be zero, and let initial inflation be zero as well. Step one refers to a decline in aggregate demand. In terms of the model there is an increase in A of 2 units and a decline in B of equally 2 units. Step two refers to the time lag. Unemployment goes from zero to 2 percent. And inflation goes from zero to – 2 percent.

Step three refers to fiscal policy. Current unemployment is two percent, and target unemployment is zero percent. So what is needed is an increase in government purchases of 2 units. Step four refers to the time lag. Unemployment goes from 2 to zero percent. And inflation goes from – 2 to zero percent. Step five refers to monetary policy. Current inflation and target inflation are zero percent each. So what is needed is no change in money supply. Step six refers to the time lag. Unemployment stays at zero percent, as does inflation. Table 1.13 presents a synopsis.

Table 1.13
Sequential Policy Decisions
A Demand Shock

Unemployment	2	Inflation	– 2
Change in Govt Purchases	2		
Unemployment	0	Inflation	0
Change in Money Supply	0		
Unemployment	0	Inflation	0

As a result, given a demand shock, sequential policy decisions produce zero unemployment and zero inflation. There is an increase in government purchases but no change in money supply. The loss functions of the central bank and the government are respectively:

$$L_1 = \pi^2 \tag{1}$$

$$L_2 = u^2 \tag{2}$$

The initial loss of the central bank is zero, as is the initial loss of the government. The demand shock causes a loss to the central bank of 4 units and a loss to the government of equally 4 units. Then sequential policy decisions bring the loss of the central bank and the government down to zero each.

2) A supply shock. Let initial unemployment and inflation be zero each. Step one refers to the supply shock. In terms of the model there is an increase in B of 2 units and an increase in A of equally 2 units. Step two refers to the time lag. Inflation goes from zero to 2 percent. And unemployment goes from zero to 2 percent as well.

Step three refers to fiscal policy. Current unemployment is 2 percent, and target unemployment is zero percent. So what is needed is an increase in government purchases of 2 units. Step four refers to the time lag. Unemployment goes from 2 to zero percent. And inflation goes from 2 to 4 percent. Step five refers to monetary policy. Current inflation is 4 percent, and target inflation is zero percent. So what is needed is a reduction in money supply of 4 units. Step six refers to the time lag. Unemployment goes from zero to 4 percent. And inflation goes from 4 to zero percent.

Step seven refers to fiscal policy. Current unemployment is 4 percent, and target unemployment is zero percent. So what is needed is an increase in government purchases of 4 units. Step eight refers to the time lag. Unemployment goes from 4 to zero percent. And inflation goes from zero to 4 percent. Step nine refers to monetary policy. Current inflation is 4 percent, and target inflation is zero percent. So what is needed is a reduction in money supply of 4 units. Step ten refers to the time lag. Unemployment goes from zero to 4 percent. And inflation goes from 4 to zero percent. And so on. Table 1.14 gives an overview.

As a result, given a supply shock, sequential policy decisions cause uniform oscillations in unemployment and inflation. The economy oscillates between unemployment and full employment. Correspondingly, the economy oscillates between price stability and inflation. And what is more, there is an explosion of government purchases and an implosion of money supply.

Table 1.14
Sequential Policy Decisions
A Supply Shock

Unemployment	2	Inflation	2
Change in Govt Purchases	2		
Unemployment	0	Inflation	4
Change in Money Supply	– 4		
Unemployment	4	Inflation	0
Change in Govt Purchases	4		
Unemployment	0	Inflation	4
Change in Money Supply	– 4		
Unemployment	4	Inflation	0
and so on			

3) A mixed shock. Let initial unemployment and inflation be zero each. Step one refers to the mixed shock. In terms of the model there is an increase in B of 4 units. Step two refers to the time lag. Inflation goes from zero to 4 percent. And unemployment stays at zero percent.

Step three refers to fiscal policy. Current unemployment is zero percent, and target unemployment is the same. So what is needed is no change in government purchases. Step four refers to the time lag. Unemployment stays at zero percent, and inflation stays at 4 percent. Step five refers to monetary policy. Current inflation is 4 percent, and target inflation is zero percent. So what is needed is a reduction in money supply of 4 units. Step six refers to the time lag. Unemployment goes from zero to 4 percent. And inflation goes from 4 to zero percent.

Step seven refers to fiscal policy. Current unemployment is 4 percent, and target unemployment is zero percent. So what is needed is an increase in government purchases of 4 units. Step eight refers to the time lag. Unemployment goes from 4 to zero percent. And inflation goes from zero to 4 percent. Step nine refers to monetary policy. Current inflation is 4 percent, and target inflation is zero percent. So what is needed is a reduction in money supply of 4 units. Step ten refers to the time lag. Unemployment goes from zero to 4 percent. And inflation goes from 4 to zero percent. And so on. For a synopsis see Table 1.15.

Table 1.15
Sequential Policy Decisions
A Mixed Shock

Unemployment	0	Inflation	4
Change in Govt Purchases	0		
Unemployment	0	Inflation	4
Change in Money Supply	– 4		
Unemployment	4	Inflation	0
Change in Govt Purchases	4		
Unemployment	0	Inflation	4
Change in Money Supply	– 4		
Unemployment	4	Inflation	0
and so on			

As a result, given a mixed shock, sequential policy decisions cause uniform oscillations in unemployment and inflation. The economy oscillates between unemployment and full employment. Correspondingly, the economy oscillates between price stability and inflation. And what is more, there is an explosion of government purchases and an implosion of money supply.

4) Another type of a mixed shock. Let initial unemployment and inflation be zero each. Step one refers to the mixed shock. In terms of the model there is an increase in A of 4 units. Step two refers to the time lag. Unemployment goes from zero to 4 percent. And inflation stays at zero percent.

Step three refers to fiscal policy. Current unemployment is 4 percent, and target unemployment is zero percent. So what is needed is an increase in government purchases of 4 units. Step four refers to the time lag. Unemployment goes from 4 to zero percent. And inflation goes from zero to 4 percent. Step five refers to monetary policy. Current inflation is 4 percent, and target inflation is zero percent. So what is needed is a reduction in money supply of 4 units. Step six refers to the time lag. Unemployment goes from zero to 4 percent. And inflation goes from 4 to zero percent. And so on. For an overview see table 1.16.

Table 1.16
Sequential Policy Decisions
Another Mixed Shock

Unemployment	4	Inflation	0
Change in Govt Purchases	4		
Unemployment	0	Inflation	4
Change in Money Supply	– 4		
Unemployment	4	Inflation	0
and so on			

As a result, given another type of a mixed shock, sequential policy decisions cause uniform oscillations in unemployment and inflation. The economy oscillates between unemployment and full employment. Correspondingly, the economy oscillates between price stability and inflation. And what is more, there is an explosion of government purchases and an implosion of money supply.

5) Summary. Given a demand shock, sequential policy decisions produce zero unemployment and zero inflation. There is an increase in government purchases but no change in money supply. Given a supply shock, sequential policy decisions cause uniform oscillations in unemployment and inflation. And what is more, there is an explosion of government purchases and an implosion of money supply. And much the same applies to mixed shocks.

2. Target System B

2.1. The Model

1) The static model. The central bank has two targets, that is zero inflation and zero unemployment. By contrast, the government has a single target, that is zero unemployment. The model of unemployment and inflation can be characterized by a system of two equations:

$$u = A - M - G \tag{1}$$

$$\pi = B + M + G \tag{2}$$

An increase in money supply lowers unemployment. On the other hand, it raises inflation. Correspondingly, an increase in government purchases lowers unemployment. On the other hand, it raises inflation.

The targets of the central bank are zero inflation and zero unemployment. The instrument of the central bank is money supply. There are two targets but only one instrument, so what is needed is a loss function. We assume that the central bank has a quadratic loss function:

$$L_1 = \pi^2 + u^2 \tag{3}$$

L_1 is the loss to the central bank caused by inflation and unemployment. For ease of exposition we assume equal weights in the loss function. The specific target of the central bank is to minimize the loss, given the inflation function and the unemployment function. Taking account of equations (1) and (2), the loss function of the central bank can be written as follows:

$$L_1 = (B + M + G)^2 + (A - M - G)^2 \tag{4}$$

Then the first-order condition for a minimum loss gives the reaction function of the central bank:

$$2M = A - B - 2G \tag{5}$$

An increase in A requires an increase in money supply. An increase in B requires a cut in money supply. And an increase in government purchases requires a cut in money supply too.

The target of the government is zero unemployment. The instrument of the government is its purchases. By equation (1), the reaction function of the government is:

$$G = A - M \tag{6}$$

An increase in A requires an increase in government purchases. An increase in B requires no change in government purchases. And a cut in money supply requires an increase in government purchases.

The Nash equilibrium is determined by the reaction functions of the central bank and the government. From the reaction function of the central bank follows:

$$\frac{dM}{dG} = -1 \tag{7}$$

And from the reaction function of the government follows:

$$\frac{dG}{dM} = -1 \tag{8}$$

That is to say, the reaction curves do not intersect. As a result there is no Nash equilibrium.

2) The dynamic model. We assume that the government and the central bank decide sequentially. First the government decides, then the central bank decides. Step 1 refers to a specific shock. Step 2 refers to the time lag. Step 3 refers to fiscal policy. Step 4 refers to the time lag. Step 5 refers to monetary policy. Step 6 refers to the time lag. Step 7 refers to fiscal policy. Step 8 refers to the time lag. Step 9 refers to monetary policy. Step 10 refers to the time lag. And so on.

Now take a closer look at the dynamic model. Step 1 refers to a specific shock. Step 2 refers to the time lag. Step 3 refers to fiscal policy. The government sets its purchases so as to achieve zero unemployment. The reaction function of the government is:

$$G = A - M \tag{9}$$

Step 4 refers to the time lag. Step 5 refers to monetary policy. The central bank sets its money supply so as to reduce its loss. The reaction function of the central bank is:

$$2M = A - B - 2G \tag{10}$$

Step 6 refers to the time lag. Step 7 refers to fiscal policy. The government sets its purchases so as to achieve zero unemployment. The reaction function of the government is:

$$G = A - M \tag{11}$$

Step 8 refers to the time lag. Step 9 refers to monetary policy. The central bank sets its money supply so as to reduce its loss. The reaction function of the central bank is:

$$2M = A - B - 2G \tag{12}$$

Step 10 refers to the time lag. And so on. Then what are the dynamic characteristics of this process?

2.2. Some Numerical Examples

Here are four distinct cases:

- a demand shock
- a supply shock
- a mixed shock
- another mixed shock.

The government has a single target, that is zero unemployment. By contrast, the central bank has two targets, that is zero inflation and zero unemployment.

1) A demand shock. Let initial unemployment be zero, and let initial inflation be zero as well. Step one refers to a decline in aggregate demand. In terms of the model there is an increase in A of 2 units and a decline in B of equally 2 units. Step two refers to the time lag. Unemployment goes from zero to 2 percent. And inflation goes from zero to – 2 percent.

Step three refers to fiscal policy. Current unemployment is 2 percent, and target unemployment is zero percent. So what is needed is an increase in government purchases of 2 units. Step four refers to the time lag. Unemployment goes from 2 to zero percent. And inflation goes from – 2 to zero percent. Step five refers to monetary policy. Current unemployment and current inflation are zero percent each. Accordingly, target unemployment and target inflation are zero percent each. So what is needed is no change in money supply. Step six refers to the time lag. Unemployment stays at zero percent, as does inflation. Table 1.17 presents a synopsis.

As a result, given a demand shock, sequential policy decisions produce zero unemployment and zero inflation. There is an increase in government purchases but no change in money supply. The loss functions of the central bank and the government are respectively:

$$L_1 = \pi^2 + u^2 \tag{1}$$

$$L_2 = u^2 \tag{2}$$

The initial loss of the central bank is zero, as is the initial loss of the government. The demand shock causes a loss to the central bank of 8 units and a loss to the government of 4 units. Then sequential policy decisions bring the loss of the central bank and the government down to zero each.

Table 1.17
Sequential Policy Decisions
A Demand Shock

Unemployment	2	Inflation	– 2
Change in Govt Purchases	2		
Unemployment	0	Inflation	0
Change in Money Supply	0		
Unemployment	0	Inflation	0

2) A supply shock. Let initial unemployment and inflation be zero each. Step one refers to the supply shock. In terms of the model there is an increase in B of 2 units and an increase in A of equally 2 units. Step two refers to the time lag. Inflation goes from zero to 2 percent. And unemployment goes from zero to 2 percent as well.

Step three refers to fiscal policy. Current unemployment is 2 percent, and target unemployment is zero percent. So what is needed is an increase in government purchases of 2 units. Step four refers to the time lag. Unemployment goes from 2 to zero percent. And inflation goes from 2 to 4 percent. Step five refers to monetary policy. Current unemployment is zero percent, and current inflation is 4 percent. Accordingly, target unemployment and target inflation are 2 percent each. So what is needed is a reduction in money supply of 2 units. Step six refers to the time lag. Unemployment goes from zero to 2 percent. And inflation goes from 4 to 2 percent. And so on. Table 1.18 gives an overview.

As a result, given a supply shock, sequential policy decisions cause uniform oscillations in unemployment and inflation. The economy oscillates between unemployment and full employment. Correspondingly, the economy oscillates between low and high inflation. And what is more, there is an explosion of government purchases and an implosion of money supply.

Table 1.18
Sequential Policy Decisions
A Supply Shock

Unemployment	2	Inflation	2
Change in Govt Purchases	2		
Unemployment	0	Inflation	4
Change in Money Supply	– 2		
Unemployment	2	Inflation	2
and so on			

3) A mixed shock. Let initial unemployment and inflation be zero each. Step one refers to the mixed shock. In terms of the model there is an increase in B of 4 units. Step two refers to the time lag. Inflation goes from zero to 4 percent. And unemployment stays at zero percent.

Step three refers to fiscal policy. Current unemployment is zero percent, and target unemployment is the same. So what is needed is no change in government purchases. Step four refers to the time lag. Unemployment stays at zero percent, and inflation stays at 4 percent. Step five refers to monetary policy. Current unemployment is zero percent, and current inflation is 4 percent. Accordingly, target unemployment and target inflation are 2 percent each. So what is needed is a reduction in money supply of 2 units. Step six refers to the time lag. Unemployment goes from zero to 2 percent. And inflation goes from 4 to 2 percent.

Step seven refers to fiscal policy. Current unemployment is 2 percent, and target unemployment is zero percent. So what is needed is an increase in government purchases of 2 units. Step eight refers to the time lag. Unemployment goes from 2 to zero percent. And inflation goes from 2 to 4 percent. Step nine refers to monetary policy. Current unemployment is zero percent, and current inflation is 4 percent. Accordingly, target unemployment and target inflation are 2 percent each. So what is needed is a reduction in money supply of 2 units. Step ten refers to the time lag. Unemployment goes from zero to 2 percent. And inflation goes from 4 to 2 percent. And so on. For a synopsis see Table 1.19.

Table 1.19
Sequential Policy Decisions
A Mixed Shock

Unemployment	0	Inflation	4
Change in Govt Purchases	0		
Unemployment	0	Inflation	4
Change in Money Supply	– 2		
Unemployment	2	Inflation	2
Change in Govt Purchases	2		
Unemployment	0	Inflation	4
Change in Money Supply	– 2		
Unemployment	2	Inflation	2
and so on			

As a result, given a mixed shock, sequential policy decisions cause uniform oscillations in unemployment and inflation. The economy oscillates between unemployment and full employment. Correspondingly, the economy oscillates between low and high inflation. And what is more, there is an explosion of government purchases and an implosion of money supply.

4) Another type of a mixed shock. Let initial unemployment and inflation be zero each. Step one refers to the mixed shock. In terms of the model there is an increase in A of 4 units. Step two refers to the time lag. Unemployment goes from zero to 4 percent. And inflation stays at zero percent.

Step three refers to fiscal policy. Current unemployment is 4 percent, and target unemployment is zero percent. So what is needed is an increase in government purchases of 4 units. Step four refers to the time lag. Unemployment goes from 4 to zero percent. And inflation goes from zero to 4 percent. Step five refers to monetary policy. Current unemployment is zero percent, and current inflation is 4 percent. Accordingly, target unemployment and target inflation are 2 percent each. So what is needed is a reduction in money supply of 2 units. Step six refers to the time lag. Unemployment goes from zero to 2 percent. And inflation goes from 4 to 2 percent.

Step seven refers to fiscal policy. Current unemployment is 2 percent, and target unemployment is zero percent. So what is needed is an increase in government purchases of 2 units. Step eight refers to the time lag. Unemployment goes from 2 to zero percent. And inflation goes from 2 to 4 percent. Step nine refers to monetary policy. Current unemployment is zero percent, and current inflation is 4 percent. Accordingly, target unemployment and target inflation are 2 percent each. So what is needed is a reduction in money supply of 2 units. Step ten refers to the time lag. Unemployment goes from zero to 2 percent. And inflation goes from 4 to 2 percent. And so on. For an overview see Table 1.20.

As a result, given another type of a mixed shock, sequential policy decisions cause uniform oscillations in unemployment and inflation. The economy oscillates between unemployment and full employment. Correspondingly, the economy oscillates between low and high inflation. And what is more, there is an explosion of government purchases and an implosion of money supply.

5) Summary. Given a demand shock, sequential policy decisions produce zero unemployment and zero inflation. There is an increase in government

purchases and no change in money supply. Given a supply shock, sequential policy decisions cause uniform oscillations in unemployment and inflation. And what is more, there is an explosion of government purchases and an implosion of money supply. And much the same applies to mixed shocks.

Table 1.20
Sequential Policy Decisions
Another Mixed Shock

Unemployment	4	Inflation	0
Change in Govt Purchases	4		
Unemployment	0	Inflation	4
Change in Money Supply	– 2		
Unemployment	2	Inflation	2
Change in Govt Purchases	2		
Unemployment	0	Inflation	4
Change in Money Supply	– 2		
Unemployment	2	Inflation	2
and so on			

3. Target System C

3.1. The Model

1) The static model. The targets of the central bank are zero inflation and zero unemployment. And the targets of the government are the same. The model of unemployment and inflation can be represented by a system of two equations:

$$u = A - M - G \tag{1}$$

$$\pi = B + M + G \tag{2}$$

An increase in money supply lowers unemployment. On the other hand, it raises inflation. Correspondingly, an increase in government purchases lowers unemployment. On the other hand, it raises inflation.

The targets of the central bank are zero inflation and zero unemployment. The instrument of the central bank is money supply. There are two targets but only one instrument, so what is needed is a loss function. We assume that the central bank has a quadratic loss function:

$$L_1 = \pi^2 + u^2 \tag{3}$$

L_1 is the loss to the central bank caused by inflation and unemployment. We assume equal weights in the loss function. The specific target of the central bank is to minimize the loss, given the inflation function and the unemployment function. Taking account of equations (1) and (2), the loss function of the central bank can be written as follows:

$$L_1 = (B + M + G)^2 + (A - M - G)^2 \tag{4}$$

Then the first-order condition for a minimum loss gives the reaction function of the central bank:

$$2M = A - B - 2G \tag{5}$$

An increase in A requires an increase in money supply. An increase in B requires a cut in money supply. And an increase in government purchases requires a cut in money supply too.

The targets of the government are zero unemployment and zero inflation. The instrument of the government is its purchases. There are two targets but only one instrument, so what is needed is a loss function. We assume that the government has a quadratic loss function:

$$L_2 = u^2 + \pi^2 \tag{6}$$

L_2 is the loss to the government caused by unemployment and inflation. We assume equal weights in the loss function. The specific target of the government is to minimize the loss, given the unemployment function and the inflation function. Taking account of equations (1) and (2), the loss function of the government can be written as follows:

$$L_2 = (A - M - G)^2 + (B + M + G)^2 \tag{7}$$

Then the first-order condition for a minimum loss gives the reaction function of the government:

$$2G = A - B - 2M \tag{8}$$

An increase in A requires an increase in government purchases. An increase in B requires a cut in government purchases. And a cut in money supply requires an increase in government purchases.

The Nash equilibrium is determined by the reaction functions of the central bank and the government. Obviously, equations (5) and (8) are identical. There are two endogenous variables, money supply and government purchases. On the other hand, there is only one independent equation. As a result there are multiple Nash equilibria.

2) The dynamic model. We assume that the government and the central bank decide sequentially. First the government decides, then the central bank decides.

Step 1 refers to a specific shock. Step 2 refers to the time lag. Step 3 refers to fiscal policy. Step 4 refers to the time lag. Step 5 refers to monetary policy. Step 6 refers to the time lag. Step 7 refers to fiscal policy. Step 8 refers to the time lag. Step 9 refers to monetary policy. Step 10 refers to the time lag. And so on.

Now have a closer look at the dynamic model. Step 1 refers to a specific shock. Step 2 refers to the time lag. Step 3 refers to fiscal policy. The government sets its purchases so as to reduce its loss. The reaction function of the government is:

$$2G = A - B - 2M \tag{9}$$

Step 4 refers to the time lag. Step 5 refers to monetary policy. The central bank sets its money supply so as to reduce its loss. The reaction function of the central bank is:

$$2M = A - B - 2G \tag{10}$$

Step 6 refers to the time lag. Step 7 refers to fiscal policy. The government sets its purchases so as to reduce its loss. The reaction function of the government is:

$$2G = A - B - 2M \tag{11}$$

Step 8 refers to the time lag. Step 9 refers to monetary policy. The central bank sets its money supply so as to reduce its loss. The reaction function of the central bank is:

$$2M = A - B - 2G \tag{12}$$

Step 10 refers to the time lag. And so on. Then what are the dynamic characteristics of this process?

3.2. Some Numerical Examples

Here are four distinct cases:

- a demand shock
- a supply shock
- a mixed shock
- another mixed shock.

The targets of the government are zero unemployment and zero inflation. And the targets of the central bank are the same.

1) A demand shock. Let initial unemployment be zero, and let initial inflation be zero as well. Step one refers to a decline in aggregate demand. In terms of the model there is an increase in A of 2 units and a decline in B of equally 2 units. Step two refers to the time lag. Unemployment goes from zero to 2 percent. And inflation goes from zero to – 2 percent.

Step three refers to fiscal policy. Current unemployment is 2 percent, and current inflation is – 2 percent. Accordingly, target unemployment and target inflation are zero percent each. So what is needed is an increase in government purchases of 2 units. Step four refers to the time lag. Unemployment goes from 2 to zero percent. And inflation goes from – 2 to zero percent. Step five refers to monetary policy. Current unemployment and current inflation are zero percent each. Accordingly, target unemployment and target inflation are zero percent each. So what is needed is no change in money supply. Step six refers to the time lag. Unemployment stays at zero percent, as does inflation. Table 1.21 presents a synopsis.

As a result, given a demand shock, sequential policy decisions produce zero unemployment and zero inflation. There is an increase in government purchases but no change in money supply. The loss functions of the central bank and the government are respectively:

$$L_1 = \pi^2 + u^2 \tag{1}$$

$$L_2 = \pi^2 + u^2 \tag{2}$$

The initial loss of the central bank is zero, as is the initial loss of the government. The demand shock causes a loss to the central bank of 8 units and a loss to the government of equally 8 units. Then sequential policy decisions bring the loss of the central bank and the government down to zero each.

Table 1.21
Sequential Policy Decisions
A Demand Shock

Unemployment	2	Inflation	– 2
Change in Govt Purchases	2		
Unemployment	0	Inflation	0
Change in Money Supply	0		
Unemployment	0	Inflation	0

2) A supply shock. Let initial unemployment and inflation be zero each. Step one refers to the supply shock. In terms of the model there is an increase in B of 2 units and an increase in A of equally 2 units. Step two refers to the time lag. Inflation goes from zero to 2 percent. And unemployment goes from zero to 2 percent as well.

Step three refers to fiscal policy. Current unemployment and current inflation are 2 percent each. Accordingly, target unemployment and target inflation are 2 percent each. So what is needed is no change in government purchases. Step four refers to the time lag. Unemployment stays at 2 percent, as does inflation. Step five refers to monetary policy. Current unemployment and current inflation are 2 percent each. Accordingly, target unemployment and target inflation are 2 percent each. So what is needed is no change in money supply. Step six refers to the time lag. Unemployment stays at 2 percent, as does inflation. Table 1.22 gives an overview.

As a result, given a supply shock, sequential policy decisions are ineffective. There is no change in government purchases and money supply. Correspondingly, there is no change in unemployment and inflation. The initial loss of the central bank is zero, as is the initial loss of the government. The supply shock causes a loss to the central bank of 8 units and a loss to the government of equally 8 units. Then sequential policy decisions keep the loss of the central bank and the government at 8 units each.

Table 1.22
Sequential Policy Decisions
A Supply Shock

Unemployment	2	Inflation	2
Change in Govt Purchases	0		
Unemployment	2	Inflation	2
Change in Money Supply	0		
Unemployment	2	Inflation	2

3) A mixed shock. Let initial unemployment and inflation be zero each. Step one refers to the mixed shock. In terms of the model there is an increase in B of 4 units. Step two refers to the time lag. Inflation goes from zero to 4 percent. And unemployment stays at zero percent.

Step three refers to fiscal policy. Current unemployment is zero percent, and current inflation is 4 percent. Accordingly, target unemployment and target inflation are 2 percent each. So what is needed is a reduction in government purchases of 2 units. Step four refers to the time lag. Unemployment goes from zero to 2 percent. And inflation goes from 4 to 2 percent. Step five refers to monetary policy. Current unemployment and current inflation are 2 percent each. Accordingly, target unemployment and target inflation are 2 percent each. So what is needed is no change in money supply. Step six refers to the time lag.

Unemployment stays at 2 percent, as does inflation. For a synopsis see Table 1.23.

As a result, given a mixed shock, sequential policy decisions lower inflation. On the other hand, they raise unemployment. There is a reduction in government purchases but no change in money supply. The initial loss of the central bank is zero, as is the initial loss of the government. The mixed shock causes a loss to the central bank of 16 units and a loss to the government of equally 16 units. Then sequential policy decisions bring the loss of the central bank and the government down to 8 units each.

Table 1.23
Sequential Policy Decisions
A Mixed Shock

Unemployment	0	Inflation	4
Change in Govt Purchases	– 2		
Unemployment	2	Inflation	2
Change in Money Supply	0		
Unemployment	2	Inflation	2

4) Another type of a mixed shock. Let initial unemployment and inflation be zero each. Step one refers to the mixed shock. In terms of the model there is an increase in A of 4 units. Step two refers to the time lag. Unemployment goes from zero to 4 percent. And inflation stays at zero percent.

Step three refers to fiscal policy. Current unemployment is 4 percent, and current inflation is zero percent. Accordingly, target unemployment and target inflation are 2 percent each. So what is needed is an increase in government purchases of 2 units. Step four refers to the time lag. Unemployment goes from 4 to 2 percent. And inflation goes from zero to 2 percent. Step five refers to monetary policy. Current unemployment and current inflation are 2 percent each.

Accordingly, target unemployment and target inflation are 2 percent each. So what is needed is no change in money supply. Step six refers to the time lag. Unemployment stays at 2 percent, as does inflation. For an overview see Table 1.24.

As a result, given another type of a mixed shock, sequential policy decisions lower unemployment. On the other hand, they raise inflation. There is an increase in government purchases but no change in money supply. The initial loss of the central bank is zero, as is the initial loss of the government. The mixed shock causes a loss to the central bank of 16 units and a loss to the government of equally 16 units. Then sequential policy decisions bring the loss of the central bank and the government down to 8 units each.

Table 1.24
Sequential Policy Decisions
Another Mixed Shock

Unemployment	4	Inflation	0
Change in Govt Purchases	2		
Unemployment	2	Inflation	2
Change in Money Supply	0		
Unemployment	2	Inflation	2

5) Summary. Given a demand shock, sequential policy decisions produce zero unemployment and zero inflation. There is an increase in government purchases but no change in money supply. Given a supply shock, sequential policy decisions are ineffective. There is no change in government purchases or money supply. Correspondingly, there is no change in unemployment or inflation. Given a mixed shock, sequential policy decisions lower inflation. On the other hand, they raise unemployment. There is a reduction in government purchases but no change in money supply. Given another type of a mixed shock, sequential policy decisions lower unemployment. On the other hand, they raise

inflation. There is an increase in government purchases but no change in money supply.

Chapter 3
Central Bank and Government Decide Simultaneously and Independently: Cold-Turkey Policies

1. Target System A

1.1. The Model

1) The static model. The target of the central bank is zero inflation. By contrast, the target of the government is zero unemployment. The model of unemployment and inflation can be represented by a system of two equations:

$$u = A - M - G \tag{1}$$

$$\pi = B + M + G \tag{2}$$

An increase in money supply lowers unemployment. On the other hand, it raises inflation. Correspondingly, an increase in government purchases lowers unemployment. On the other hand, it raises inflation.

The target of the central bank is zero inflation. The instrument of the central bank is money supply. By equation (2), the reaction function of the central bank is:

$$M = - B - G \tag{3}$$

An increase in B requires a cut in money supply. And an increase in government purchases requires a cut in money supply too.

The target of the government is zero unemployment. The instrument of the government is its purchases. By equation (1), the reaction function of the government is:

M. Carlberg, *Dynamic Policy Interactions in a Monetary Union*,
DOI 10.1007/978-3-642-18228-0_4, © Springer-Verlag Berlin Heidelberg 2011

$$G = A - M \tag{4}$$

An increase in A requires an increase in government purchases. And a cut in money supply requires an increase in government purchases as well.

The Nash equilibrium is determined by the reaction functions of the central bank and the government. From the reaction function of the central bank follows:

$$\frac{dM}{dG} = -1 \tag{5}$$

And from the reaction function of the government follows:

$$\frac{dG}{dM} = -1 \tag{6}$$

That is to say, the reaction curves do not intersect. As a result there is no Nash equilibrium.

2) The dynamic model. We assume that the central bank and the government decide simultaneously and independently. Step 1 refers to a specific shock. Step 2 refers to the time lag. Step 3 refers to monetary and fiscal policies. Step 4 refers to the time lag. Step 5 refers to monetary and fiscal policies. Step 6 refers to the time lag. And so on.

Now have a closer look at the dynamic model. Step 1 refers to a specific shock. This could be a demand shock, a supply shock, or a mixed shock. Step 2 refers to the time lag. This includes both the inside lag and the outside lag. In step 3, the central bank and the government decide simultaneously and independently. The central bank sets its money supply so as to achieve zero inflation. The reaction function of the central bank is:

$$M = -B - G \tag{7}$$

The government sets its purchases so as to achieve zero unemployment. The reaction function of the government is:

$$G = A - M \tag{8}$$

Step 4 refers to the time lag. In step 5, the central bank and the government decide simultaneously and independently. The central bank sets its money supply so as to achieve zero inflation. The reaction function of the central bank is:

$$M = - B - G \tag{9}$$

The government sets its purchases so as to achieve zero unemployment. The reaction function of the government is:

$$G = A - M \tag{10}$$

Step 6 refers to the time lag. And so on. Then what are the dynamic characteristics of this process?

1.2. Some Numerical Examples

It proves useful to study four distinct cases:

- a demand shock
- a supply shock
- a mixed shock
- another mixed shock.

The target of the central bank is zero inflation. By contrast, the target of the government is zero unemployment.

1) A demand shock. Let initial unemployment be zero, and let initial inflation be zero as well. Step one refers to a decline in aggregate demand. In terms of the model there is an increase in A of 2 units and a decline in B of equally 2 units. Step two refers to the time lag. Unemployment goes from zero to 2 percent. And inflation goes from zero to – 2 percent.

In step three, the central bank and the government decide simultaneously and independently. First consider monetary policy. Current inflation is – 2 percent, and target inflation is zero percent. So what is needed is an increase in money supply of 2 units. Second consider fiscal policy. Current unemployment is 2 percent, and target unemployment is zero percent. So what is needed is an increase in government purchases of 2 units. Step four refers to the time lag. Unemployment goes from 2 to – 2 percent. And inflation goes from – 2 to 2 percent.

In step five, the central bank and the government decide simultaneously and independently. First consider monetary policy. Current inflation is 2 percent, and target inflation is zero percent. So what is needed is a reduction in money supply of 2 units. Second consider fiscal policy. Current unemployment is – 2 percent, and target unemployment is zero percent. So what is needed is a reduction in government purchases of 2 units. Step six refers to the time lag. Unemployment goes from – 2 to 2 percent. And inflation goes from 2 to – 2 percent. And so on. Table 1.25 presents a synopsis.

Table 1.25
Simultaneous and Independent Policy Decisions
A Demand Shock

Unemployment	2	Inflation	– 2
Change in Money Supply	2	Change in Govt Purchases	2
Unemployment	– 2	Inflation	2
Change in Money Supply	– 2	Change in Govt Purchases	– 2
Unemployment	2	Inflation	– 2
and so on			

As a result, given a demand shock, simultaneous and independent policy decisions cause uniform oscillations in unemployment and inflation. The economy oscillates between unemployment and overemployment. Correspondingly, the economy oscillates between deflation and inflation. And what is more, there are uniform oscillations in money supply and government purchases.

2) A supply shock. Let initial unemployment and inflation be zero each. Step one refers to the supply shock. In terms of the model there is an increase in B of 2 units and an increase in A of equally 2 units. Step two refers to the time lag. Inflation goes from zero to 2 percent. And unemployment goes from zero to 2 percent as well.

In step three, the central bank and the government decide simultaneously and independently. First consider monetary policy. Current inflation is 2 percent, and target inflation is zero percent. So what is needed is a reduction in money supply of 2 units. Second consider fiscal policy. Current unemployment is 2 percent, and target unemployment is zero percent. So what is needed is an increase in government purchases of 2 units. Step four refers to the time lag. Unemployment stays at 2 percent, as does inflation.

In step five, the central bank and the government decide simultaneously and independently. First consider monetary policy. Current inflation is 2 percent, and target inflation is zero percent. So what is needed is a reduction in money supply of 2 units. Second consider fiscal policy. Current unemployment is 2 percent, and target unemployment is zero percent. So what is needed is an increase in government purchases of 2 units. Step six refers to the time lag. Unemployment stays at 2 percent, as does inflation. And so on. Table 1.26 gives an overview.

As a result, given a supply shock, simultaneous and independent policy decisions have no effect on unemployment and inflation. And what is more, there is an explosion of government purchases and an implosion of money supply.

Table 1.26
Simultaneous and Independent Policy Decisions
A Supply Shock

Unemployment	2	Inflation	2
Change in Money Supply	– 2	Change in Govt Purchases	2
Unemployment	2	Inflation	2
Change in Money Supply	– 2	Change in Govt Purchases	2
Unemployment	2	Inflation	2
and so on			

3) A mixed shock. Let initial unemployment and inflation be zero each. Step one refers to the mixed shock. In terms of the model there is an increase in B of 2 units. Step two refers to the time lag. Inflation goes from zero to 2 percent. And unemployment stays at zero percent.

In step three, the central bank and the government decide simultaneously and independently. First consider monetary policy. Current inflation is 2 percent, and target inflation is zero percent. So what is needed is a reduction in money supply of 2 units. Second consider fiscal policy. Current unemployment and target unemployment are zero percent each. So what is needed is no change in government purchases. Step four refers to the time lag. Unemployment goes from zero to 2 percent. And inflation goes from 2 to zero percent.

In step five, the central bank and the government decide simultaneously and independently. First consider monetary policy. Current inflation and target inflation are zero percent each. So what is needed is no change in money supply. Second consider fiscal policy. Current unemployment is 2 percent, and target unemployment is zero percent. So what is needed is an increase in government purchases of 2 units. Step six refers to the time lag. Unemployment goes from 2 to zero percent. And inflation goes from zero to 2 percent. And so on. For a synopsis see Table 1.27.

As a result, given a mixed shock, simultaneous and independent policy decisions cause uniform oscillations in unemployment and inflation. The economy oscillates between unemployment and full employment. Correspondingly, the economy oscillates between price stability and inflation. And what is more, there is an explosion of government purchases and an implosion of money supply.

Table 1.27
Simultaneous and Independent Policy Decisions
A Mixed Shock

Unemployment	0	Inflation	2
Change in Money Supply	– 2	Change in Govt Purchases	0
Unemployment	2	Inflation	0
Change in Money Supply	0	Change in Govt Purchases	2
Unemployment	0	Inflation	2
and so on			

4) Another type of a mixed shock. Let initial unemployment and inflation be zero each. Step one refers to the mixed shock. In terms of the model there is an increase in A of 2 units. Step two refers to the time lag. Unemployment goes from zero to 2 percent. And inflation stays at zero percent.

In step three, the central bank and the government decide simultaneously and independently. First consider monetary policy. Current inflation and target inflation are zero percent each. So what is needed is no change in money supply. Second consider fiscal policy. Current unemployment is 2 percent, and target unemployment is zero percent. So what is needed is an increase in government purchases of 2 units. Step four refers to the time lag. Unemployment goes from 2 to zero percent. And inflation goes from zero to 2 percent.

In step five, the central bank and the government decide simultaneously and independently. First consider monetary policy. Current inflation is 2 percent, and target inflation is zero percent. So what is needed is a reduction in money supply of 2 units. Second consider fiscal policy. Current unemployment and target unemployment are zero percent each. So what is needed is no change in government purchases. Step six refers to the time lag. Unemployment goes from zero to 2 percent. And inflation goes from 2 to zero percent. And so on. For an overview see Table 1.28.

As a result, given another type of a mixed shock, simultaneous and independent policy decisions cause uniform oscillations in unemployment and inflation. The economy oscillates between unemployment and full employment. Accordingly, the economy oscillates between price stability and inflation. And what is more, there is an explosion of government purchases and an implosion of money supply.

Table 1.28
Simultaneous and Independent Policy Decisions
Another Mixed Shock

Unemployment	2	Inflation	0
Change in Money Supply	0	Change in Govt Purchases	2
Unemployment	0	Inflation	2
Change in Money Supply	– 2	Change in Govt Purchases	0
Unemployment	2	Inflation	0
and so on			

5) Summary. Given a demand shock, simultaneous and independent policy decisions cause uniform oscillations in unemployment and inflation. And what is more, there are uniform oscillations in government purchases and money supply.

Given a supply shock, simultaneous and independent policy decisions have no effect on unemployment and inflation. And what is more, there is an explosion of government purchases and an implosion of money supply. Given a mixed shock, simultaneous and independent policy decisions cause uniform oscillations in unemployment and inflation. And what is more, there is an explosion of government purchases and an implosion of money supply.

2. Target System B

2.1. The Model

1) The static model. The central bank has two targets, that is zero inflation and zero unemployment. By contrast, the government has a single target, that is zero unemployment. The model of unemployment and inflation can be characterized by a system of two equations:

$$u = A - M - G \tag{1}$$

$$\pi = B + M + G \tag{2}$$

An increase in money supply lowers unemployment. On the other hand, it raises inflation. Correspondingly, an increase in government purchases lowers unemployment. On the other hand, it raises inflation.

The targets of the central bank are zero inflation and zero unemployment. The instrument of the central bank is money supply. There are two targets but only one instrument, so what is needed is a loss function. We assume that the central bank has a quadratic loss function:

$$L_1 = \pi^2 + u^2 \tag{3}$$

L_1 is the loss to the central bank caused by inflation and unemployment. For ease of exposition we assume equal weights in the loss function. The specific target of the central bank is to minimize the loss, given the inflation function and the unemployment function. Taking account of equations (1) and (2), the loss function of the central bank can be written as follows:

$$L_1 = (B + M + G)^2 + (A - M - G)^2 \tag{4}$$

Then the first-order condition for a minimum loss gives the reaction function of the central bank:

$$2M = A - B - 2G \tag{5}$$

An increase in A requires an increase in money supply. An increase in B requires a cut in money supply. And an increase in government purchases requires a cut in money supply too.

The target of the government is zero unemployment. The instrument of the government is its purchases. By equation (1), the reaction function of the government is:

$$G = A - M \tag{6}$$

An increase in A requires an increase in government purchases. An increase in B requires no change in government purchases. And a cut in money supply requires an increase in government purchases.

The Nash equilibrium is determined by the reaction functions of the central bank and the government. From the reaction function of the central bank follows:

$$\frac{dM}{dG} = -1 \tag{7}$$

And from the reaction function of the government follows:

$$\frac{dG}{dM} = -1 \tag{8}$$

That is to say, the reaction curves do not intersect. As a result there is no Nash equilibrium.

2) The dynamic model. We assume that the central bank and the government decide simultaneously and independently. Step 1 refers to a specific shock. Step 2 refers to the time lag. Step 3 refers to monetary and fiscal policies. Step 4 refers to the time lag. Step 5 refers to monetary and fiscal policies. Step 6 refers to the time lag. And so on.

Now take a closer look at the dynamic model. Step 1 refers to a specific shock. Step 2 refers to the time lag. In step 3, the central bank and the government decide simultaneously and independently. The central bank sets its money supply so as to reduce its loss. The reaction function of the central bank is:

$$2M = A - B - 2G \tag{9}$$

The government sets its purchases so as to achieve zero unemployment. The reaction function of the government is:

$$G = A - M \tag{10}$$

Step 4 refers to the time lag. In step 5, the central bank and the government decide simultaneously and independently. The central bank sets its money supply so as to reduce its loss. The reaction function of the central bank is:

$$2M = A - B - 2G \tag{11}$$

The government sets its purchases so as to achieve zero unemployment. The reaction function of the government is:

$$G = A - M \tag{12}$$

Step 6 refers to the time lag. And so on. Then what are the dynamic characteristics of this process?

2.2. Some Numerical Examples

Here are four distinct cases:

- a demand shock
- a supply shock
- a mixed shock
- another mixed shock.

The central bank has two targets, that is zero inflation and zero unemployment. By contrast, the government has a single target, that is zero unemployment.

1) A demand shock. Let initial unemployment be zero, and let initial inflation be zero as well. Step one refers to a decline in aggregate demand. In terms of the model there is an increase in A of 2 units and a decline in B of equally 2 units. Step two refers to the time lag. Unemployment goes from zero to 2 percent. And inflation goes from zero to – 2 percent.

In step three, the central bank and the government decide simultaneously and independently. First consider monetary policy. Current unemployment is 2 percent, and current inflation is – 2 percent. Accordingly, target unemployment and target inflation are zero percent each. So what is needed is an increase in money supply of 2 units. Second consider fiscal policy. Current unemployment is 2 percent, and target unemployment is zero percent. So what is needed is an increase in government purchases of 2 units. Step four refers to the time lag. Unemployment goes from 2 to – 2 percent. And inflation goes from – 2 to 2 percent.

In step five, the central bank and the government decide simultaneously and independently. First consider monetary policy. Current unemployment is – 2 percent, and current inflation is 2 percent. Accordingly, target unemployment and target inflation are zero percent each. So what is needed is a reduction in money supply of 2 units. Second consider fiscal policy. Current unemployment is – 2 percent, and target unemployment is zero percent. So what is needed is a reduction in government purchases of 2 units. Step six refers to the time lag. Unemployment goes from – 2 to 2 percent. And inflation goes from 2 to – 2 percent. And so on. Table 1.29 presents a synopsis.

As a result, given a demand shock, simultaneous and independent policy decisions cause uniform oscillations in unemployment and inflation. The economy oscillates between underemployment and overemployment. Correspondingly, the economy oscillates between deflation and inflation. And what is more, there are uniform oscillations in money supply and government purchases.

Table 1.29
Simultaneous and Independent Policy Decisions
A Demand Shock

Unemployment	2	Inflation	− 2
Change in Money Supply	2	Change in Govt Purchases	2
Unemployment	− 2	Inflation	2
Change in Money Supply	− 2	Change in Govt Purchases	− 2
Unemployment	2	Inflation	− 2
and so on			

2) A supply shock. Let initial unemployment and inflation be zero each. Step one refers to the supply shock. In terms of the model there is an increase in B of 2 units and an increase in A of equally 2 units. Step two refers to the time lag. Inflation goes from zero to 2 percent. And unemployment goes from zero to 2 percent as well.

In step three, the central bank and the government decide simultaneously and independently. First consider monetary policy. Current unemployment and current inflation are 2 percent each. Accordingly, target unemployment and target inflation are 2 percent each. So what is needed is no change in money supply. Second consider fiscal policy. Current unemployment is 2 percent, and target unemployment is zero percent. So what is needed is an increase in government purchases of 2 units. Step four refers to the time lag. Unemployment goes from 2 to zero percent. And inflation goes from 2 to 4 percent.

In step five, the central bank and the government decide simultaneously and independently. First consider monetary policy. Current unemployment is zero percent, and current inflation is 4 percent. Accordingly, target unemployment and target inflation are 2 percent each. So what is needed is a reduction in money supply of 2 units. Second consider fiscal policy. Current unemployment and target unemployment are zero percent each. So what is needed is no change in government purchases. Step six refers to the time lag. Unemployment goes from zero to 2 percent. And inflation goes from 4 to 2 percent. And so on. Table 1.30 gives an overview.

As a result, given a supply shock, simultaneous and independent policy decisions cause uniform oscillations in unemployment and inflation. The economy oscillates between unemployment and full employment. Correspondingly, the economy oscillates between low and high inflation. And what is more, there is an explosion of government purchases and an implosion of money supply.

Table 1.30
Simultaneous and Independent Policy Decisions
A Supply Shock

Unemployment	2	Inflation	2
Change in Money Supply	0	Change in Govt Purchases	2
Unemployment	0	Inflation	4
Change in Money Supply	– 2	Change in Govt Purchases	0
Unemployment	2	Inflation	2
and so on			

3) A mixed shock. Let initial unemployment and inflation be zero each. Step one refers to the mixed shock. In terms of the model there is an increase in B of 2 units. Step two refers to the time lag. Inflation goes from zero to 2 percent. And unemployment stays at zero percent.

In step three, the central bank and the government decide simultaneously and independently. First consider monetary policy. Current unemployment is zero percent, and current inflation is 2 percent. Accordingly, target unemployment and target inflation are 1 percent each. So what is needed is a reduction in money supply of 1 unit. Second consider fiscal policy. Current unemployment and target unemployment are zero percent each. So what is needed is no change in government purchases. Step four refers to the time lag. Unemployment goes from zero to 1 percent. And inflation goes from 2 to 1 percent.

In step five, the central bank and the government decide simultaneously and independently. First consider monetary policy. Current unemployment and current inflation are 1 percent each. Accordingly, target unemployment and target inflation are 1 percent each. So what is needed is no change in money supply. Second consider fiscal policy. Current unemployment is 1 percent, and target unemployment is zero percent. So what is needed is an increase in government purchases of 1 unit. Step six refers to the time lag. Unemployment goes from 1 to zero percent. And inflation goes from 1 to 2 percent. And so on. For a synopsis see Table 1.31.

As a result, given a mixed shock, simultaneous and independent policy decisions cause uniform oscillations in unemployment and inflation. The economy oscillates between unemployment and full employment. Correspondingly, the economy oscillates between low and high inflation. And what is more, there is an explosion of government purchases and an implosion of money supply.

Table 1.31
Simultaneous and Independent Policy Decisions
A Mixed Shock

Unemployment	0	Inflation	2
Change in Money Supply	– 1	Change in Govt Purchases	0
Unemployment	1	Inflation	1
Change in Money Supply	0	Change in Govt Purchases	1
Unemployment	0	Inflation	2
and so on			

4) Another type of a mixed shock. Let initial unemployment and inflation be zero each. Step one refers to the mixed shock. In terms of the model there is an increase in A of 2 units. Step two refers to the time lag. Unemployment goes from zero to 2 percent. And inflation stays at zero percent.

In step three, the central bank and the government decide simultaneously and independently. First consider monetary policy. Current unemployment is 2 percent, and current inflation is zero percent. Accordingly, target unemployment and target inflation are 1 percent each. So what is needed is an increase in money supply of 1 unit. Second consider fiscal policy. Current unemployment is 2 percent, and target unemployment is zero percent. So what is needed is an increase in government purchases of 2 units. Step four refers to the time lag. Unemployment goes from 2 to – 1 percent. And inflation goes from zero to 3 percent.

In step five, the central bank and the government decide simultaneously and independently. First consider monetary policy. Current unemployment is – 1 percent, and current inflation is 3 percent. Accordingly, target unemployment and target inflation are 1 percent each. So what is needed is a reduction in money supply of 2 units. Second consider fiscal policy. Current unemployment is – 1 percent, and target unemployment is zero percent. So what is needed is a reduction in government purchases of 1 unit. Step six refers to the time lag. Unemployment goes from – 1 to 2 percent. And inflation goes from 3 to zero percent. And so on. For an overview see Table 1.32.

As a result, given another type of a mixed shock, simultaneous and independent policy decisions cause uniform oscillations in unemployment and inflation. The economy oscillates between underemployment and overemployment. Correspondingly, the economy oscillates between price stability and inflation. And what is more, there is an explosion of government purchases and an implosion of money supply.

Table 1.32
Simultaneous and Independent Policy Decisions
Another Mixed Shock

Unemployment	2	Inflation	0
Change in Money Supply	1	Change in Govt Purchases	2
Unemployment	– 1	Inflation	3
Change in Money Supply	– 2	Change in Govt Purchases	– 1
Unemployment	2	Inflation	0
and so on			

5) Summary. Given a demand shock, simultaneous and independent policy decisions cause uniform oscillations in unemployment and inflation. And what is more, there are uniform oscillations in government purchases and money supply. Given a supply shock, simultaneous and independent policy decisions cause uniform oscillations in unemployment and inflation. And what is more, there is an explosion of government purchases and an implosion of money supply. And much the same applies to a mixed shock.

3. Target System C

3.1. The Model

1) The static model. The targets of the central bank are zero inflation and zero unemployment. And the targets of the government are the same. The model of unemployment and inflation can be represented by a system of two equations:

$$u = A - M - G \tag{1}$$

$$\pi = B + M + G \tag{2}$$

An increase in money supply lowers unemployment. On the other hand, it raises inflation. Correspondingly, an increase in government purchases lowers unemployment. On the other hand, it raises inflation.

The targets of the central bank are zero inflation and zero unemployment. The instrument of the central bank is money supply. There are two targets but only one instrument, so what is needed is a loss function. We assume that the central bank has a quadratic loss function:

$$L_1 = \pi^2 + u^2 \tag{3}$$

L_1 is the loss to the central bank caused by inflation and unemployment. We assume equal weights in the loss function. The specific target of the central bank is to minimize the loss, given the inflation function and the unemployment function. Taking account of equations (1) and (2), the loss function of the central bank can be written as follows:

$$L_1 = (B + M + G)^2 + (A - M - G)^2 \tag{4}$$

Then the first-order condition for a minimum loss gives the reaction function of the central bank:

$$2M = A - B - 2G \tag{5}$$

An increase in A requires an increase in money supply. An increase in B requires a cut in money supply. And an increase in government purchases requires a cut in money supply too.

The targets of the government are zero unemployment and zero inflation. The instrument of the government is its purchases. There are two targets but only one instrument, so what is needed is a loss function. We assume that the government has a quadratic loss function:

$$L_2 = u^2 + \pi^2 \tag{6}$$

L_2 is the loss to the government caused by unemployment and inflation. We assume equal weights in the loss function. The specific target of the government is to minimize the loss, given the unemployment function and the inflation function. Taking account of equations (1) and (2), the loss function of the government can be written as follows:

$$L_2 = (A - M - G)^2 + (B + M + G)^2 \tag{7}$$

Then the first-order condition for a minimum loss gives the reaction function of the government:

$$2G = A - B - 2M \tag{8}$$

An increase in A requires an increase in government purchases. An increase in B requires a cut in government purchases. And a cut in money supply requires an increase in government purchases.

The Nash equilibrium is determined by the reaction functions of the central bank and the government. Obviously, equations (5) and (8) are identical. There are two endogenous variables, money supply and government purchases. On the other hand, there is only one independent equation. As a result there are multiple Nash equilibria.

2) The dynamic model. We assume that the central bank and the government decide simultaneously and independently. Step 1 refers to a specific shock. Step

2 refers to the time lag. Step 3 refers to monetary and fiscal policies. Step 4 refers to the time lag. Step 5 refers to monetary and fiscal policies. Step 6 refers to the time lag. And so on.

Now have a closer look at the dynamic model. Step 1 refers to a specific shock. Step 2 refers to the time lag. In step 3, the central bank and the government decide simultaneously and independently. The central bank sets its money supply so as to reduce its loss. The reaction function of the central bank is:

$$2M = A - B - 2G \tag{9}$$

The government sets its purchases so as to reduce its loss. The reaction function of the government is:

$$2G = A - B - 2M \tag{10}$$

Step 4 refers to the time lag. In step 5, the central bank and the government decide simultaneously and independently. The central bank sets its money supply so as to reduce its loss. The reaction function of the central bank is:

$$2M = A - B - 2G \tag{11}$$

The government sets its purchases so as to reduce its loss. The reaction function of the government is:

$$2G = A - B - 2M \tag{12}$$

Step 6 refers to the time lag. And so on. Then what are the dynamic characteristics of this process?

3.2. Some Numerical Examples

Here are four distinct cases:

- a demand shock
- a supply shock
- a mixed shock
- another mixed shock.

The targets of the central bank are zero inflation and zero unemployment. And the targets of the government are the same.

1) A demand shock. Let initial unemployment be zero, and let initial inflation be zero as well. Step one refers to a decline in aggregate demand. In terms of the model there is an increase in A of 2 units and a decline in B of equally 2 units. Step two refers to the time lag. Unemployment goes from zero to 2 percent. And inflation goes from zero to – 2 percent.

In step three, the central bank and the government decide simultaneously and independently. First consider monetary policy. Current unemployment is 2 percent, and current inflation is – 2 percent. Accordingly, target unemployment and target inflation are zero percent each. So what is needed is an increase in money supply of 2 units. Second consider fiscal policy. Current unemployment is 2 percent, and current inflation is – 2 percent. Accordingly, target unemployment and target inflation are zero percent each. So what is needed is an increase in government purchases of 2 units. Step four refers to the time lag. Unemployment goes from 2 to – 2 percent. And inflation goes from – 2 to 2 percent.

In step five, the central bank and the government decide simultaneously and independently. First consider monetary policy. Current unemployment is – 2 percent, and current inflation is 2 percent. Accordingly, target unemployment and target inflation are zero percent each. So what is needed is a reduction in money supply of 2 units. Second consider fiscal policy. Current unemployment is – 2 percent, and current inflation is 2 percent. Accordingly, target unemployment and target inflation are zero percent each. So what is needed is a reduction in government purchases of 2 units. Step six refers to the time lag. Unemployment goes from – 2 to 2 percent. And inflation goes from 2 to – 2 percent. And so on. Table 1.33 presents a synopsis.

As a result, given a demand shock, simultaneous and independent policy decisions cause uniform oscillations in unemployment and inflation. The economy oscillates between underemployment and overemployment. Correspondingly, the economy oscillates between deflation and inflation. And what is more, there are uniform oscillations in money supply and government purchases.

Table 1.33
Simultaneous and Independent Policy Decisions
A Demand Shock

Unemployment	2	Inflation	– 2
Change in Money Supply	2	Change in Govt Purchases	2
Unemployment	– 2	Inflation	2
Change in Money Supply	– 2	Change in Govt Purchases	– 2
Unemployment	2	Inflation	– 2
and so on			

2) A supply shock. Let initial unemployment and inflation be zero each. Step one refers to the supply shock. In terms of the model there is an increase in B of 2 units and an increase in A of equally 2 units. Step two refers to the time lag. Inflation goes from zero to 2 percent. And unemployment goes from zero to 2 percent as well.

In step three, the central bank and the government decide simultaneously and independently. First consider monetary policy. Current unemployment and current inflation are 2 percent each. Accordingly, target unemployment and target inflation are 2 percent each. So what is needed is no change in money supply. Second consider fiscal policy. Current unemployment and current inflation are 2 percent each. Accordingly, target unemployment and target inflation are 2 percent each. So what is needed is no change in government purchases. Step four refers to the time lag. Unemployment stays at 2 percent, as does inflation. Table 1.34 gives an overview.

As a result, given a supply shock, simultaneous and independent policy decisions are ineffective. There is no change in money supply and government purchases. Correspondingly, there is no change in unemployment and inflation.

Table 1.34
Simultaneous and Independent Policy Decisions
A Supply Shock

Unemployment	2	Inflation	2
Change in Money Supply	0	Change in Govt Purchases	0
Unemployment	2	Inflation	2

3) A mixed shock. Let initial unemployment and inflation be zero each. Step one refers to the mixed shock. In terms of the model there is an increase in B of 2 units. Step two refers to the time lag. Inflation goes from zero to 2 percent. And unemployment stays at zero percent.

In step three, the central bank and the government decide simultaneously and independently. First consider monetary policy. Current unemployment is zero percent, and current inflation is 2 percent. Accordingly, target unemployment and target inflation are 1 percent each. So what is needed is a reduction in money supply of 1 unit. Second consider fiscal policy. Current unemployment is zero percent, and current inflation is 2 percent. Accordingly, target unemployment and target inflation are 1 percent each. So what is needed is a reduction in government purchases of 1 unit. Step four refers to the time lag. Unemployment goes from zero to 2 percent. And inflation goes from 2 to zero percent.

In step five, the central bank and the government decide simultaneously and independently. First consider monetary policy. Current unemployment is 2 percent, and current inflation is zero percent. Accordingly, target unemployment and target inflation are 1 percent each. So what is needed is an increase in money supply of 1 unit. Second consider fiscal policy. Current unemployment is 2 percent, and current inflation is zero percent. Accordingly, target unemployment and target inflation are 1 percent each. So what is needed is an increase in government purchases of 1 unit. Step six refers to the time lag. Unemployment goes from 2 to zero percent. And inflation goes from zero to 2 percent. And so on. For a synopsis see Table 1.35.

Table 1.35
Simultaneous and Independent Policy Decisions
A Mixed Shock

Unemployment	0	Inflation	2
Change in Money Supply	– 1	Change in Govt Purchases	– 1
Unemployment	2	Inflation	0
Change in Money Supply	1	Change in Govt Purchases	1
Unemployment	0	Inflation	2
and so on			

As a result, given a mixed shock, simultaneous and independent policy decisions cause uniform oscillations in unemployment and inflation. The economy oscillates between unemployment and full employment. Correspondingly, the economy oscillates between price stability and inflation. And what is more, there are uniform oscillations in money supply and government purchases.

4) Another type of a mixed shock. Let initial unemployment and inflation be zero each. Step one refers to the mixed shock. In terms of the model there is an increase in A of 2 units. Step two refers to the time lag. Unemployment goes from zero to 2 percent. And inflation stays at zero percent.

In step three, the central bank and the government decide simultaneously and independently. First consider monetary policy. Current unemployment is 2 percent, and current inflation is zero percent. Accordingly, target unemployment and target inflation are 1 percent each. So what is needed is an increase in money supply of 1 unit. Second consider fiscal policy. Current unemployment is 2 percent, and current inflation is zero percent. Accordingly, target unemployment and target inflation are 1 percent each. So what is needed is an increase in government purchases of 1 unit. Step four refers to the time lag. Unemployment goes from 2 to zero percent. And inflation goes from zero to 2 percent.

In step five, the central bank and the government decide simultaneously and independently. First consider monetary policy. Current unemployment is zero percent, and current inflation is 2 percent. Accordingly, target unemployment and target inflation are 1 percent each. So what is needed is a reduction in money supply of 1 unit. Second consider fiscal policy. Current unemployment is zero percent, and current inflation is 2 percent. Accordingly, target unemployment and target inflation are 1 percent each. So what is needed is a reduction in government purchases of 1 unit. Step six refers to the time lag. Unemployment goes from zero to 2 percent. And inflation goes from 2 to zero percent. And so on. For an overview see Table 1.36.

As a result, given another type of a mixed shock, simultaneous and independent policy decisions cause uniform oscillations in unemployment and inflation. The economy oscillates between unemployment and full employment. Correspondingly, the economy oscillates between price stability and inflation. And what is more, there are uniform oscillations in money supply and government purchases.

5) Summary. Given a demand shock, simultaneous and independent policy decisions cause uniform oscillations in unemployment and inflation. And what is more, there are uniform oscillations in money supply and government purchases. Given a supply shock, simultaneous and independent policy decisions are

ineffective. There is no change in money supply and government purchases. Correspondingly, there is no change in unemployment and inflation. Given a mixed shock, simultaneous and independent policy decisions cause uniform oscillations in unemployment and inflation. And what is more, there are uniform oscillations in money supply and government purchases.

Table 1.36
Simultaneous and Independent Policy Decisions
Another Mixed Shock

Unemployment	2	Inflation	0
Change in Money Supply	1	Change in Govt Purchases	1
Unemployment	0	Inflation	2
Change in Money Supply	– 1	Change in Govt Purchases	– 1
Unemployment	2	Inflation	0
and so on			

Chapter 4
Central Bank and Government Decide Simultaneously and Independently: Gradualist Policies

1. The Model

1) The static model. The target of the central bank is zero inflation. By contrast, the target of the government is zero unemployment. The model of unemployment and inflation can be characterized by a system of two equations:

$$u = A - M - G \tag{1}$$

$$\pi = B + M + G \tag{2}$$

An increase in money supply lowers unemployment. On the other hand, it raises inflation. Correspondingly, an increase in government purchases lowers unemployment. On the other hand, it raises inflation.

The target of the central bank is zero inflation. The instrument of the central bank is money supply. By equation (2), the reaction function of the central bank is:

$$M = -B - G \tag{3}$$

An increase in B requires a cut in money supply. And an increase in government purchases requires a cut in money supply too.

The target of the government is zero unemployment. The instrument of the government is its purchases. By equation (1), the reaction function of the government is:

$$G = A - M \tag{4}$$

M. Carlberg, *Dynamic Policy Interactions in a Monetary Union*,
DOI 10.1007/978-3-642-18228-0_5, © Springer-Verlag Berlin Heidelberg 2011

An increase in A requires an increase in government purchases. And a cut in money supply requires an increase in government purchases as well.

The Nash equilibrium is determined by the reaction functions of the central bank and the government. From the reaction function of the central bank follows:

$$\frac{dM}{dG} = -1 \tag{5}$$

And from the reaction function of the government follows:

$$\frac{dG}{dM} = -1 \tag{6}$$

That is to say, the reaction curves do not intersect. As a result there is no Nash equilibrium.

2) The dynamic model. The target of the central bank is to cut inflation by half. By contrast, the target of the government is to cut unemployment by half. We assume that the central bank and the government decide simultaneously and independently. Step 1 refers to a specific shock. Step 2 refers to the time lag. Step 3 refers to monetary and fiscal policies. Step 4 refers to the time lag. Step 5 refers to monetary and fiscal policies. Step 6 refers to the time lag. And so on.

Now take a closer look at the dynamic model. Step 1 refers to a specific shock. This could be a demand shock, a supply shock, or a mixed shock. Step 2 refers to the time lag. This includes both the inside lag and the outside lag. In step 3, the central bank and the government decide simultaneously and independently. The central bank sets its money supply so as to cut inflation by half. The reaction function of the central bank is:

$$2M = -B - G \tag{7}$$

The government sets its purchases so as to cut unemployment by half. The reaction function of the government is:

$$2G = A - M \quad (8)$$

Step 4 refers to the time lag. In step 5, the central bank and the government decide simultaneously and independently. The central bank sets its money supply so as to cut inflation by half. The reaction function of the central bank is:

$$2M = - B - G \quad (9)$$

The government sets its purchases so as to cut unemployment by half. The reaction function of the government is:

$$2G = A - M \quad (10)$$

Step 6 refers to the time lag. And so on. Then what are the dynamic characteristics of this process?

2. Some Numerical Examples

It proves useful to study four distinct cases:
- a demand shock
- a supply shock
- a mixed shock
- another mixed shock.

The target of the central bank is to cut inflation by half. By contrast, the target of the government is to cut unemployment by half.

1) A demand shock. Let initial unemployment be zero, and let initial inflation be zero as well. Step one refers to a decline in aggregate demand. In terms of the model there is an increase in A of 4 units and a decline in B of equally 4 units. Step two refers to the time lag. Unemployment goes from zero to 4 percent. And inflation goes from zero to – 4 percent.

In step three, the central bank and the government decide simultaneously and independently. First consider monetary policy. The central bank sets its money supply so as to cut inflation by half. Current inflation is – 4 percent, and target inflation is – 2 percent. So what is needed is an increase in money supply of 2 units. Second consider fiscal policy. The government sets its purchases so as to cut unemployment by half. Current unemployment is 4 percent, and target unemployment is 2 percent. So what is needed is an increase in government purchases of 2 units. Step four refers to the time lag. Unemployment goes from 4 to zero percent. And inflation goes from – 4 to zero percent. Table 1.37 presents a synopsis.

As a result, given a demand shock, simultaneous and independent policy decisions produce zero unemployment and zero inflation. There is an increase in both money supply and government purchases.

Table 1.37
Gradualist Policies
A Demand Shock

Unemployment	4	Inflation	– 4
Change in Money Supply	2	Change in Govt Purchases	2
Unemployment	0	Inflation	0

2) A supply shock. Let initial unemployment and inflation be zero each. Step one refers to the supply shock. In terms of the model there is an increase in B of 4 units and an increase in A of equally 4 units. Step two refers to the time lag. Inflation goes from zero to 4 percent. And unemployment goes from zero to 4 percent as well.

In step three, the central bank and the government decide simultaneously and independently. First consider monetary policy. The central bank sets its money supply so as to cut inflation by half. Current inflation is 4 percent, and target inflation is 2 percent. So what is needed is a reduction in money supply of 2 units. Second consider fiscal policy. The government sets its purchases so as to cut unemployment by half. Current unemployment is 4 percent, and target unemployment is 2 percent. So what is needed is an increase in government purchases of 2 units. Step four refers to the time lag. Unemployment stays at 4 percent, and the same holds for inflation. And so on. Table 1.38 gives an overview.

As a result, given a supply shock, simultaneous and independent policy decisions do not reduce unemployment and inflation. And what is more, there is an explosion of government purchases and an implosion of money supply.

Table 1.38
Gradualist Policies
A Supply Shock

Unemployment	4	Inflation	4
Change in Money Supply	– 2	Change in Govt Purchases	2
Unemployment	4	Inflation	4
and so on			

3) A mixed shock. Let initial unemployment and inflation be zero each. Step one refers to the mixed shock. In terms of the model there is an increase in B of 4 units. Step two refers to the time lag. Inflation goes from zero to 4 percent. And unemployment stays at zero percent.

In step three, the central bank and the government decide simultaneously and independently. First consider monetary policy. The central bank sets its money supply so as to cut inflation by half. Current inflation is 4 percent, and target inflation is 2 percent. So what is needed is a reduction in money supply of 2 units. Second consider fiscal policy. The government sets its purchases so as to cut unemployment by half. Current unemployment and target unemployment are zero percent each. So what is needed is no change in government purchases. Step four refers to the time lag. Unemployment goes from zero to 2 percent. And inflation goes from 4 to 2 percent.

In step five, the central bank and the government decide simultaneously and independently. First consider monetary policy. The central bank sets its money supply so as to cut inflation by half. Current inflation is 2 percent, and target inflation is 1 percent. So what is needed is a reduction in money supply of 1 unit. Second consider fiscal policy. The government sets its purchases so as to cut unemployment by half. Current unemployment is 2 percent, and target unemployment is 1 percent. So what is needed is an increase in government purchases of 1 unit. Step six refers to the time lag. Unemployment stays at 2 percent, and the same holds for inflation. And so on. For a synopsis see Table 1.39.

Table 1.39
Gradualist Policies
A Mixed Shock

Unemployment	0	Inflation	4
Change in Money Supply	– 2	Change in Govt Purchases	0
Unemployment	2	Inflation	2
Change in Money Supply	– 1	Change in Govt Purchases	1
Unemployment	2	Inflation	2
and so on			

As a result, given a mixed shock, simultaneous and independent policy decisions lower inflation. On the other hand, they raise unemployment. And what is more, there is an explosion of government purchases and an implosion of money supply.

4) Another type of a mixed shock. Let initial unemployment and inflation be zero each. Step one refers to the mixed shock. In terms of the model there is an increase in A of 4 units. Step two refers to the time lag. Unemployment goes from zero to 4 percent. And inflation stays at zero percent.

In step three, the central bank and the government decide simultaneously and independently. First consider monetary policy. The central bank sets its money supply so as to cut inflation by half. Current inflation and target inflation are zero percent each. So what is needed is no change in money supply. Second consider fiscal policy. The government sets its purchases so as to cut unemployment by half. Current unemployment is 4 percent, and target unemployment is 2 percent. So what is needed is an increase in government purchases of 2 units. Step four refers to the time lag. Unemployment goes from 4 to 2 percent. And inflation goes from zero to 2 percent.

In step five, the central bank and the government decide simultaneously and independently. First consider monetary policy. The central bank sets its money supply so as to cut inflation by half. Current inflation is 2 percent, and target inflation is 1 percent. So what is needed is a reduction in money supply of 1 unit. Second consider fiscal policy. The government sets its purchases so as to cut unemployment by half. Current unemployment is 2 percent, and target unemployment is 1 percent. So what is needed is an increase in government purchases of 1 unit. Step six refers to the time lag. Unemployment stays at 2 percent, as does inflation. And so on. For an overview see Table 1.40.

As a result, given another type of a mixed shock, simultaneous and independent policy decisions lower unemployment. On the other hand, they raise inflation. And what is more, there is an explosion of government purchases and an implosion of money supply.

5) Summary. Given a demand shock, simultaneous and independent policy decisions produce zero unemployment and zero inflation. There is an increase in both money supply and government purchases. Given a supply shock, simultaneous and independent policy decisions do not reduce unemployment and inflation. And what is more, there is an explosion of government purchases and an implosion of money supply.

Given a mixed shock, simultaneous and independent policy decisions lower inflation. On the other hand, they raise unemployment. And what is more, there is an explosion of government purchases and an implosion of money supply. Given another type of a mixed shock, simultaneous and independent policy decisions lower unemployment. On the other hand, they raise inflation. And what is more, there is an explosion of government purchases and an implosion of money supply.

Table 1.40
Gradualist Policies
Another Mixed Shock

Unemployment	4	Inflation	0
Change in Money Supply	0	Change in Govt Purchases	2
Unemployment	2	Inflation	2
Change in Money Supply	– 1	Change in Govt Purchases	1
Unemployment	2	Inflation	2
and so on			

Chapter 5
Central Bank and Government Cooperate

1. The Model

The model of unemployment and inflation can be represented by a system of two equations:

$$u = A - M - G \tag{1}$$

$$\pi = B + M + G \tag{2}$$

An increase in money supply lowers unemployment. On the other hand, it raises inflation. Correspondingly, an increase in government purchases lowers unemployment. On the other hand, it raises inflation.

The policy makers are the central bank and the government. The targets of policy cooperation are zero inflation and zero unemployment. The instruments of policy cooperation are money supply and government purchases. Thus there are two targets and two instruments. We assume that the policy makers agree on a common loss function:

$$L = \pi^2 + u^2 \tag{3}$$

L is the loss caused by inflation and unemployment. For ease of exposition we assume equal weights in the loss function. Of course this is a plausible assumption. Other plausible assumptions could be:

$$L = 1.5\pi^2 + 0.5u^2 \tag{4}$$

or

$$L = 0.5\pi^2 + 1.5u^2 \tag{5}$$

The specific target of policy cooperation is to minimize the loss, given the inflation function and the unemployment function. Taking account of equations (1) and (2), the loss function under policy cooperation can be written as follows:

M. Carlberg, *Dynamic Policy Interactions in a Monetary Union*,
DOI 10.1007/978-3-642-18228-0_6, © Springer-Verlag Berlin Heidelberg 2011

$$L = (B + M + G)^2 + (A - M - G)^2 \tag{6}$$

Then the first-order conditions for a minimum loss are:

$$2M = A - B - 2G \tag{7}$$

$$2G = A - B - 2M \tag{8}$$

Equation (7) shows the first-order condition with respect to money supply. And equation (8) shows the first-order condition with respect to government purchases. Obviously, equations (7) and (8) are identical. There are two endogenous variables, money supply and government purchases. On the other hand, there is only one independent equation. Thus there is an infinite number of solutions.

The cooperative equilibrium is determined by the first-order conditions for a minimum loss. The solution to this problem is as follows:

$$2M + 2G = A - B \tag{9}$$

Equation (9) yields the optimum combinations of money supply and government purchases. As a result, policy cooperation can reduce the loss caused by inflation and unemployment.

2. Some Numerical Examples

Here are four distinct cases:

- a demand shock
- a supply shock
- a mixed shock
- another mixed shock.

The targets of policy cooperation are zero inflation and zero unemployment.

1) A demand shock. Let initial unemployment be zero, and let initial inflation be zero as well. Step one refers to a decline in aggregate demand. In terms of the model there is an increase in A of 2 units and a decline in B of equally 2 units. Step two refers to the time lag. Unemployment goes from zero to 2 percent. And inflation goes from zero to – 2 percent. Step three refers to the policy response. According to the model, a first solution is an increase in money supply of 2 units and no change in government purchases. Step four refers to the time lag. Unemployment goes from 2 to zero percent. And inflation goes from – 2 to zero percent. Table 1.41 presents a synopsis.

Table 1.41
Policy Cooperation
A Demand Shock

Unemployment	2	Inflation	– 2
Change in Money Supply	2	Change in Govt Purchases	0
Unemployment	0	Inflation	0

As a result, given a demand shock, policy cooperation achieves both zero inflation and zero unemployment. A second solution is an increase in money supply of 1 unit and an increase in government purchases of equally 1 unit. A third solution is no change in money supply and an increase in government purchases of 2 units. And so on. The loss function under policy cooperation is:

$$L = \pi^2 + u^2 \tag{1}$$

The initial loss is zero. The demand shock causes a loss of 8 units. Then policy cooperation brings the loss down to zero again.

2) A supply shock. Let initial unemployment and inflation be zero each. Step one refers to the supply shock. In terms of the model there is an increase in B of 2 units and an increase in A of equally 2 units. Step two refers to the time lag. Inflation goes from zero to 2 percent. And unemployment goes from zero to 2 percent as well. Step three refers to the policy response. According to the model, a first solution is to keep money supply and government purchases constant. Step four refers to the time lag. Obviously, inflation stays at 2 percent, and unemployment stays at 2 percent as well. Table 1.42 gives an overview.

Table 1.42
Policy Cooperation
A Supply Shock

Unemployment	2	Inflation	2
Change in Money Supply	0	Change in Govt Purchases	0
Unemployment	2	Inflation	2

As a result, given a supply shock, policy cooperation is ineffective. There is no change in money supply and government purchases. Correspondingly, there is no change in unemployment and inflation. A second solution is an increase in money supply of 1 unit and a reduction in government purchases of equally 1 unit. A third solution is a reduction in money supply of 1 unit and an increase in government purchases of equally 1 unit. And so on. The initial loss is zero. The supply shock causes a loss of 8 units. However, policy cooperation cannot reduce the loss.

3) A mixed shock. Let initial unemployment and inflation be zero each. Step one refers to the mixed shock. In terms of the model there is an increase in B of 4 units. Step two refers to the time lag. Inflation goes from zero to 4 percent. And unemployment stays at zero percent. Step three refers to the policy response. According to the model, a first solution is a reduction in money supply of 2 units and no change in government purchases. Step four refers to the time lag. Unemployment goes from zero to 2 percent. And inflation goes from 4 to 2 percent. For a synopsis see Table 1.43.

Table 1.43
Policy Cooperation
A Mixed Shock

Unemployment	0	Inflation	4
Change in Money Supply	– 2	Change in Govt Purchases	0
Unemployment	2	Inflation	2

As a result, given a mixed shock, policy cooperation lowers inflation. On the other hand, it raises unemployment. A second solution is a reduction in money supply of 1 unit and a reduction in government purchases of equally 1 unit. A third solution is no change in money supply and a reduction in government purchases of 2 units. And so on. The initial loss is zero. The mixed shock causes a loss of 16 units. Then policy cooperation brings the loss down to 8 units.

4) Another type of a mixed shock. Let initial unemployment and inflation be zero each. Step one refers to the mixed shock. In terms of the model there is an increase in A of 4 units. Step two refers to the time lag. Unemployment goes from zero to 4 percent. And inflation stays at zero percent. Step three refers to the policy response. According to the model, a first solution is an increase in money

supply of 2 units and no change in government purchases. Step four refers to the time lag. Unemployment goes from 4 to 2 percent. And inflation goes from zero to 2 percent. For an overview see Table 1.44.

As a result, given another type of a mixed shock, policy cooperation lowers unemployment. On the other hand, it raises inflation. A second solution is an increase in money supply of 1 unit and an increase in government purchases of equally 1 unit. A third solution is no change in money supply and an increase in government purchases of 2 units. And so on. The initial loss is zero. The mixed shock causes a loss of 16 units. Then policy cooperation brings the loss down to 8 units.

Table 1.44
Policy Cooperation
Another Mixed Shock

Unemployment	4	Inflation	0
Change in Money Supply	2	Change in Govt Purchases	0
Unemployment	2	Inflation	2

5) Summary. Given a demand shock, policy cooperation achieves both zero unemployment and zero inflation. There is an increase in money supply or government purchases. Given a supply shock, policy cooperation is ineffective. There is no change in the sum of money supply and government purchases. Correspondingly, there is no change in unemployment and inflation. Given a mixed shock, policy cooperation lowers inflation. On the other hand, it raises unemployment. There is a reduction in money supply or government purchases. Given another type of a mixed shock, policy cooperation lowers unemployment. On the other hand, it raises inflation. There is an increase in money supply or government purchases.

6) Comparing policy cooperation with policy interaction. As a rule, policy interaction causes uniform oscillations in unemployment and inflation. And what is more, it causes an explosion of government purchases and an implosion of money supply. As a rule, policy cooperation reduces the loss caused by unemployment and inflation. There is a one-time change in unemployment and inflation. And there is a one-time change in money supply and government purchases. Judging from this point of view, policy cooperation seems to be superior to policy interaction.

Part Two

Monetary Policy in Europe

Chapter 1
Target System A

1. The Model

For ease of exposition we assume that the monetary union consists of two countries, say Germany and France. The member countries are the same size and have the same behavioural functions. This chapter is based on target system A. The targets of the European central bank are zero inflation in Germany and France respectively. An increase in European money supply lowers unemployment in Germany and France. On the other hand, it raises producer inflation there. Here producer inflation in Germany refers to the price of German goods. Similarly, producer inflation in France refers to the price of French goods.

The model of unemployment and inflation can be represented by a system of four equations:

$$u_1 = A_1 - M \tag{1}$$

$$u_2 = A_2 - M \tag{2}$$

$$\pi_1 = B_1 + M \tag{3}$$

$$\pi_2 = B_2 + M \tag{4}$$

Of course this is a reduced form. Here u_1 denotes the rate of unemployment in Germany, u_2 is the rate of unemployment in France, π_1 is the rate of inflation in Germany, π_2 is the rate of inflation in France, M is European money supply, A_1 is some other factors bearing on the rate of unemployment in Germany, A_2 is some other factors bearing on the rate of unemployment in France, B_1 is some other factors bearing on the rate of inflation in Germany, and B_2 is some other factors bearing on the rate of inflation in France. The endogenous variables are the rate of unemployment in Germany, the rate of unemployment in France, the rate of inflation in Germany, and the rate of inflation in France.

M. Carlberg, *Dynamic Policy Interactions in a Monetary Union*,
DOI 10.1007/978-3-642-18228-0_7, © Springer-Verlag Berlin Heidelberg 2011

According to equation (1), the rate of unemployment in Germany is a positive function of A_1 and a negative function of European money supply. According to equation (2), the rate of unemployment in France is a positive function of A_2 and a negative function of European money supply. According to equation (3), the rate of inflation in Germany is a positive function of B_1 and a positive function of European money supply. According to equation (4), the rate of inflation in France is a positive function of B_2 and a positive function of European money supply.

A unit increase in European money supply lowers the rates of unemployment in Germany and France by 1 percentage point each. On the other hand, it raises the rates of inflation there by 1 percentage point each. For instance, let initial unemployment in Germany be 3 percent, and let initial unemployment in France be 1 percent. Further let initial inflation in Germany be 3 percent, and let initial inflation in France be 1 percent. Now consider a unit increase in European money supply. Then unemployment in Germany goes from 3 to 2 percent, and unemployment in France goes from 1 to zero percent. On the other hand, inflation in Germany goes from 3 to 4 percent, and inflation in France goes from 1 to 2 percent.

The targets of the European central bank are zero inflation in Germany and France respectively. The instrument of the European central bank is European money supply. There are two targets but only one instrument, so what is needed is a loss function. We assume that the European central bank has a quadratic loss function:

$$L = \pi_1^2 + \pi_2^2 \qquad (5)$$

L is the loss to the European central bank caused by inflation in Germany and France. We assume equal weights in the loss function. The specific target of the European central bank is to minimize the loss, given the inflation functions. Taking account of equations (3) and (4), the loss function of the European central bank can be written as follows:

$$L = (B_1 + M)^2 + (B_2 + M)^2 \qquad (6)$$

Then the first-order condition for a minimum loss is:

$$2M = -B_1 - B_2 \tag{7}$$

Here M is the optimum level of European money supply. An increase in A_1 or A_2 requires no change in European money supply. And an increase in B_1 or B_2 requires a cut in European money supply.

2. Some Numerical Examples

It proves useful to study eight distinct cases:

- a demand shock in Germany
- a supply shock in Germany
- a mixed shock in Germany
- another mixed shock in Germany
- a common demand shock in Europe
- a common supply shock in Europe
- a common mixed shock in Europe
- another common mixed shock in Europe.

1) A demand shock in Germany. In each of the member countries, let initial unemployment be zero, and let initial inflation be zero as well. Step one refers to a decline in the demand for German goods. In terms of the model there is an increase in A_1 of 2 units and a decline in B_1 of equally 2 units. Step two refers to the time lag. Unemployment in Germany goes from zero to 2 percent. Unemployment in France stays at zero percent. Thus unemployment in Europe goes from zero to 1 percent. Inflation in Germany goes from zero to – 2 percent. Inflation in France stays at zero percent. Thus inflation in Europe goes from zero to – 1 percent.

Step three refers to monetary policy in Europe. Current inflation in Europe is – 1 percent, and target inflation in Europe is zero percent. So what is needed is an increase in European money supply of 1 unit. Step four refers to the time lag.

Unemployment in Germany goes from 2 to 1 percent. Unemployment in France goes from zero to – 1 percent. Thus unemployment in Europe goes from 1 to zero percent. Inflation in Germany goes from – 2 to – 1 percent. Inflation in France goes from zero to 1 percent. Thus inflation in Europe goes from – 1 to zero percent. Table 2.1 presents a synopsis.

Table 2.1
Monetary Policy in Europe
A Demand Shock in Germany

Germany		France	
Unemployment	2	Unemployment	0
Inflation	– 2	Inflation	0
Δ European Money Supply	1		
Unemployment	1	Unemployment	– 1
Inflation	– 1	Inflation	1

As a result, given a demand shock in Germany, monetary policy in Europe achieves zero inflation in Europe as a whole. However, it does not achieve zero inflation in Germany and France. The loss function of the European central bank is:

$$L = \pi_1^2 + \pi_2^2 \tag{1}$$

The initial loss is zero. The demand shock in Germany causes a loss of 4 units. Then monetary policy in Europe brings the loss down to 2 units.

2) A supply shock in Germany. In each of the member countries, let initial unemployment be zero, and let initial inflation be zero as well. Step one refers to the supply shock in Germany. In terms of the model there is an increase in B_1 of 2 units and an increase in A_1 of equally 2 units. Step two refers to the time lag.

Inflation in Germany goes from zero to 2 percent. Inflation in France stays at zero percent. Hence inflation in Europe goes from zero to 1 percent. Unemployment in Germany goes from zero to 2 percent. Unemployment in France stays at zero percent. Hence unemployment in Europe goes from zero to 1 percent.

Step three refers to monetary policy in Europe. Current inflation in Europe is 1 percent, and target inflation in Europe is zero percent. So what is needed is a reduction in European money supply of 1 unit. Step four refers to the time lag. Unemployment in Germany goes from 2 to 3 percent. Unemployment in France goes from zero to 1 percent percent. Hence unemployment in Europe goes from 1 to 2 percent. Inflation in Germany goes from 2 to 1 percent. Inflation in France goes from zero to – 1 percent. Hence inflation in Europe goes from 1 to zero percent. Table 2.2 gives an overview.

Table 2.2
Monetary Policy in Europe
A Supply Shock in Germany

Germany		France	
Unemployment	2	Unemployment	0
Inflation	2	Inflation	0
Δ European Money Supply	– 1		
Unemployment	3	Unemployment	1
Inflation	1	Inflation	– 1

As a result, given a supply shock in Germany, monetary policy in Europe achieves zero inflation in Europe as a whole. However, it does not achieve zero inflation in Germany and France. And what is more, it causes an increase in European unemployment. The supply shock in Germany causes a loss of 4 units. Then monetary policy in Europe brings the loss down to 2 units.

3) A mixed shock in Germany. In each of the member countries, let initial unemployment be zero, and let initial inflation be zero as well. Step one refers to the mixed shock in Germany. In terms of the model there is an increase in B_1 of 4 units. Step two refers to the time lag. Inflation in Germany goes from zero to 4 percent. Inflation in France stays at zero percent. Thus inflation in Europe goes from zero to 2 percent. Unemployment in Germany stays at zero percent, as does unemployment in France. Thus unemployment in Europe stays at zero percent too.

Step three refers to monetary policy in Europe. Current inflation in Europe is 2 percent, and target inflation in Europe is zero percent. So what is needed is a reduction in European money supply of 2 units. Step four refers to the time lag. Unemployment in Germany goes from zero to 2 percent. And the same applies to unemployment in France. Thus unemployment in Europe goes from zero to 2 percent as well. Inflation in Germany goes from 4 to 2 percent. Inflation in France goes from zero to – 2 percent. Thus inflation in Europe goes from 2 to zero percent. For a synopsis see Table 2.3.

Table 2.3
Monetary Policy in Europe
A Mixed Shock in Germany

Germany		France	
Unemployment	0	Unemployment	0
Inflation	4	Inflation	0
Δ European Money Supply	– 2		
Unemployment	2	Unemployment	2
Inflation	2	Inflation	– 2

As a result, given a mixed shock in Germany, monetary policy in Europe achieves zero inflation in Europe as a whole. However, it does not achieve zero inflation in Germany and France. The mixed shock in Germany causes a loss of 16 units. Then monetary policy in Europe brings the loss down to 8 units.

4) Another type of a mixed shock in Germany. In each of the member countries, let initial unemployment be zero, and let initial inflation be zero as well. Step one refers to the mixed shock in Germany. In terms of the model there is an increase in A_1 of 4 units. Step two refers to the time lag. Unemployment in Germany goes from zero to 4 percent. Unemployment in France stays at zero percent. Hence unemployment in Europe goes from zero to 2 percent. Inflation in Germany stays at zero percent, as does inflation in France. Hence inflation in Europe stays at zero percent too.

Step three refers to monetary policy in Europe. Current inflation in Europe and target inflation in Europe are zero percent each. So what is needed is no change in European money supply. Step four refers to the time lag. Unemployment in Germany stays at 4 percent. Unemployment in France stays at zero percent. Hence unemployment in Europe stays at 2 percent. Inflation in Germany stays at zero percent. And the same applies to inflation in France. Hence inflation in Europe stays at zero percent as well. For an overview see Table 2.4.

Table 2.4
Monetary Policy in Europe
Another Mixed Shock in Germany

Germany		France	
Unemployment	4	Unemployment	0
Inflation	0	Inflation	0
Δ European Money Supply	0		
Unemployment	4	Unemployment	0
Inflation	0	Inflation	0

As a result, given another type of a mixed shock in Germany, monetary policy in Europe achieves zero inflation in Germany and France. The mixed shock in Germany causes a loss of zero units. Then monetary policy in Europe keeps the loss at zero units.

5) A common demand shock in Europe. In each of the member countries, let initial unemployment be zero, and let initial inflation be zero as well. Step one refers to a decline in the common demand for European goods. In terms of the model there is an increase in A_1 of 2 units, an increase in A_2 of 2 units, a decline in B_1 of 2 units, and a decline in B_2 of equally 2 units. Step two refers to the time lag. Unemployment in Germany goes from zero to 2 percent, as does unemployment in France. Thus unemployment in Europe goes from zero to 2 percent as well. Inflation in Germany goes from zero to – 2 percent, as does inflation in France. Thus inflation in Europe goes from zero to – 2 percent as well.

Step three refers to monetary policy in Europe. Current inflation in Europe is – 2 percent, and target inflation in Europe is zero percent. So what is needed is an increase in European money supply of 2 units. Step four refers to the time lag. Unemployment in Germany goes from 2 to zero percent, as does unemployment in France. Thus unemployment in Europe goes from 2 to zero percent as well. Inflation in Germany goes from – 2 to zero percent, as does inflation in France. Thus inflation in Europe goes from – 2 to zero percent as well. Table 2.5 presents a synopsis.

As a result, given a common demand shock, monetary policy in Europe achieves zero inflation in Germany and France. And what is more, it achieves zero unemployment there. The common demand shock causes a loss of 8 units. Then monetary policy in Europe brings the loss down to zero again.

Table 2.5
Monetary Policy in Europe
A Common Demand Shock

Germany		France	
Unemployment	2	Unemployment	2
Inflation	− 2	Inflation	− 2
Δ European Money Supply	2		
Unemployment	0	Unemployment	0
Inflation	0	Inflation	0

6) A common supply shock in Europe. In each of the member countries, let initial unemployment be zero, and let initial inflation be zero as well. Step one refers to the common supply shock in Europe. In terms of the model there is an increase in B_1 of 2 units, an increase in B_2 of 2 units, an increase in A_1 of 2 units, and an increase in A_2 of 2 units. Step two refers to the time lag. Inflation in Germany goes from zero to 2 percent, as does inflation in France. Hence inflation in Europe goes from zero to 2 percent too. Unemployment in Germany goes from zero to 2 percent, as does unemployment in France. Hence unemployment in Europe goes from zero to 2 percent too.

Step three refers to monetary policy in Europe. Current inflation in Europe is 2 percent, and target inflation in Europe is zero percent. So what is needed is a reduction in European money supply of 2 units. Step four refers to the time lag. Unemployment in Germany goes from 2 to 4 percent, as does unemployment in France. Hence unemployment in Europe goes from 2 to 4 percent too. Inflation in Germany goes from 2 to zero percent, as does inflation in France. Hence inflation in Europe goes from 2 to zero percent too. Table 2.6 gives an overview.

As a result, given a common supply shock, monetary policy in Europe achieves zero inflation in Germany and France. However, it raises unemployment there. The common supply shock causes a loss of 8 units. Then monetary policy in Europe brings the loss down to zero again.

Table 2.6
Monetary Policy in Europe
A Common Supply Shock

Germany		France	
Unemployment	2	Unemployment	2
Inflation	2	Inflation	2
Δ European Money Supply	– 2		
Unemployment	4	Unemployment	4
Inflation	0	Inflation	0

7) A common mixed shock in Europe. In each of the member countries, let initial unemployment be zero, and let initial inflation be zero as well. Step one refers to the common mixed shock in Europe. In terms of the model there is an increase in B_1 of 4 units and an increase in B_2 of equally 4 units. Step two refers to the time lag. Inflation in Germany goes from zero to 4 percent, as does inflation in France. Thus inflation in Europe goes from zero to 4 percent as well. Unemployment in Germany stays at zero percent, as does unemployment in France. Thus unemployment in Europe stays at zero percent as well.

Step three refers to monetary policy in Europe. Current inflation in Europe is 4 percent, and target inflation in Europe is zero percent. So what is needed is a reduction in European money supply of 4 units. Step four refers to the time lag. Unemployment in Germany goes from zero to 4 percent, as does unemployment in France. Thus unemployment in Europe goes from zero to 4 percent as well. Inflation in Germany goes from 4 to zero percent, as does inflation in France. Thus inflation in Europe goes from 4 to zero percent as well. For a synopsis see Table 2.7.

As a result, given a common mixed shock, monetary policy in Europe achieves zero inflation in Germany and France. However, it produces unemployment there. The common mixed shock causes a loss of 32 units. Then monetary policy in Europe brings the loss down to zero again.

Table 2.7
Monetary Policy in Europe
A Common Mixed Shock

Germany		France	
Unemployment	0	Unemployment	0
Inflation	4	Inflation	4
Δ European Money Supply	– 4		
Unemployment	4	Unemployment	4
Inflation	0	Inflation	0

8) Another type of a common mixed shock in Europe. In each of the member countries, let initial unemployment be zero, and let initial inflation be zero as well. Step one refers to the common mixed shock in Europe. In terms of the model there is an increase in A_1 of 4 units and an increase in A_2 of equally 4 units. Step two refers to the time lag. Unemployment in Germany goes from zero to 4 percent, as does unemployment in France. Hence unemployment in Europe goes from zero to 4 percent too. Inflation in Germany stays at zero percent, as does inflation in France. Hence inflation in Europe stays at zero percent too.

Step three refers to monetary policy in Europe. Current inflation in Europe and target inflation in Europe are zero percent each. So what is needed is no change in European money supply. Step four refers to the time lag. Unemployment in Germany stays at 4 percent, as does unemployment in France. Hence unemployment in Europe stays at 4 percent too. Inflation in Germany stays at zero percent, as does inflation in France. Hence inflation in Europe stays at zero percent too. For an overview see Table 2.8.

As a result, given another type of a common mixed shock, monetary policy in Europe achieves zero inflation in Germany and France. The common mixed shock causes a loss of zero units. Then monetary policy in Europe keeps the loss at zero units.

Table 2.8
Monetary Policy in Europe
Another Common Mixed Shock

Germany		France	
Unemployment	4	Unemployment	4
Inflation	0	Inflation	0
Δ European Money Supply	0		
Unemployment	4	Unemployment	4
Inflation	0	Inflation	0

9) Summary. Given a demand shock in Germany, monetary policy in Europe achieves zero inflation in Europe as a whole. However, it does not achieve zero inflation in Germany and France. Much the same is true of a supply shock or a mixed shock in Germany. Given a common demand shock in Europe, monetary policy in Europe achieves zero inflation in Germany and France. Much the same is true of a common supply shock or a common mixed shock in Europe.

Chapter 2
Target System B

1. The Model

This chapter is based on target system B. The targets of the European central bank are zero inflation and zero unemployment in each of the member countries. The model of unemployment and inflation can be characterized by a system of four equations:

$$u_1 = A_1 - M \tag{1}$$

$$u_2 = A_2 - M \tag{2}$$

$$\pi_1 = B_1 + M \tag{3}$$

$$\pi_2 = B_2 + M \tag{4}$$

An increase in European money supply lowers unemployment in Germany and France. On the other hand, it raises inflation there.

The targets of the European central bank are zero inflation and zero unemployment in each of the member countries. The instrument of the European central bank is European money supply. There are four targets but only one instrument, so what is needed is a loss function. We assume that the European central bank has a quadratic loss function:

$$L = \pi_1^2 + \pi_2^2 + u_1^2 + u_2^2 \tag{5}$$

L is the loss to the European central bank caused by inflation and unemployment in each of the member countries. We assume equal weights in the loss function. The specific target of the European central bank is to minimize the loss, given the inflation functions and the unemployment functions. Taking account of equations (1), (2), (3) and (4), the loss function of the European central bank can be written as follows:

M. Carlberg, *Dynamic Policy Interactions in a Monetary Union*,
DOI 10.1007/978-3-642-18228-0_8, © Springer-Verlag Berlin Heidelberg 2011

$$L = (B_1 + M)^2 + (B_2 + M)^2 + (A_1 - M)^2 + (A_2 - M)^2 \quad (6)$$

Then the first-order condition for a minimum loss is:

$$4M = A_1 + A_2 - B_1 - B_2 \quad (7)$$

Here M is the optimum level of European money supply. An increase in A_1 or A_2 requires an increase in European money supply. And an increase in B_1 or B_2 requires a cut in European money supply.

2. Some Numerical Examples

Here are eight distinct cases:

- a demand shock in Germany
- a supply shock in Germany
- a mixed shock in Germany
- another mixed shock in Germany
- a common demand shock in Europe
- a common supply shock in Europe
- a common mixed shock in Europe
- another common mixed shock in Europe.

1) A demand shock in Germany. In each of the member countries, let initial unemployment be zero, and let initial inflation be zero as well. Step one refers to a decline in the demand for German goods. In terms of the model there is an increase in A_1 of 2 units and a decline in B_1 of equally 2 units. Step two refers to the time lag. Unemployment in Germany goes from zero to 2 percent. Unemployment in France stays at zero percent. Thus unemployment in Europe goes from zero to 1 percent. Inflation in Germany goes from zero to – 2 percent. Inflation in France stays at zero percent. Thus inflation in Europe goes from zero to – 1 percent.

Step three refers to monetary policy in Europe. Current unemployment in Europe is 1 percent, and current inflation in Europe is – 1 percent. Accordingly, target unemployment in Europe and target inflation in Europe are zero percent each. So what is needed is an increase in European money supply of 1 unit. Step four refers to the time lag. Unemployment in Germany goes from 2 to 1 percent. Unemployment in France goes from zero to – 1 percent. Thus unemployment in Europe goes from 1 to zero percent. Inflation in Germany goes from – 2 to – 1 percent. Inflation in France goes from zero to 1 percent. Thus inflation in Europe goes from – 1 to zero percent. Table 2.9 presents a synopsis.

As a result, given a demand shock in Germany, monetary policy in Europe achieves zero inflation and zero unemployment in Europe as a whole. However, it does not do so in Germany and France. The loss function of the European central bank is:

$$L = \pi_1^2 + \pi_2^2 + u_1^2 + u_2^2 \tag{1}$$

The initial loss is zero. The demand shock in Germany causes a loss of 8 units. Then monetary policy in Europe brings the loss down to 4 units.

Table 2.9
Monetary Policy in Europe
A Demand Shock in Germany

Germany		France	
Unemployment	2	Unemployment	0
Inflation	– 2	Inflation	0
Δ European Money Supply	1		
Unemployment	1	Unemployment	– 1
Inflation	– 1	Inflation	1

2) A supply shock in Germany. In each of the member countries, let initial unemployment be zero, and let initial inflation be zero as well. Step one refers to the supply shock in Germany. In terms of the model there is an increase in B_1 of 2 units and an increase in A_1 of equally 2 units. Step two refers to the time lag. Inflation in Germany goes from zero to 2 percent. Inflation in France stays at zero percent. Hence inflation in Europe goes from zero to 1 percent. Unemployment in Germany goes from zero to 2 percent. Unemployment in France stays at zero percent. Hence unemployment in Europe goes from zero to 1 percent.

Step three refers to monetary policy in Europe. Current unemployment in Europe and current inflation in Europe are 1 percent each. Accordingly, target unemployment in Europe and target inflation in Europe are 1 percent each. So what is needed is no change in European money supply. Step four refers to the time lag. Unemployment in Germany stays at 2 percent, and unemployment in France stays at zero percent. Hence unemployment in Europe stays at 1 percent. Inflation in Germany stays at 2 percent, and inflation in France stays at zero percent. Hence inflation in Europe stays at 1 percent. Table 2.10 gives an overview.

Table 2.10
Monetary Policy in Europe
A Supply Shock in Germany

Germany		France	
Unemployment	2	Unemployment	0
Inflation	2	Inflation	0
Δ European Money Supply	0		
Unemployment	2	Unemployment	0
Inflation	2	Inflation	0

As a result, given a supply shock in Germany, monetary policy in Europe is ineffective. There is no change in money supply. Correspondingly, there is no change in unemployment and inflation. The supply shock in Germany causes a loss of 8 units. However, monetary policy in Europe does not bring down the loss.

3) A mixed shock in Germany. In each of the member countries, let initial unemployment be zero, and let initial inflation be zero well. Step one refers to the mixed shock in Germany. In terms of the model there is an increase in B_1 of 4 units. Step two refers to the time lag. Inflation in Germany goes from zero to 4 percent. Inflation in France stays at zero percent. Thus inflation in Europe goes from zero to 2 percent. Unemployment in Germany stays at zero percent, as does unemployment in France. Thus unemployment in Europe stays at zero percent too.

Step three refers to monetary policy in Europe. Current unemployment in Europe is zero percent, and current inflation in Europe is 2 percent. Accordingly, target unemployment in Europe and target inflation in Europe are 1 percent each. So what is needed is a reduction in European money supply of 1 unit. Step four refers to the time lag. Unemployment in Germany goes from zero to 1 percent, as does unemployment in France. Thus unemployment in Europe goes from zero to 1 percent as well. Inflation in Germany goes from 4 to 3 percent. Inflation in France goes from zero to – 1 percent. Thus inflation in Europe goes from 2 to 1 percent. For a synopsis see Table 2.11.

As a result, given a mixed shock in Germany, monetary policy in Europe lowers inflation in Europe as a whole. On the other hand, it raises unemployment there. The mixed shock in Germany causes a loss of 16 units. Then monetary policy in Europe brings the loss down to 12 units.

Table 2.11
Monetary Policy in Europe
A Mixed Shock in Germany

Germany		France	
Unemployment	0	Unemployment	0
Inflation	4	Inflation	0
Δ European Money Supply	− 1		
Unemployment	1	Unemployment	1
Inflation	3	Inflation	− 1

4) Another type of a mixed shock in Germany. In each of the member countries, let initial unemployment be zero, and let initial inflation be zero as well. Step one refers to the mixed shock in Germany. In terms of the model there is an increase in A_1 of 4 units. Step two refers to the time lag. Unemployment in Germany goes from zero to 4 percent. Unemployment in France stays at zero percent. Hence unemployment in Europe goes from zero to 2 percent. Inflation in Germany stays at zero percent, as does inflation in France. Hence inflation in Europe stays at zero percent too.

Step three refers to monetary policy in Europe. Current unemployment in Europe is 2 percent, and current inflation in Europe is zero percent. Accordingly, target unemployment in Europe and target inflation in Europe are 1 percent each. So what is needed is an increase in European money supply of 1 unit. Step four refers to the time lag. Unemployment in Germany goes from 4 to 3 percent. Unemployment in France goes from zero to – 1 percent. Hence unemployment in Europe goes from 2 to 1 percent. Inflation in Germany goes from zero to 1 percent, as does inflation in France. Hence inflation in Europe goes from zero to 1 percent as well. For an overview see Table 2.12.

Table 2.12
Monetary Policy in Europe
Another Mixed Shock in Germany

Germany		France	
Unemployment	4	Unemployment	0
Inflation	0	Inflation	0
Δ European Money Supply	1		
Unemployment	3	Unemployment	– 1
Inflation	1	Inflation	1

As a result, given another type of a mixed shock in Germany, monetary policy in Europe lowers unemployment in Europe as a whole. On the other hand, it raises inflation there. The mixed shock in Germany causes a loss of 16 units. Then monetary policy in Europe brings the loss down to 12 units.

5) A common demand shock in Europe. In each of the member countries, let initial unemployment be zero, and let initial inflation be zero as well. Step one refers to a decline in the common demand for European goods. In terms of the model there is an increase in A_1 of 2 units, an increase in A_2 of 2 units, a decline in B_1 of 2 units, and a decline in B_2 of equally 2 units. Step two refers to the time lag. Unemployment in Germany goes from zero to 2 percent, as does unemployment in France. Thus unemployment in Europe goes from zero to 2 percent as well. Inflation in Germany goes from zero to – 2 percent, as does inflation in France. Thus inflation in Europe goes from zero to – 2 percent as well.

Step three refers to monetary policy in Europe. Current unemployment in Europe is 2 percent, and current inflation in Europe is – 2 percent. Accordingly, target unemployment in Europe and target inflation in Europe are zero percent each. So what is needed is an increase in European money supply of 2 units. Step four refers to the time lag. Unemployment in Germany goes from 2 to zero percent, as does unemployment in France. Thus unemployment in Europe goes from 2 to zero percent as well. Inflation in Germany goes from – 2 to zero percent, as does inflation in France. Thus inflation in Europe goes from – 2 to zero percent as well. Table 2.13 presents a synopsis.

As a result, given a common demand shock, monetary policy in Europe achieves zero unemployment and zero inflation in each of the member countries. The common demand shock causes a loss of 16 units. Then monetary policy in Europe brings the loss down to zero again.

Table 2.13
Monetary Policy in Europe
A Common Demand Shock

Germany		France	
Unemployment	2	Unemployment	2
Inflation	– 2	Inflation	– 2
Δ European Money Supply	2		
Unemployment	0	Unemployment	0
Inflation	0	Inflation	0

6) A common supply shock in Europe. In each of the member countries, let initial unemployment be zero, and let initial inflation be zero as well. Step one refers to the common supply shock in Europe. In terms of the model there is an increase in B_1 of 2 units, an increase in B_2 of 2 units, an increase in A_1 of 2 units, and an increase in A_2 of 2 units. Step two refers to the time lag. Inflation in Germany goes from zero to 2 percent, as does inflation in France. Hence inflation in Europe goes from zero to 2 percent too. Unemployment in Germany goes from zero to 2 percent, as does unemployment in France. Hence unemployment in Europe goes from zero to 2 percent too.

Step three refers to monetary policy in Europe. Current unemployment in Europe and current inflation in Europe are 2 percent each. Accordingly, target unemployment in Europe and target inflation in Europe are 2 percent each. So what is needed is no change in European money supply. Step four refers to the time lag. Unemployment in Germany stays at 2 percent, as does unemployment in France. Hence unemployment in Europe stays at 2 percent too. Inflation in Germany stays at 2 percent, as does inflation in France. Hence inflation in Europe stays at 2 percent too. Table 2.14 gives an overview.

As a result, given a common supply shock, monetary policy in Europe is ineffective. There is no change in money supply. Correspondingly, there is no change in unemployment and inflation. The common supply shock causes a loss of 16 units. Then monetary policy in Europe keeps the loss at 16 units.

Table 2.14
Monetary Policy in Europe
A Common Supply Shock

Germany		France	
Unemployment	2	Unemployment	2
Inflation	2	Inflation	2
Δ European Money Supply	0		
Unemployment	2	Unemployment	2
Inflation	2	Inflation	2

7) A common mixed shock in Europe. In each of the member countries, let initial unemployment be zero, and let initial inflation be zero as well. Step one refers to the common mixed shock in Europe. In terms of the model there is an increase in B_1 of 4 units and an increase in B_2 of equally 4 units. Step two refers to the time lag. Inflation in Germany goes from zero to 4 percent, as does inflation in France. Thus inflation in Europe goes from zero to 4 percent as well.

Unemployment in Germany stays at zero percent, as does unemployment in France. Thus unemployment in Europe stays at zero percent as well.

Step three refers to monetary policy in Europe. Current unemployment in Europe is zero percent, and current inflation in Europe is 4 percent. Accordingly, target unemployment in Europe and target inflation in Europe are 2 percent each. So what is needed is a reduction in European money supply of 2 units. Step four refers to the time lag. Unemployment in Germany goes from zero to 2 percent, as does unemployment in France. Thus unemployment in Europe goes from zero to 2 percent as well. Inflation in Germany goes from 4 to 2 percent, as does inflation in France. Thus inflation in Europe goes from 4 to 2 percent as well. For a synopsis see Table 2.15.

As a result, given a common mixed shock, monetary policy in Europe lowers inflation in Germany and France. On the other hand, it raises unemployment there. The common mixed shock causes a loss of 32 units. Then monetary policy in Europe brings the loss down to 16 units.

Table 2.15
Monetary Policy in Europe
A Common Mixed Shock

Germany		France	
Unemployment	0	Unemployment	0
Inflation	4	Inflation	4
Δ European Money Supply	– 2		
Unemployment	2	Unemployment	2
Inflation	2	Inflation	2

8) Another type of a common mixed shock in Europe. In each of the member countries, let initial unemployment be zero, and let initial inflation be zero as

well. Step one refers to the common mixed shock. In terms of the model there is an increase in A_1 of 4 units and an increase in A_2 of equally 4 units. Step two refers to the time lag. Unemployment in Germany goes from zero to 4 percent, as does unemployment in France. Hence unemployment in Europe goes from zero to 4 percent too. Inflation in Germany stays at zero percent, as does inflation in France. Hence inflation in Europe stays at zero percent too.

Step three refers to monetary policy in Europe. Current unemployment in Europe is 4 percent, and current inflation in Europe is zero percent. Accordingly, target unemployment in Europe and target inflation in Europe are two percent each. So what is needed is an increase in European money supply of 2 units. Step four refers to the time lag. Unemployment in Germany goes from 4 to 2 percent, as does unemployment in France. Hence unemployment in Europe goes from 4 to 2 percent too. Inflation in Germany goes from zero to 2 percent, as does inflation in France. Hence inflation in Europe goes from zero to 2 percent too. For an overview see Table 2.16.

As a result, given another type of a common mixed shock, monetary policy in Europe lowers unemployment in Germany and France. On the other hand, it raises inflation there. The common mixed shock causes a loss of 32 units. Then monetary policy in Europe brings the loss down to 16 units.

Table 2.16
Monetary Policy in Europe
Another Common Mixed Shock

Germany		France	
Unemployment	4	Unemployment	4
Inflation	0	Inflation	0
Δ European Money Supply	2		
Unemployment	2	Unemployment	2
Inflation	2	Inflation	2

9) Summary. Given a demand shock in Germany, monetary policy in Europe achieves zero unemployment and zero inflation in Europe as a whole. However, it does not do so in Germany and France. Given a supply shock in Germany, monetary policy in Europe is ineffective. There is no change in money supply. Correspondingly, there is no change in unemployment and inflation. Given a mixed shock in Germany, monetary policy in Europe lowers inflation in Europe as a whole. On the other hand, it raises unemployment there. Given another type of a mixed shock in Germany, monetary policy in Europe lowers unemployment in Europe as a whole. On the other hand, it raises inflation there.

Given a common demand shock in Europe, monetary policy achieves zero unemployment and zero inflation in each of the member countries. Given a common supply shock in Europe, monetary policy is ineffective. There is no change in money supply. Correspondingly, there is no change in unemployment and inflation. Given a common mixed shock in Europe, monetary policy lowers inflation in Germany and France. On the other hand, it raises unemployment there. Given another type of a common mixed shock in Europe, monetary policy lowers unemployment in Germany and France. On the other hand, it raises inflation there.

Part Three

Fiscal Policy in Germany

Chapter 1
Target System A

1. The Model

The monetary union consists of two countries, say Germany and France. The member countries are the same size and have the same behavioural functions. This chapter is based on target system A. The target of the German government is zero unemployment in Germany. An increase in German government purchases lowers unemployment in Germany. On the other hand, it raises producer inflation there. For ease of exposition we assume that fiscal policy in one of the countries has no effect on unemployment or producer inflation in the other country.

The model of unemployment and inflation can be represented by a system of two equations:

$$u_1 = A_1 - G_1 \tag{1}$$

$$\pi_1 = B_1 + G_1 \tag{2}$$

Here u_1 denotes the rate of unemployment in Germany, π_1 is the rate of inflation in Germany, G_1 is German government purchases, A_1 is some other factors bearing on the rate of unemployment in Germany, and B_1 is some other factors bearing on the rate of inflation in Germany. The endogenous variables are the rate of unemployment and the rate of inflation in Germany.

According to equation (1), the rate of unemployment in Germany is a positive function of A_1 and a negative function of German government purchases. According to equation (2), the rate of inflation in Germany is a positive function of B_1 and a positive function of German government purchases.

A unit increase in government purchases lowers the rate of unemployment by 1 percentage point. On the other hand, it raises the rate of inflation by 1 percentage point. For instance, let initial unemployment be 2 percent, and let

M. Carlberg, *Dynamic Policy Interactions in a Monetary Union*,
DOI 10.1007/978-3-642-18228-0_9, © Springer-Verlag Berlin Heidelberg 2011

initial inflation be 2 percent as well. Now consider a unit increase in government purchases. Then unemployment goes from 2 to 1 percent. On the other hand, inflation goes from 2 to 3 percent.

The target of the German government is zero unemployment in Germany. The instrument of the German government is its purchases. By equation (1), the optimum level of German government purchases is:

$$G_1 = A_1 \tag{3}$$

That is, an increase in A_1 requires an increase in German government purchases. And an increase in B_1 requires no change in German government purchases.

2. Some Numerical Examples

It proves useful to study four distinct cases:

- a demand shock in Germany
- a supply shock in Germany
- a mixed shock in Germany
- another mixed shock in Germany.

1) A demand shock in Germany. At the start, let German unemployment be zero, and let German inflation be zero as well. Step one refers to a decline in the demand for German goods. In terms of the model there is an increase in A_1 of 1 unit and a decline in B_1 of equally 1 unit. Step two refers to the time lag. German unemployment goes from zero to 1 percent. And German inflation goes from zero to – 1 percent.

Step three refers to fiscal policy in Germany. Current unemployment in Germany is 1 percent, and target unemployment in Germany is zero percent. So what is needed is an increase in German government purchases of 1 unit. Step four refers to the time lag. German unemployment goes from 1 to zero percent.

And German inflation goes from – 1 to zero percent. Table 3.1 presents a synopsis.

As a result, given a demand shock in Germany, fiscal policy in Germany achieves zero unemployment. And what is more, as a side effect, it achieves zero inflation. The loss function of the German government is:

$$L_1 = u_1^2 \tag{1}$$

The initial loss is zero. The demand shock in Germany causes a loss of 1 unit. Then fiscal policy in Germany brings the loss down to zero again.

Table 3.1
Fiscal Policy in Germany
A Demand Shock

Unemployment	1	Inflation	– 1
Change in Govt Purchases	1		
Unemployment	0	Inflation	0

2) A supply shock in Germany. At the start, let German unemployment and German inflation be zero each. Step one refers to the supply shock. In terms of the model there is an increase in B_1 of 1 unit and an increase in A_1 of equally 1 unit. Step two refers to the time lag. German inflation goes from zero to 1 percent. And German unemployment goes from zero to 1 percent too.

Step three refers to fiscal policy in Germany. Current unemployment in Germany is 1 percent, and target unemployment in Germany is zero percent. So what is needed is an increase in German government purchases of 1 unit. Step four refers to the time lag. German unemployment goes from 1 to zero percent. And German inflation goes from 1 to 2 percent. Table 3.2 gives an overview.

As a result, given a supply shock in Germany, fiscal policy in Germany achieves zero unemployment. However, as a side effect, it causes an increase in inflation. The supply shock in Germany causes a loss of 1 unit. Then fiscal policy in Germany brings the loss down to zero again.

Table 3.2
Fiscal Policy in Germany
A Supply Shock

Unemployment	1	Inflation	1
Change in Govt Purchases	1		
Unemployment	0	Inflation	2

3) A mixed shock in Germany. At the start, let German unemployment and German inflation be zero each. Step one refers to the mixed shock in Germany. In terms of the model there is an increase in B_1 of 2 units. Step two refers to the time lag. German inflation goes from zero to 2 percent. And German unemployment stays at zero percent.

Step three refers to fiscal policy in Germany. Current unemployment in Germany and target unemployment in Germany are zero percent each. So what is needed is no change in German government purchases. Step four refers to the time lag. German unemployment stays at zero percent, and German inflation stays at 2 percent. For a synopsis see Table 3.3. As a result, given a mixed shock in Germany, fiscal policy in Germany achieves zero unemployment. The mixed shock in Germany causes no loss.

4) Another type of a mixed shock in Germany. At the start, let German unemployment and German inflation be zero each. Step one refers to the mixed shock in Germany. In terms of the model there is an increase in A_1 of 2 units. Step two refers to the time lag. German unemployment goes from zero to 2 percent. And German inflation stays at zero percent.

Step three refers to fiscal policy in Germany. Current unemployment in Germany is 2 percent, and target unemployment in Germany is zero percent. So what is needed is an increase in German government purchases of 2 units. Step four refers to the time lag. German unemployment goes from 2 to zero percent. And German inflation goes from zero to 2 percent. For an overview see Table 3.4.

As a result, given another type of a mixed shock in Germany, fiscal policy in Germany achieves zero unemployment. However, as a side effect, it produces inflation. The mixed shock in Germany causes a loss of 4 units. Then fiscal policy in Germany brings the loss down to zero.

Table 3.3
Fiscal Policy in Germany
A Mixed Shock

Unemployment	0	Inflation	2
Change in Govt Purchases	0		
Unemployment	0	Inflation	2

Table 3.4
Fiscal Policy in Germany
Another Mixed Shock

Unemployment	2	Inflation	0
Change in Govt Purchases	2		
Unemployment	0	Inflation	2

5) Summary. Given a demand shock in Germany, fiscal policy in Germany achieves zero unemployment. And what is more, as a side effect, it achieves zero inflation. Given a supply shock in Germany, fiscal policy in Germany achieves zero unemployment. However, as a side effect, it raises inflation. And much the same applies to mixed shocks.

Chapter 2
Target System B

1. The Model

This chapter is based on target system B. The targets of the German government are zero unemployment and zero inflation in Germany. The model of unemployment and inflation can be characterized by a system of two equations:

$$u_1 = A_1 - G_1 \tag{1}$$

$$\pi_1 = B_1 + G_1 \tag{2}$$

An increase in German government purchases lowers unemployment in Germany. On the other hand, it raises inflation there.

The targets of the German government are zero unemployment and zero inflation in Germany. The instrument of the German government is its purchases. There are two targets but only one instrument, so what is needed is a loss function. We assume that the German government has a quadratic loss function:

$$L_1 = u_1^2 + \pi_1^2 \tag{3}$$

L_1 is the loss to the German government caused by unemployment and inflation. We assume equal weights in the loss function. The specific target of the German government is to minimize the loss, given the unemployment function and the inflation function. Taking account of equations (1) and (2), the loss function of the German government can be written as follows:

$$L_1 = (A_1 - G_1)^2 + (B_1 + G_1)^2 \tag{4}$$

Then the first-order condition for a minimum loss is:

$$2G_1 = A_1 - B_1 \tag{5}$$

M. Carlberg, *Dynamic Policy Interactions in a Monetary Union*,
DOI 10.1007/978-3-642-18228-0_10, © Springer-Verlag Berlin Heidelberg 2011

Here G_1 is the optimum level of German government purchases. An increase in A_1 requires an increase in German government purchases. And an increase in B_1 requires a cut in German government purchases.

2. Some Numerical Examples

Here are four distinct cases:

- a demand shock in Germany
- a supply shock in Germany
- a mixed shock in Germany
- another mixed shock in Germany.

1) A demand shock in Germany. At the start, let German unemployment be zero, and let German inflation be zero as well. Step one refers to a decline in the demand for German goods. In terms of the model there is an increase in A_1 of 1 unit and a decline in B_1 of equally 1 unit. Step two refers to the time lag. German unemployment goes from zero to 1 percent. And German inflation goes from zero to – 1 percent.

Step three refers to fiscal policy in Germany. Current unemployment in Germany is 1 percent, and current inflation in Germany is – 1 percent. Accordingly, target unemployment in Germany and target inflation in Germany are zero percent each. So what is needed is an increase in German government purchases of 1 unit. Step four refers to the time lag. German unemployment goes from 1 to zero percent. And German inflation goes from – 1 to zero percent. Table 3.5 presents a synopsis.

As a result, given a demand shock in Germany, fiscal policy in Germany achieves both zero unemployment and zero inflation. The loss function of the German government is:

$$L_1 = u_1^2 + \pi_1^2 \tag{1}$$

The initial loss is zero. The demand shock in Germany causes a loss of 2 units. Then fiscal policy in Germany brings the loss down to zero again.

Table 3.5
Fiscal Policy in Germany
A Demand Shock

Unemployment	1	Inflation	− 1
Change in Govt Purchases	1		
Unemployment	0	Inflation	0

2) A supply shock in Germany. At the start, let German unemployment and German inflation be zero each. Step one refers to the supply shock in Germany. In terms of the model there is an increase in B_1 of 1 unit and an increase in A_1 of equally 1 unit. Step two refers to the time lag. German inflation goes from zero to 1 percent. And German unemployment goes from zero to 1 percent too.

Step three refers to fiscal policy in Germany. Current unemployment in Germany and current inflation in Germany are 1 percent each. Accordingly, target unemployment in Germany and target inflation in Germany are 1 percent each. So what is needed is no change in German government purchases. Step four refers to the time lag. German unemployment stays at 1 percent, as does German inflation. Table 3.6 gives an overview.

As a result, given a supply shock in Germany, fiscal policy in Germany is ineffective. There is no change in government purchases. Correspondingly, there is no change in unemployment and inflation. The supply shock in Germany causes a loss of 2 units. However, fiscal policy in Germany cannot bring down the loss.

Table 3.6
Fiscal Policy in Germany
A Supply Shock

Unemployment	1	Inflation	1
Change in Govt Purchases	0		
Unemployment	1	Inflation	1

3) A mixed shock in Germany. At the start, let German unemployment and German inflation be zero each. Step one refers to the mixed shock in Germany. In terms of the model there is an increase in B_1 of 2 units. Step two refers to the time lag. German inflation goes from zero to 2 percent. And German unemployment stays at zero percent.

Step three refers to fiscal policy in Germany. Current unemployment in Germany is zero percent, and current inflation in Germany is 2 percent. Accordingly, target unemployment in Germany and target inflation in Germany are 1 percent each. So what is needed is a reduction in German government purchases of 1 unit. Step four refers to the time lag. German unemployment goes from zero to 1 percent. And German inflation goes from 2 to 1 percent. For a synopsis see Table 3.7.

As a result, given a mixed shock in Germany, fiscal policy in Germany lowers inflation. On the other hand, it raises unemployment. The mixed shock in Germany causes a loss of 4 units. Then fiscal policy in Germany brings the loss down to 2 units.

4) Another type of a mixed shock in Germany. At the start, let German unemployment and German inflation be zero each. Step one refers to the mixed shock in Germany. In terms of the model there is an increase in A_1 of 2 units. Step two refers to the time lag. German unemployment goes from zero to 2 percent. And German inflation stays at zero percent.

Step three refers to fiscal policy in Germany. Current unemployment in Germany is 2 percent, and current inflation in Germany is zero percent. Accordingly, target unemployment in Germany and target inflation in Germany are 1 percent each. So what is needed is an increase in German government purchases of 1 unit. Step four refers to the time lag. German unemployment goes from 2 to 1 percent. And German inflation goes from zero to 1 percent. For an overview see Table 3.8.

As a result, given another type of a mixed shock in Germany, fiscal policy in Germany lowers unemployment. On the other hand, it raises inflation. The mixed shock in Germany causes a loss of 4 units. Then fiscal policy in Germany brings the loss down to 2 units.

Table 3.7
Fiscal Policy in Germany
A Mixed Shock

Unemployment	0	Inflation	2
Change in Govt Purchases	– 1		
Unemployment	1	Inflation	1

Table 3.8
Fiscal Policy in Germany
Another Mixed Shock

Unemployment	2	Inflation	0
Change in Govt Purchases	1		
Unemployment	1	Inflation	1

5) Summary. Given a demand shock in Germany, fiscal policy in Germany achieves both zero unemployment and zero inflation. Given a supply shock in Germany, fiscal policy in Germany is ineffective. There is no change in government purchases. Correspondingly, there is no change in unemployment and inflation. Given a mixed shock in Germany, fiscal policy in Germany lowers inflation. On the other hand, it raises unemployment. Given another type of a mixed shock in Germany, fiscal policy in Germany lowers unemployment. On the other hand, it raises inflation.

Part Four

First the Central Bank Decides, then the Governments Decide

Chapter 1
Target System A

1. The Model

1) The static model. The monetary union consists of two countries, say Germany and France. The member countries are the same size and have the same behavioural functions. This chapter is based on target system A. The targets of the European central bank are zero inflation in Germany and France respectively. The target of the German government is zero unemployment in Germany. And the target of the French government is zero unemployment in France.

An increase in European money supply lowers unemployment in Germany and France. On the other hand, it raises inflation there. An increase in German government purchases lowers unemployment in Germany. On the other hand, it raises inflation there. Correspondingly, an increase in French government purchases lowers unemployment in France. On the other hand, it raises inflation there. Fiscal policy in one of the member countries has no effect on unemployment or inflation in the other country.

The model of unemployment and inflation can be represented by a system of four equations:

$$u_1 = A_1 - M - G_1 \tag{1}$$

$$u_2 = A_2 - M - G_2 \tag{2}$$

$$\pi_1 = B_1 + M + G_1 \tag{3}$$

$$\pi_2 = B_2 + M + G_2 \tag{4}$$

Here u_1 denotes the rate of unemployment in Germany, u_2 is the rate of unemployment in France, π_1 is the rate of inflation in Germany, π_2 is the rate of inflation in France, M is European money supply, G_1 is German government purchases, G_2 is French government purchases, A_1 is some other factors bearing on the rate of unemployment in Germany, A_2 is some other factors

M. Carlberg, *Dynamic Policy Interactions in a Monetary Union*,
DOI 10.1007/978-3-642-18228-0_11, © Springer-Verlag Berlin Heidelberg 2011

bearing on the rate of unemployment in France, B_1 is some other factors bearing on the rate of inflation in Germany, and B_2 is some other factors bearing on the rate of inflation in France. The endogenous variables are the rate of unemployment in Germany, the rate of unemployment in France, the rate of inflation in Germany, and the rate of inflation in France.

According to equation (1), the rate of unemployment in Germany is a positive function of A_1, a negative function of European money supply, and a negative function of German government purchases. According to equation (2), the rate of unemployment in France is a positive function of A_2, a negative function of European money supply, and a negative function of French government purchases. According to equation (3), the rate of inflation in Germany is a positive function of B_1, a positive function of European money supply, and a positive function of German government purchases. According to equation (4), the rate of inflation in France is a positive function of B_2, a positive function of European money supply, and a positive function of French government purchases.

A unit increase in European money supply lowers the rates of unemployment in Germany and France by 1 percentage point each. On the other hand, it raises the rates of inflation there by 1 percentage point each. A unit increase in German government purchases lowers the rate of unemployment in Germany by 1 percentage point. On the other hand, it raises the rate of inflation there by 1 percentage point. Similarly, a unit increase in French government purchases lowers the rate of unemployment in France by 1 percentage point. On the other hand, it raises the rate of inflation there by 1 percentage point.

The targets of the European central bank are zero inflation in Germany and France respectively. The instrument of the European central bank is European money supply. There are two targets but only one instrument, so what is needed is a loss function. We assume that the European central bank has a quadratic loss function:

$$L = \pi_1^2 + \pi_2^2 \tag{5}$$

L is the loss to the European central bank caused by inflation in Germany and France. We assume equal weights in the loss function. The specific target of the

European central bank is to minimize the loss, given the inflation functions. Taking account of equations (3) and (4), the loss function of the European central bank can be written as follows:

$$L = (B_1 + M + G_1)^2 + (B_2 + M + G_2)^2 \tag{6}$$

Then the first-order condition for a minimum loss gives the reaction function of the European central bank:

$$2M = -B_1 - B_2 - G_1 - G_2 \tag{7}$$

An increase in B_1 or B_2 requires a cut in European money supply. And an increase in German or French government purchases requires a cut in European money supply too.

In a monetary union, fiscal policy is the only instrument available at the national level. Fiscal policy in Germany is the only instrument available at the German level. And fiscal policy in France is the only instrument available at the French level.

The target of the German government is zero unemployment in Germany. The instrument of the German government is German government purchases. By equation (1), the reaction function of the German government is:

$$G_1 = A_1 - M \tag{8}$$

An increase in A_1 requires an increase in German government purchases. And a cut in European money supply requires an increase in German government purchases as well.

The target of the French government is zero unemployment in France. The instrument of the French government is French government purchases. By equation (2), the reaction function of the French government is:

$$G_2 = A_2 - M \tag{9}$$

An increase in A_2 requires an increase in French government purchases. And a cut in European money supply requires an increase in French government purchases as well.

The Nash equilibrium is determined by the reaction functions of the European central bank, the German government, and the French government. From the reaction functions follows:

$$A_1 + A_2 + B_1 + B_2 = 0 \tag{10}$$

Evidently, this is in contradiction to the assumption that A_1, A_2, B_1 and B_2 are given exogenously. As a result there is no Nash equilibrium.

2) The dynamic model. We assume that the central bank and the governments decide sequentially. First the central bank decides, then the governments decide. Step 1 refers to a specific shock. Step 2 refers to the time lag. Step 3 refers to monetary policy in Europe. Step 4 refers to the time lag. Step 5 refers to fiscal policies in Germany and France. Step 6 refers to the time lag. Step 7 refers to monetary policy in Europe. Step 8 refers to the time lag. Step 9 refers to fiscal policies in Germany and France. Step 10 refers to the time lag. And so on.

Now have a closer look at the dynamic model. Step 1 refers to a specific shock. This could be a demand shock, a supply shock or a mixed shock, in Germany or France. Step 2 refers to the time lag. This includes both the inside lag and the outside lag. Step 3 refers to monetary policy in Europe. The European central bank sets European money supply so as to achieve zero inflation in Europe. The reaction function of the European central bank is:

$$2M = -B_1 - B_2 - G_1 - G_2 \tag{11}$$

Step 4 refers to the time lag. Step 5 refers to fiscal policies in Germany and France. The German government sets its purchases of German goods so as to achieve zero unemployment in Germany. The reaction function of the German government is:

$$G_1 = A_1 - M \tag{12}$$

The French government sets its purchases of French goods so as to achieve zero unemployment in France. The reaction function of the French government is:

$$G_2 = A_2 - M \tag{13}$$

Step 6 refers to the time lag. Step 7 refers to monetary policy in Europe. The European central bank sets European money supply so as to achieve zero inflation in Europe. The reaction function of the European central bank is:

$$2M = -B_1 - B_2 - G_1 - G_2 \tag{14}$$

Step 8 refers to the time lag. Step 9 refers to fiscal policies in Germany and France. The German government sets its purchases of German goods so as to achieve zero unemployment in Germany. The reaction function of the German government is:

$$G_1 = A_1 - M \tag{15}$$

The French government sets its purchases of French goods so as to achieve zero unemployment in France. The reaction function of the French government is:

$$G_2 = A_2 - M \tag{16}$$

Step 10 refers to the time lag. And so on. Then what are the dynamic characteristics of this process?

2. Some Numerical Examples

It proves useful to study three distinct cases:

- a demand shock in Germany
- a supply shock in Germany
- a mixed shock in Germany.

The targets of the European central bank are zero inflation in Germany and France respectively. The target of the German government is zero unemployment in Germany. And the target of the French government is zero unemployment in France.

1) A demand shock in Germany. In each of the member countries, let initial unemployment be zero, and let initial inflation be zero as well. Step one refers to a decline in the demand for German goods. In terms of the model there is an increase in A_1 of 2 units and a decline in B_1 of equally 2 units. Step two refers to the time lag. Unemployment in Germany goes from zero to 2 percent. Unemployment in France stays at zero percent. Thus unemployment in Europe goes from zero to 1 percent. Inflation in Germany goes from zero to – 2 percent. Inflation in France stays at zero percent. Thus inflation in Europe goes from zero to – 1 percent.

Step three refers to monetary policy in Europe. Current inflation in Europe is – 1 percent, and target inflation in Europe is zero percent. So what is needed is an increase in European money supply of 1 unit. Step four refers to the time lag. Unemployment in Germany goes from 2 to 1 percent. Unemployment in France goes from zero to – 1 percent. Thus unemployment in Europe goes from 1 to zero percent. Inflation in Germany goes from – 2 to – 1 percent. Inflation in France goes from zero to 1 percent. Thus inflation in Europe goes from – 1 to zero percent.

Step five refers to fiscal policies in Germany and France. First consider fiscal policy in Germany. Current unemployment in Germany is 1 percent, and target unemployment in Germany is zero percent. So what is needed is an increase in German government purchases of 1 unit. Second consider fiscal policy in France. Current unemployment in France is – 1 percent, and target unemployment in

France is zero percent. So what is needed is a reduction in French government purchases of 1 unit. Step six refers to the time lag. Unemployment in Germany goes from 1 to zero percent. Unemployment in France goes from – 1 to zero percent. Thus unemployment in Europe stays at zero percent. Inflation in Germany goes from – 1 to zero percent. Inflation in France goes from 1 to zero percent. Thus inflation in Europe stays at zero percent. Table 4.1 presents a synopsis.

Table 4.1
Sequential Policy Decisions
A Demand Shock in Germany

Germany		France	
Unemployment	2	Unemployment	0
Inflation	– 2	Inflation	0
Δ European Money Supply	1		
Unemployment	1	Unemployment	– 1
Inflation	– 1	Inflation	1
Δ Government Purchases	1	Δ Government Purchases	– 1
Unemployment	0	Unemployment	0
Inflation	0	Inflation	0

As a result, given a demand shock in Germany, sequential policy decisions produce zero unemployment and zero inflation in each of the member countries. There is an increase in European money supply, an increase in German government purchases, a reduction in French government purchases, and no change in European government purchases as a whole.

The loss functions of the European central bank, the German government, and the French government are respectively:

$$L = \pi_1^2 + \pi_2^2 \tag{1}$$

$$L_1 = u_1^2 \tag{2}$$

$$L_2 = u_2^2 \tag{3}$$

The initial loss of each policy maker is zero. The demand shock in Germany causes a loss to the European central bank of 4 units, a loss to the German government of equally 4 units, and a loss to the French government of zero units. Then sequential policy decisions reduce the loss of the European central bank from 4 to zero units. Correspondingly, they reduce the loss of the German government from 4 to zero units. And they keep the loss of the French government at zero units.

2) A supply shock in Germany. In each of the member countries, let initial unemployment be zero, and let initial inflation be zero as well. Step one refers to the supply shock in Germany. In terms of the model there is an increase in B_1 of 2 units and an increase in A_1 of equally 2 units. Step two refers to the time lag. Inflation in Germany goes from zero to 2 percent. Inflation in France stays at zero percent. Hence inflation in Europe goes from zero to 1 percent. Unemployment in Germany goes from zero to 2 percent. Unemployment in France stays at zero percent. Hence unemployment in Europe goes from zero to 1 percent.

Step three refers to monetary policy in Europe. Current inflation in Europe is 1 percent, and target inflation in Europe is zero percent. So what is needed is a reduction in European money supply of 1 unit. Step four refers to the time lag. Unemployment in Germany goes from 2 to 3 percent. Unemployment in France goes from zero to 1 percent. Hence unemployment in Europe goes from 1 to 2 percent. Inflation in Germany goes from 2 to 1 percent. Inflation in France goes from zero to – 1 percent. Hence inflation in Europe goes from 1 to zero percent.

Step five refers to fiscal policies in Germany and France. First consider fiscal policy in Germany. Current unemployment in Germany is 3 percent, and target unemployment in Germany is zero percent. So what is needed is an increase in German government purchases of 3 units. Second consider fiscal policy in France. Current unemployment in France is 1 percent, and target unemployment in France is zero percent. So what is needed is an increase in French government purchases of 1 unit. Step six refers to the time lag. Unemployment in Germany goes from 3 to zero percent. Unemployment in France goes from 1 to zero percent. Hence unemployment in Europe goes from 2 to zero percent. Inflation in Germany goes from 1 to 4 percent. Inflation in France goes from – 1 to zero percent. Hence inflation in Europe goes from zero to 2 percent.

Step seven refers to monetary policy in Europe. Current inflation in Europe is 2 percent, and target inflation in Europe is zero percent. So what is needed is a reduction in European money supply of 2 units. Step eight refers to the time lag. Unemployment in Germany goes from zero to 2 percent, as does unemployment in France. Hence unemployment in Europe goes from zero to 2 percent as well. Inflation in Germany goes from 4 to 2 percent. Inflation in France goes from zero to – 2 percent. Hence inflation in Europe goes from 2 to zero percent.

Step nine refers to fiscal policies in Germany and France. First consider fiscal policy in Germany. Current unemployment in Germany is 2 percent, and target unemployment in Germany is zero percent. So what is needed is an increase in German government purchases of 2 units. Second consider fiscal policy in France. Current unemployment in France is 2 percent, and target unemployment in France is zero percent. So what is needed is an increase in French government purchases of 2 units. Step ten refers to the time lag. Unemployment in Germany goes from 2 to zero percent, as does unemployment in France. Hence unemployment in Europe goes from 2 to zero percent as well. Inflation in Germany goes from 2 to 4 percent. Inflation in France goes from – 2 to zero percent. Hence inflation in Europe goes from zero to 2 percent. And so on. Table 4.2 gives an overview.

As a result, given a supply shock in Germany, sequential policy decisions cause uniform oscillations in unemployment and inflation. And what is more, there is an explosion of government purchases and an implosion of money supply.

Table 4.2
Sequential Policy Decisions
A Supply Shock in Germany

Germany		France	
Unemployment	2	Unemployment	0
Inflation	2	Inflation	0
Δ European Money Supply	– 1		
Unemployment	3	Unemployment	1
Inflation	1	Inflation	– 1
Δ Government Purchases	3	Δ Government Purchases	1
Unemployment	0	Unemployment	0
Inflation	4	Inflation	0
Δ European Money Supply	– 2		
Unemployment	2	Unemployment	2
Inflation	2	Inflation	– 2
Δ Government Purchases	2	Δ Government Purchases	2
Unemployment	0	Unemployment	0
Inflation	4	Inflation	0
and so on			

3) A mixed shock in Germany. In each of the member countries, let initial unemployment be zero, and let initial inflation be zero as well. Step one refers to the mixed shock in Germany. In terms of the model there is an increase in B_1 of 4 units. Step two refers to the time lag. Inflation in Germany goes from zero to 4 percent. Inflation in France stays at zero percent. Thus inflation in Europe goes from zero to 2 percent. Unemployment in Germany stays at zero percent, as does unemployment in France. Thus unemployment in Europe stays at zero percent too.

Step three refers to monetary policy in Europe. Current inflation in Europe is 2 percent, and target inflation in Europe is zero percent. So what is needed is a reduction in European money supply of 2 units. Step four refers to the time lag. Unemployment in Germany goes from zero to 2 percent, as does unemployment in France. Thus unemployment in Europe goes from zero to 2 percent as well. Inflation in Germany goes from 4 to 2 percent. Inflation in France goes from zero to – 2 percent. Thus inflation in Europe goes from 2 to zero percent.

Step five refers to fiscal policies in Germany and France. First consider fiscal policy in Germany. Current unemployment in Germany is 2 percent, and target unemployment in Germany is zero percent. So what is needed is an increase in German government purchases of 2 units. Second consider fiscal policy in France. Current unemployment in France is 2 percent, and target unemployment in France is zero percent. So what is needed is an increase in French government purchases of 2 units. Step six refers to the time lag. Unemployment in Germany goes from 2 to zero percent, as does unemployment in France. Thus unemployment in Europe goes from 2 to zero percent as well. Inflation in Germany goes from 2 to 4 percent. Inflation in France goes from – 2 to zero percent. Thus inflation in Europe goes from zero to 2 percent. And so on. For a synopsis see Table 4.3.

As a result, given a mixed shock in Germany, sequential policy decisions cause uniform oscillations in unemployment and inflation. And what is more, there is an explosion of government purchases and an implosion of money supply.

4) Summary. Given a demand shock in Germany, sequential policy decisions produce zero unemployment and zero inflation in each of the member countries. There is an increase in European money supply, an increase in German government purchases, a reduction in French government purchases, and no change in European government purchases as a whole. Given a supply shock in Germany, sequential policy decisions cause uniform oscillations in unemployment and inflation. What is more, there is an explosion of government purchases and an implosion of money supply. And much the same applies to a mixed shock in Germany.

Table 4.3
Sequential Policy Decisions
A Mixed Shock in Germany

Germany		France	
Unemployment	0	Unemployment	0
Inflation	4	Inflation	0
Δ European Money Supply	– 2		
Unemployment	2	Unemployment	2
Inflation	2	Inflation	– 2
Δ Government Purchases	2	Δ Government Purchases	2
Unemployment	0	Unemployment	0
Inflation	4	Inflation	0
and so on			

Chapter 2
Target System B

1. The Model

1) The static model. This chapter is based on target system B. The targets of the European central bank are zero inflation and zero unemployment in each of the member countries. The target of the German government is zero unemployment in Germany. And the target of the French government is zero unemployment in France.

The model of unemployment and inflation can be characterized by a system of four equations:

$$u_1 = A_1 - M - G_1 \tag{1}$$

$$u_2 = A_2 - M - G_2 \tag{2}$$

$$\pi_1 = B_1 + M + G_1 \tag{3}$$

$$\pi_2 = B_2 + M + G_2 \tag{4}$$

An increase in European money supply lowers unemployment in Germany and France. On the other hand, it raises inflation there. An increase in German government purchases lowers unemployment in Germany. On the other hand, it raises inflation there. Correspondingly, an increase in French government purchases lowers unemployment in France. On the other hand, it raises inflation there.

The targets of the European central bank are zero inflation and zero unemployment in each of the member countries. The instrument of the European central bank is European money supply. There are four targets but only one instrument, so what is needed is a loss function. We assume that the European central bank has a quadratic loss function:

$$L = \pi_1^2 + \pi_2^2 + u_1^2 + u_2^2 \tag{5}$$

M. Carlberg, *Dynamic Policy Interactions in a Monetary Union*,
DOI 10.1007/978-3-642-18228-0_12, © Springer-Verlag Berlin Heidelberg 2011

L is the loss to the European central bank caused by inflation and unemployment in each of the member countries. We assume equal weights in the loss function. The specific target of the European central bank is to minimize the loss, given the inflation functions and the unemployment functions. Taking account of equations (1), (2), (3) and (4), the loss function of the European central bank can be written as follows:

$$\begin{aligned} L &= (B_1 + M + G_1)^2 + (B_2 + M + G_2)^2 \\ &\quad + (A_1 - M - G_1)^2 + (A_2 - M - G_2)^2 \end{aligned} \tag{6}$$

Then the first-order condition for a minimum loss gives the reaction function of the European central bank:

$$4M = A_1 + A_2 - B_1 - B_2 - 2G_1 - 2G_2 \tag{7}$$

An increase in A_1 or A_2 requires an increase in European money supply. An increase in B_1 or B_2 requires a cut in European money supply. And an increase in German or French government purchases requires a cut in European money supply too.

The target of the German government is zero unemployment in Germany. The instrument of the German government is German government purchases. By equation (1), the reaction function of the German government is:

$$G_1 = A_1 - M \tag{8}$$

An increase in A_1 requires an increase in German government purchases. And a cut in European money supply requires an increase in German government purchases as well.

The target of the French government is zero unemployment in France. The instrument of the French government is French government purchases. By equation (2), the reaction function of the French government is:

$$G_2 = A_2 - M \tag{9}$$

An increase in A_2 requires an increase in French government purchases. And a cut in European money supply requires an increase in French government purchases as well.

The Nash equilibrium is determined by the reaction functions of the European central bank, the German government, and the French government. From the reaction functions follows:

$$A_1 + A_2 + B_1 + B_2 = 0 \tag{10}$$

Evidently, this is in contradiction to the assumption that A_1, A_2, B_1 and B_2 are given exogenously. As a result there is no Nash equilibrium.

2) The dynamic model. We assume that the central bank and the governments decide sequentially. First the central bank decides, then the governments decide. Step 1 refers to a specific shock. Step 2 refers to the time lag. Step 3 refers to monetary policy in Europe. Step 4 refers to the time lag. Step 5 refers to fiscal policies in Germany and France. Step 6 refers to the time lag. Step 7 refers to monetary policy in Europe. Step 8 refers to the time lag. Step 9 refers to fiscal policies in Germany and France. Step 10 refers to the time lag. And so on.

Now take a closer look at the dynamic model. Step 1 refers to a specific shock. Step 2 refers to the time lag. Step 3 refers to monetary policy in Europe. The European central bank sets European money supply so as to reduce its loss. The reaction function of the European central bank is:

$$4M = A_1 + A_2 - B_1 - B_2 - 2G_1 - 2G_2 \tag{11}$$

Step 4 refers to the time lag. Step 5 refers to fiscal policies in Germany and France. The German government sets its purchases of German goods so as to achieve zero unemployment in Germany. The reaction function of the German government is:

$$G_1 = A_1 - M \tag{12}$$

The French government sets its purchases of French goods so as to achieve zero unemployment in France. The reaction function of the French government is:

$$G_2 = A_2 - M \tag{13}$$

Step 6 refers to the time lag. Step 7 refers to monetary policy in Europe. The European central bank sets European money supply so as to reduce its loss. The reaction function of the European central bank is:

$$4M = A_1 + A_2 - B_1 - B_2 - 2G_1 - 2G_2 \tag{14}$$

Step 8 refers to the time lag. Step 9 refers to fiscal policies in Germany and France. The German government sets its purchases of German goods so as to achieve zero unemployment in Germany. The reaction function of the German government is:

$$G_1 = A_1 - M \tag{15}$$

The French government sets its purchases of French goods so as to achieve zero unemployment in France. The reaction function of the French government is:

$$G_2 = A_2 - M \tag{16}$$

Step 10 refers to the time lag. And so on. Then what are the dynamic characteristics of this process?

2. Some Numerical Examples

Here are three distinct cases:

- a demand shock in Germany
- a supply shock in Germany
- a mixed shock in Germany.

The targets of the European central bank are zero inflation and zero unemployment in each of the member countries. The target of the German government is zero unemployment in Germany. And the target of the French government is zero unemployment in France.

1) A demand shock in Germany. In each of the member countries, let initial unemployment be zero, and let initial inflation be zero as well. Step one refers to a decline in the demand for German goods. In terms of the model there is an increase in A_1 of 2 units and a decline in B_1 of equally 2 units. Step two refers to the time lag. Unemployment in Germany goes from zero to 2 percent. Unemployment in France stays at zero percent. Thus unemployment in Europe goes from zero to 1 percent. Inflation in Germany goes from zero to – 2 percent. Inflation in France stays at zero percent. Thus inflation in Europe goes from zero to – 1 percent.

Step three refers to monetary policy in Europe. Current unemployment in Europe is 1 percent, and current inflation in Europe is – 1 percent. Accordingly, target unemployment in Europe and target inflation in Europe are zero percent each. So what is needed is an increase in European money supply of 1 unit. Step four refers to the time lag. Unemployment in Germany goes from 2 to 1 percent. Unemployment in France goes from zero to – 1 percent. Thus unemployment in Europe goes from 1 to zero percent. Inflation in Germany goes from – 2 to – 1 percent. Inflation in France goes from zero to 1 percent. Thus inflation in Europe goes from – 1 to zero percent.

Step five refers to fiscal policies in Germany and France. First consider fiscal policy in Germany. Current unemployment in Germany is 1 percent, and target unemployment in Germany is zero percent. So what is needed is an increase in German government purchases of 1 unit. Second consider fiscal policy in France.

Current unemployment in France is – 1 percent, and target unemployment in France is zero percent. So what is needed is a reduction in French government purchases of 1 unit. Step six refers to the time lag. Unemployment in Germany goes from 1 to zero percent. Unemployment in France goes from – 1 to zero percent. Thus unemployment in Europe stays at zero percent. Inflation in Germany goes from – 1 to zero percent. Inflation in France goes from 1 to zero percent. Thus inflation in Europe stays at zero percent. Table 4.4 presents a synopsis.

Table 4.4
Sequential Policy Decisions
A Demand Shock in Germany

Germany		France	
Unemployment	2	Unemployment	0
Inflation	– 2	Inflation	0
Δ European Money Supply	1		
Unemployment	1	Unemployment	– 1
Inflation	– 1	Inflation	1
Δ Government Purchases	1	Δ Government Purchases	– 1
Unemployment	0	Unemployment	0
Inflation	0	Inflation	0

As a result, given a demand shock in Germany, sequential policy decisions produce zero unemployment and zero inflation in each of the member countries. There is an increase in European money supply, an increase in German government purchases, a reduction in French government purchases, and no change in European government purchases as a whole.

The loss functions of the European central bank, the German government, and the French government are respectively:

$$L = \pi_1^2 + \pi_2^2 + u_1^2 + u_2^2 \tag{1}$$

$$L_1 = u_1^2 \tag{2}$$

$$L_2 = u_2^2 \tag{3}$$

The initial loss of each policy maker is zero. The demand shock in Germany causes a loss to the European central bank of 8 units, a loss to the German government of 4 units, and a loss to the French government of zero units. Then sequential policy decisions reduce the loss of the European central bank from 8 to zero units. Correspondingly, they reduce the loss of the German government from 4 to zero units. And they keep the loss of the French government at zero units.

2) A supply shock in Germany. In each of the member countries, let initial unemployment be zero, and let initial inflation be zero as well. Step one refers to the supply shock in Germany. In terms of the model there is an increase in B_1 of 2 units and an increase in A_1 of equally 2 units. Step two refers to the time lag. Inflation in Germany goes from zero to 2 percent. Inflation in France stays at zero percent. Hence inflation in Europe goes from zero to 1 percent. Unemployment in Germany goes from zero to 2 percent. Unemployment in France stays at zero percent. Hence unemployment in Europe goes from zero to 1 percent.

Step three refers to monetary policy in Europe. Current unemployment in Europe and current inflation in Europe are 1 percent each. Accordingly, target unemployment in Europe and target inflation Europe are 1 percent each. So what is needed is no change in European money supply. Step four refers to the time lag. Unemployment in Germany stays at 2 percent, and unemployment in France stays at zero percent. Hence unemployment in Europe stays at 1 percent. Inflation in Germany stays at 2 percent, and inflation in France stays at zero percent. Hence inflation in Europe stays at 1 percent.

Step five refers to fiscal policies in Germany and France. First consider fiscal policy in Germany. Current unemployment in Germany is 2 percent, and target unemployment in Germany is zero percent. So what is needed is an increase in German government purchases of 2 units. Second consider fiscal policy in

France. Current unemployment in France and target unemployment in France are zero percent each. So what is needed is no change in French government purchases. Step six refers to the time lag. Unemployment in Germany goes from 2 to zero percent. Unemployment in France stays at zero percent. Hence unemployment in Europe goes from 1 to zero percent. Inflation in Germany goes from 2 to 4 percent. Inflation in France stays at zero percent. Hence inflation in Europe goes from 1 to 2 percent.

Step seven refers to monetary policy in Europe. Current unemployment in Europe is zero percent, and current inflation in Europe is 2 percent. Accordingly, target unemployment in Europe and target inflation in Europe are 1 percent each. So what is needed is a reduction in European money supply of 1 unit. Step eight refers to the time lag. Unemployment in Germany goes from zero to 1 percent, as does unemployment in France. Hence unemployment in Europe goes from zero to 1 percent as well. Inflation in Germany goes from 4 to 3 percent. Inflation in France goes from zero to – 1 percent. Hence inflation in Europe goes from 2 to 1 percent.

Step nine refers to fiscal policies in Germany and France. First consider fiscal policy in Germany. Current unemployment in Germany is 1 percent, and target unemployment in Germany is zero percent. So what is needed is an increase in German government purchases of 1 unit. Second consider fiscal policy in France. Current unemployment in France is 1 percent, and target unemployment in France is zero percent. So what is needed is an increase in French government purchases of 1 unit. Step ten refers to the time lag. Unemployment in Germany goes from 1 to zero percent, as does unemployment in France. Hence unemployment in Europe goes from 1 to zero percent as well. Inflation in Germany goes from 3 to 4 percent. Inflation in France goes from – 1 to zero percent. Hence inflation in Europe goes from 1 to 2 percent. And so on. Table 4.5 gives an overview.

As a result, given a supply shock in Germany, sequential policy decisions cause uniform oscillations in unemployment and inflation. And what is more, there is an explosion of government purchases and an implosion of money supply.

Table 4.5
Sequential Policy Decisions
A Supply Shock in Germany

Germany		France	
Unemployment	2	Unemployment	0
Inflation	2	Inflation	0
Δ European Money Supply	0		
Unemployment	2	Unemployment	0
Inflation	2	Inflation	0
Δ Government Purchases	2	Δ Government Purchases	0
Unemployment	0	Unemployment	0
Inflation	4	Inflation	0
Δ European Money Supply	– 1		
Unemployment	1	Unemployment	1
Inflation	3	Inflation	– 1
Δ Government Purchases	1	Δ Government Purchases	1
Unemployment	0	Unemployment	0
Inflation	4	Inflation	0
and so on			

3) A mixed shock in Germany. In each of the member countries, let initial unemployment be zero, and let initial inflation be zero as well. Step one refers to the mixed shock in Germany. In terms of the model there is an increase in B_1 of 4 units. Step two refers to the time lag. Inflation in Germany goes from zero to 4 percent. Inflation in France stays at zero percent. Thus inflation in Europe goes from zero to 2 percent. Unemployment in Germany stays at zero percent, as does unemployment in France. Thus unemployment in Europe stays at zero percent too.

Step three refers to monetary policy in Europe. Current unemployment in Europe is zero percent, and current inflation in Europe is 2 percent. Accordingly, target unemployment in Europe and target inflation in Europe are 1 percent each. So what is needed is a reduction in European money supply of 1 unit. Step four refers to the time lag. Unemployment in Germany goes from zero to 1 percent, as does unemployment in France. Thus unemployment in Europe goes from zero to 1 percent as well. Inflation in Germany goes from 4 to 3 percent. Inflation in France goes from zero to – 1 percent. Thus inflation in Europe goes from 2 to 1 percent.

Step five refers to fiscal policies in Germany and France. First consider fiscal policy in Germany. Current unemployment in Germany is 1 percent, and target unemployment in Germany is zero percent. So what is needed is an increase in German government purchases of 1 unit. Second consider fiscal policy in France. Current unemployment in France is 1 percent, and target unemployment in France is zero percent. So what is needed is an increase in French government purchases of 1 unit. Step six refers to the time lag. Unemployment in Germany goes from 1 to zero percent, as does unemployment in France. Thus unemployment in Europe goes from 1 to zero percent as well. Inflation in Germany goes from 3 to 4 percent. Inflation in France goes from – 1 to zero percent. Thus inflation in Europe goes from 1 to 2 percent. And so on. For a synopsis see Table 4.6.

As a result, given a mixed shock in Germany, sequential policy decisions cause uniform oscillations in unemployment and inflation. And what is more, there is an explosion of government purchases and an implosion of money supply.

4) Summary. Given a demand shock in Germany, sequential policy decisions produce zero unemployment and zero inflation in each of the member countries. There is an increase in European money supply, an increase in German government purchases, a reduction in French government purchases, and no change in European government purchases as a whole. Given a supply shock in Germany, sequential policy decisions cause uniform oscillations in unemployment and inflation. What is more, there is an explosion of government

purchases and an implosion of money supply. And much the same applies to a mixed shock in Germany.

Table 4.6
Sequential Policy Decisions
A Mixed Shock in Germany

Germany		France	
Unemployment	0	Unemployment	0
Inflation	4	Inflation	0
Δ European Money Supply	– 1		
Unemployment	1	Unemployment	1
Inflation	3	Inflation	– 1
Δ Government Purchases	1	Δ Government Purchases	1
Unemployment	0	Unemployment	0
Inflation	4	Inflation	0
and so on			

Chapter 3
Target System C

1. The Model

1) The static model. This chapter is based on target system C. The targets of the European central bank are zero inflation and zero unemployment in each of the member countries. The targets of the German government are zero unemployment and zero inflation in Germany. And the targets of the French government are zero unemployment and zero inflation in France.

The model of unemployment and inflation can be represented by a system of four equations:

$$u_1 = A_1 - M - G_1 \qquad (1)$$

$$u_2 = A_2 - M - G_2 \qquad (2)$$

$$\pi_1 = B_1 + M + G_1 \qquad (3)$$

$$\pi_2 = B_2 + M + G_2 \qquad (4)$$

An increase in European money supply lowers unemployment in Germany and France. On the other hand, it raises inflation there. An increase in German government purchases lowers unemployment in Germany. On the other hand, it raises inflation there. Correspondingly, an increase in French government purchases lowers unemployment in France. On the other hand, it raises inflation there.

The targets of the European central bank are zero inflation and zero unemployment in each of the member countries. The instrument of the European central bank is European money supply. There are four targets but only one instrument, so what is needed is a loss function. We assume that the European central bank has a quadratic loss function:

$$L = \pi_1^2 + \pi_2^2 + u_1^2 + u_2^2 \qquad (5)$$

M. Carlberg, *Dynamic Policy Interactions in a Monetary Union*,
DOI 10.1007/978-3-642-18228-0_13, © Springer-Verlag Berlin Heidelberg 2011

L is the loss to the European central bank caused by inflation and unemployment in each of the member countries. We assume equal weights in the loss function. The specific target of the European central bank is to minimize the loss, given the inflation functions and the unemployment functions. Taking account of equations (1), (2), (3) and (4), the loss function of the European central bank can be written as follows:

$$\begin{aligned} L &= (B_1 + M + G_1)^2 + (B_2 + M + G_2)^2 \\ &+ (A_1 - M - G_1)^2 + (A_2 - M - G_2)^2 \end{aligned} \tag{6}$$

Then the first-order condition for a minimum loss gives the reaction function of the European central bank:

$$4M = A_1 + A_2 - B_1 - B_2 - 2G_1 - 2G_2 \tag{7}$$

An increase in A_1 or A_2 requires an increase in European money supply. An increase in B_1 or B_2 requires a cut in European money supply. And an increase in German or French government purchases requires a cut in European money supply too.

The targets of the German government are zero unemployment and zero inflation in Germany. The instrument of the German government is German government purchases. There are two targets but only one instrument, so what is needed is a loss function. We assume that the German government has a quadratic loss function:

$$L_1 = \pi_1^2 + u_1^2 \tag{8}$$

L_1 is the loss to the German government caused by inflation and unemployment in Germany. We assume equal weights in the loss function. The specific target of the German government is to minimize the loss, given the inflation function and the unemployment function. Taking account of equations (1) and (3), the loss function of the German government can be written as follows:

$$L_1 = (B_1 + M + G_1)^2 + (A_1 - M - G_1)^2 \tag{9}$$

Then the first-order condition for a minimum loss gives the reaction function of the German government:

$$2G_1 = A_1 - B_1 - 2M \tag{10}$$

An increase in A_1 requires an increase in German government purchases. An increase in B_1 requires a cut in German government purchases. And a cut in European money supply requires an increase in German government purchases.

The targets of the French government are zero unemployment and zero inflation in France. The instrument of the French government is French government purchases. There are two targets but only one instrument, so what is needed is a loss function. We assume that the French government has a quadratic loss function:

$$L_2 = \pi_2^2 + u_2^2 \tag{11}$$

L_2 is the loss to the French government caused by inflation and unemployment in France. We assume equal weights in the loss function. The specific target of the French government is to minimize the loss, given the inflation function and the unemployment function. Taking account of equations (2) and (4), the loss function of the French government can be written as follows:

$$L_2 = (B_2 + M + G_2)^2 + (A_2 - M - G_2)^2 \tag{12}$$

Then the first-order condition for a minimum loss gives the reaction function of the French government:

$$2G_2 = A_2 - B_2 - 2M \tag{13}$$

An increase in A_2 requires an increase in French government purchases. An increase in B_2 requires a cut in French government purchases. And a cut in European money supply requires an increase in French government purchases.

The Nash equilibrium is determined by the reaction functions of the European central bank, the German government, and the French government:

$$4M = A_1 + A_2 - B_1 - B_2 - 2G_1 - 2G_2 \tag{14}$$

$$2G_1 = A_1 - B_1 - 2M \tag{15}$$

$$2G_2 = A_2 - B_2 - 2M \tag{16}$$

Now take the sum of equations (15) and (16) to find out:

$$4M = A_1 + A_2 - B_1 - B_2 - 2G_1 - 2G_2 \tag{17}$$

Clearly, equations (14) and (17) are identical. There are three endogenous variables (M, G_1, G_2). On the other hand, there are only two independent equations. As a result there are multiple Nash equilibria.

Finally compare the target systems A, B and C. Under target system A there is no Nash equilibrium. Under target system B there is no Nash equilibrium either. And under target system C there are multiple Nash equilibria.

2) The dynamic model. We assume that the central bank and the governments decide sequentially. First the central bank decides, then the governments decide. Step 1 refers to a specific shock. Step 2 refers to the time lag. Step 3 refers to monetary policy in Europe. Step 4 refers to the time lag. Step 5 refers to fiscal policies in Germany and France. Step 6 refers to the time lag. Step 7 refers to monetary policy in Europe. Step 8 refers to the time lag. Step 9 refers to fiscal policies in Germany and France. Step 10 refers to the time lag. And so on.

Now have a closer look at the dynamic model. Step 1 refers to a specific shock. Step 2 refers to the time lag. Step 3 refers to monetary policy in Europe. The European central bank sets European money supply so as to reduce its loss. The reaction function of the European central bank is:

$$4M = A_1 + A_2 - B_1 - B_2 - 2G_1 - 2G_2 \tag{18}$$

Step 4 refers to the time lag. Step 5 refers to fiscal policies in Germany and France. The German government sets its purchases of German goods so as to reduce its loss. The reaction function of the German government is:

$$2G_1 = A_1 - B_1 - 2M \tag{19}$$

The French government sets its purchases of French goods so as to reduce its loss. The reaction function of the French government is:

$$2G_2 = A_2 - B_2 - 2M \tag{20}$$

Step 6 refers to the time lag. Step 7 refers to monetary policy in Europe. The European central bank sets European money supply so as to reduce its loss. The reaction function of the European central bank is:

$$4M = A_1 + A_2 - B_1 - B_2 - 2G_1 - 2G_2 \tag{21}$$

Step 8 refers to the time lag. Step 9 refers to fiscal policies in Germany and France. The German government sets its purchases of German goods so as to reduce its loss. The reaction function of the German government is:

$$2G_1 = A_1 - B_1 - 2M \tag{22}$$

The French government sets its purchases of French goods so as to reduce its loss. The reaction function of the French government is:

$$2G_2 = A_2 - B_2 - 2M \tag{23}$$

Step 10 refers to the time lag. And so on. Then what are the dynamic characteristics of this process?

2. Some Numerical Examples

Here are three distinct cases:

- a demand shock in Germany
- a supply shock in Germany
- a mixed shock in Germany.

The targets of the European central bank are zero inflation and zero unemployment in each of the member countries. The targets of the German government are zero unemployment and zero inflation in Germany. And the targets of the French government are zero unemployment and zero inflation in France.

1) A demand shock in Germany. In each of the member countries, let initial unemployment be zero, and let initial inflation be zero as well. Step one refers to a decline in the demand for German goods. In terms of the model there is an increase in A_1 of 2 units and a decline in B_1 of equally 2 units. Step two refers to the time lag. Unemployment in Germany goes from zero to 2 percent. Unemployment in France stays at zero percent. Thus unemployment in Europe goes from zero to 1 percent. Inflation in Germany goes from zero to – 2 percent. Inflation in France stays at zero percent. Thus inflation in Europe goes from zero to – 1 percent.

Step three refers to monetary policy in Europe. Current unemployment in Europe is 1 percent, and current inflation in Europe is – 1 percent. Accordingly, target unemployment in Europe and target inflation in Europe are zero percent each. So what is needed is an increase in European money supply of 1 unit. Step four refers to the time lag. Unemployment in Germany goes from 2 to 1 percent. Unemployment in France goes from zero to – 1 percent. Thus unemployment in Europe goes from 1 to zero percent. Inflation in Germany goes from – 2 to – 1 percent. Inflation in France goes from zero to 1 percent. Thus inflation in Europe goes from – 1 to zero percent.

Step five refers to fiscal policies in Germany and France. First consider fiscal policy in Germany. Current unemployment in Germany is 1 percent, and current inflation in Germany is – 1 percent. Accordingly, target unemployment in

Germany and target inflation in Germany are zero percent each. So what is needed is an increase in German government purchases of 1 unit. Second consider fiscal policy in France. Current unemployment in France is – 1 percent, and current inflation in France is 1 percent. Accordingly, target unemployment in France and target inflation in France are zero percent each. So what is needed is a reduction in French government purchases of 1 unit.

Step six refers to the time lag. Unemployment in Germany goes from 1 to zero percent. Unemployment in France goes from – 1 to zero percent. Thus unemployment in Europe stays at zero percent. Inflation in Germany goes from – 1 to zero percent. Inflation in France goes from 1 to zero percent. Thus inflation in Europe stays at zero percent. Table 4.7 presents a synopsis.

As a result, given a demand shock in Germany, sequential policy decisions produce zero unemployment and zero inflation in each of the member countries. There is an increase in European money supply, an increase in German government purchases, a reduction in French government purchases, and no change in European government purchases as a whole.

The loss functions of the European central bank, the German government, and the French government are respectively:

$$L = \pi_1^2 + \pi_2^2 + u_1^2 + u_2^2 \tag{1}$$

$$L_1 = u_1^2 + \pi_1^2 \tag{2}$$

$$L_2 = u_2^2 + \pi_2^2 \tag{3}$$

The initial loss of each policy maker is zero. The demand shock in Germany causes a loss to the European central bank of 8 units, a loss to the German government of equally 8 units, and a loss to the French government of zero units. Then sequential policy decisions reduce the loss of the European central bank from 8 to zero units. Correspondingly, they reduce the loss of the German government from 8 to zero units. And they keep the loss of the French government at zero units.

Table 4.7
Sequential Policy Decisions
A Demand Shock in Germany

Germany		France	
Unemployment	2	Unemployment	0
Inflation	– 2	Inflation	0
Δ European Money Supply	1		
Unemployment	1	Unemployment	– 1
Inflation	– 1	Inflation	1
Δ Government Purchases	1	Δ Government Purchases	– 1
Unemployment	0	Unemployment	0
Inflation	0	Inflation	0

2) A supply shock in Germany. In each of the member countries, let initial unemployment be zero, and let initial inflation be zero as well. Step one refers to the supply shock in Germany. In terms of the model there is an increase in B_1 of 2 units and an increase in A_1 of equally 2 units. Step two refers to the time lag. Inflation in Germany goes from zero to 2 percent. Inflation in France stays at zero percent. Hence inflation in Europe goes from zero to 1 percent. Unemployment in Germany goes from zero to 2 percent. Unemployment in France stays at zero percent. Hence unemployment in Europe goes from zero to 1 percent.

Step three refers to monetary policy in Europe. Current unemployment in Europe and current inflation in Europe are 1 percent each. Accordingly, target unemployment in Europe and target inflation Europe are 1 percent each. So what is needed is no change in European money supply. Step four refers to the time lag. Unemployment in Germany stays at 2 percent, and unemployment in France stays at zero percent. Hence unemployment in Europe stays at 1 percent. Inflation in Germany stays at 2 percent, and inflation in France stays at zero percent. Hence inflation in Europe stays at 1 percent.

Step five refers to fiscal policies in Germany and France. First consider fiscal policy in Germany. Current unemployment in Germany and current inflation in Germany are 2 percent each. Accordingly, target unemployment in Germany and target inflation in Germany are 2 percent each. So what is needed is no change in German government purchases. Second consider fiscal policy in France. Current unemployment in France and current inflation in France are zero percent each. Accordingly, target unemployment in France and target inflation in France are zero percent each. So what is needed is no change in French government purchases.

Step six refers to the time lag. Unemployment in Germany stays at 2 percent, and unemployment in France stays at zero percent. Hence unemployment in Europe stays at 1 percent. Inflation in Germany stays at 2 percent, and inflation in France stays at zero percent. Hence inflation in Europe stays at 1 percent. Table 4.8 gives an overview.

Table 4.8
Sequential Policy Decisions
A Supply Shock in Germany

Germany		France	
Unemployment	2	Unemployment	0
Inflation	2	Inflation	0
Δ European Money Supply	0		
Unemployment	2	Unemployment	0
Inflation	2	Inflation	0
Δ Government Purchases	0	Δ Government Purchases	0
Unemployment	2	Unemployment	0
Inflation	2	Inflation	0

As a result, given a supply shock in Germany, sequential policy decisions are ineffective. There is no change in money supply and government purchases. Correspondingly, there is no change in unemployment and inflation. The initial loss of each policy maker is zero. The supply shock in Germany causes a loss to the European central bank of 8 units, a loss to the German government of equally 8 units, and a loss to the French government of zero units. Then sequential policy decisions keep the loss of the European central bank at 8 units. Similarly, they keep the loss of the German government at 8 units. And they keep the loss of the French government at zero units.

3) A mixed shock in Germany. In each of the member countries, let initial unemployment be zero, and let initial inflation be zero as well. Step one refers to the mixed shock in Germany. In terms of the model there is an increase in B_1 of 4 units. Step two refers to the time lag. Inflation in Germany goes from zero to 4 percent. Inflation in France stays at zero percent. Thus inflation in Europe goes from zero to 2 percent. Unemployment in Germany stays at zero percent, as does unemployment in France. Thus unemployment in Europe stays at zero percent too.

Step three refers to monetary policy in Europe. Current unemployment in Europe is zero percent, and current inflation in Europe is 2 percent. Accordingly, target unemployment in Europe and target inflation in Europe are 1 percent each. So what is needed is a reduction in European money supply of 1 unit. Step four refers to the time lag. Unemployment in Germany goes from zero to 1 percent, as does unemployment in France. Thus unemployment in Europe goes from zero to 1 percent as well. Inflation in Germany goes from 4 to 3 percent. Inflation in France goes from zero to – 1 percent. Thus inflation in Europe goes from 2 to 1 percent.

Step five refers to fiscal policies in Germany and France. First consider fiscal policy in Germany. Current unemployment in Germany is 1 percent, and current inflation in Germany is 3 percent. Accordingly, target unemployment in Germany and target inflation in Germany are 2 percent each. So what is needed is a reduction in German government purchases of 1 unit. Second consider fiscal policy in France. Current unemployment in France is 1 percent, and current inflation in France is – 1 percent. Accordingly, target unemployment in France and target inflation in France are zero percent each. So what is needed is an increase in French government purchases of 1 unit.

Step six refers to the time lag. Unemployment in Germany goes from 1 to 2 percent. Unemployment in France goes from 1 to zero percent. Thus unemployment in Europe stays at 1 percent. Inflation in Germany goes from 3 to 2 percent. Inflation in France goes from – 1 to zero percent. Thus inflation in Europe stays at 1 percent. For a synopsis see Table 4.9.

Table 4.9
Sequential Policy Decisions
A Mixed Shock in Germany

Germany		France	
Unemployment	0	Unemployment	0
Inflation	4	Inflation	0
Δ European Money Supply	– 1		
Unemployment	1	Unemployment	1
Inflation	3	Inflation	– 1
Δ Government Purchases	– 1	Δ Government Purchases	1
Unemployment	2	Unemployment	0
Inflation	2	Inflation	0

As a result, given a mixed shock in Germany, sequential policy decisions lower German inflation. On the other hand, they raise German unemployment. And what is more, sequential policy decisions keep up zero unemployment and zero inflation in France. There is a reduction in European money supply, a reduction in German government purchases, an increase in French government purchases, and no change in European government purchases as a whole.

The initial loss of each policy maker is zero. The mixed shock in Germany causes a loss to the European central bank of 16 units, a loss to the German government of equally 16 units, and a loss to the French government of zero units. Then sequential policy decisions reduce the loss of the European central bank from 16 to 8 units. Similarly, they reduce the loss of the German government from 16 to 8 units. And they keep the loss of the French government at zero units.

4) Summary. Given a demand shock in Germany, sequential policy decisions produce zero unemployment and zero inflation in each of the member countries. There is an increase in European money supply, an increase in German government purchases, a reduction in French government purchases, and no change in European government purchases as a whole. Given a supply shock in Germany, sequential policy decisions are ineffective. There is no change in money supply and government purchases. Correspondingly, there is no change in unemployment and inflation. Given a mixed shock in Germany, sequential policy decisions lower German inflation. On the other hand, they raise German unemployment. And what is more, sequential policy decisions keep up zero unemployment and zero inflation in France. There is a reduction in European money supply, a reduction in German government purchases, an increase in French government purchases, and no change in European government purchases as a whole.

Part Five

First the Governments Decide, then the Central Bank Decides

Chapter 1
Target System A

1. The Model

1) The static model. The monetary union consists of two countries, say Germany and France. The member countries are the same size and have the same behavioural functions. This chapter is based on target system A. The targets of the European central bank are zero inflation in Germany and France respectively. The target of the German government is zero unemployment in Germany. And the target of the French government is zero unemployment in France.

The model of unemployment and inflation can be represented by a system of four equations:

$$u_1 = A_1 - M - G_1 \tag{1}$$

$$u_2 = A_2 - M - G_2 \tag{2}$$

$$\pi_1 = B_1 + M + G_1 \tag{3}$$

$$\pi_2 = B_2 + M + G_2 \tag{4}$$

Here u_1 denotes the rate of unemployment in Germany, u_2 is the rate of unemployment in France, π_1 is the rate of inflation in Germany, π_2 is the rate of inflation in France, M is European money supply, G_1 is German government purchases, G_2 is French government purchases, A_1 is some other factors bearing on the rate of unemployment in Germany, A_2 is some other factors bearing on the rate of unemployment in France, B_1 is some other factors bearing on the rate of inflation in Germany, and B_2 is some other factors bearing on the rate of inflation in France. The endogenous variables are the rate of unemployment in Germany, the rate of unemployment in France, the rate of inflation in Germany, and the rate of inflation in France.

An increase in European money supply lowers unemployment in Germany and France. On the other hand, it raises inflation there. An increase in German

M. Carlberg, *Dynamic Policy Interactions in a Monetary Union*,
DOI 10.1007/978-3-642-18228-0_14, © Springer-Verlag Berlin Heidelberg 2011

government purchases lowers unemployment in Germany. On the other hand, it raises inflation there. Correspondingly, an increase in French government purchases lowers unemployment in France. On the other hand, it raises inflation there. Fiscal policy in one of the member countries has no effect on unemployment or inflation in the other country.

The targets of the European central bank are zero inflation in Germany and France respectively. The instrument of the European central bank is European money supply. There are two targets but only one instrument, so what is needed is a loss function. We assume that the European central bank has a quadratic loss function:

$$L = \pi_1^2 + \pi_2^2 \tag{5}$$

L is the loss to the European central bank caused by inflation in Germany and France. We assume equal weights in the loss function. The specific target of the European central bank is to minimize the loss, given the inflation functions. Taking account of equations (3) and (4), the loss function of the European central bank can be written as follows:

$$L = (B_1 + M + G_1)^2 + (B_2 + M + G_2)^2 \tag{6}$$

Then the first-order condition for a minimum loss gives the reaction function of the European central bank:

$$2M = -B_1 - B_2 - G_1 - G_2 \tag{7}$$

An increase in B_1 or B_2 requires a cut in European money supply. And an increase in German or French government purchases requires a cut in European money supply too.

The target of the German government is zero unemployment in Germany. The instrument of the German government is German government purchases. By equation (1), the reaction function of the German government is:

$$G_1 = A_1 - M \tag{8}$$

An increase in A_1 requires an increase in German government purchases. And a cut in European money supply requires an increase in German government purchases as well.

The target of the French government is zero unemployment in France. The instrument of the French government is French government purchases. By equation (2), the reaction function of the French government is:

$$G_2 = A_2 - M \tag{9}$$

An increase in A_2 requires an increase in French government purchases. And a cut in European money supply requires an increase in French government purchases as well.

The Nash equilibrium is determined by the reaction functions of the European central bank, the German government, and the French government. From the reaction functions follows:

$$A_1 + A_2 + B_1 + B_2 = 0 \tag{10}$$

Evidently, this is in contradiction to the assumption that A_1, A_2, B_1 and B_2 are given exogenously. As a result there is no Nash equilibrium.

2) The dynamic model. We assume that the governments and the central bank decide sequentially. First the governments decide, then the central bank decides. Step 1 refers to a specific shock. Step 2 refers to the time lag. Step 3 refers to fiscal policies in Germany and France. Step 4 refers to the time lag. Step 5 refers to monetary policy in Europe. Step 6 refers to the time lag. Step 7 refers to fiscal policies in Germany and France. Step 8 refers to the time lag. Step 9 refers to monetary policy in Europe. Step 10 refers to the time lag. And so on.

Now have a closer look at the dynamic model. Step 1 refers to a specific shock. This could be a demand shock, a supply shock or a mixed shock, in Germany or France. Step 2 refers to the time lag. This includes both the inside lag and the outside lag. Step 3 refers to fiscal policies in Germany and France. The German government sets its purchases of German goods so as to achieve zero unemployment in Germany. The reaction function of the German government is:

$$G_1 = A_1 - M \tag{11}$$

The French government sets its purchases of French goods so as to achieve zero unemployment in France. The reaction function of the French government is:

$$G_2 = A_2 - M \tag{12}$$

Step 4 refers to the time lag. Step 5 refers to monetary policy in Europe. The European central bank sets European money supply so as to achieve zero inflation in Europe. The reaction function of the European central bank is:

$$2M = -B_1 - B_2 - G_1 - G_2 \tag{13}$$

Step 6 refers to the time lag. Step 7 refers to fiscal policies in Germany and France. The German government sets its purchases of German goods so as to achieve zero unemployment in Germany. The reaction function of the German government is:

$$G_1 = A_1 - M \tag{14}$$

The French government sets its purchases of French goods so as to achieve zero unemployment in France. The reaction function of the French government is:

$$G_2 = A_2 - M \tag{15}$$

Step 8 refers to the time lag. Step 9 refers to monetary policy in Europe. The European central bank sets European money supply so as to achieve zero inflation in Europe. The reaction function of the European central bank is:

$$2M = -B_1 - B_2 - G_1 - G_2 \tag{16}$$

Step 10 refers to the time lag. And so on. Then what are the dynamic characteristics of this process?

2. Some Numerical Examples

It proves useful to study three distinct cases:

- a demand shock in Germany
- a supply shock in Germany
- a mixed shock in Germany.

The targets of the European central bank are zero inflation in Germany and France respectively. The target of the German government is zero unemployment in Germany. And the target of the French government is zero unemployment in France.

1) A demand shock in Germany. In each of the member countries, let initial unemployment be zero, and let initial inflation be zero as well. Step one refers to a decline in the demand for German goods. In terms of the model there is an increase in A_1 of 2 units and a decline in B_1 of equally 2 units. Step two refers to the time lag. Unemployment in Germany goes from zero to 2 percent. Unemployment in France stays at zero percent. Thus unemployment in Europe goes from zero to 1 percent. Inflation in Germany goes from zero to – 2 percent. Inflation in France stays at zero percent. Thus inflation in Europe goes from zero to – 1 percent.

Step three refers to fiscal policies in Germany and France. First consider fiscal policy in Germany. Current unemployment in Germany is 2 percent, and target unemployment in Germany is zero percent. So what is needed is an increase in German government purchases of 2 units. Second consider fiscal policy in France. Current unemployment in France is zero percent, and target unemployment in France is the same. So what is needed is no change in French government purchases. Step four refers to the time lag. Unemployment in Germany goes from 2 to zero percent. Unemployment in France stays at zero percent. Thus unemployment in Europe goes from 1 to zero percent. Inflation in Germany goes from – 2 to zero percent. Inflation in France stays at zero percent. Thus inflation in Europe goes from – 1 to zero percent.

Step five refers to monetary policy in Europe. Current inflation in Europe is zero percent, and target inflation in Europe is the same. So what is needed is no change in European money supply. Step six refers to the time lag. Unemployment in Germany stays at zero percent, as does unemployment in France. Thus unemployment in Europe stays at zero percent as well. Inflation in Germany stays at zero percent, as does inflation in France. Thus inflation in Europe stays at zero percent as well. Table 5.1 presents a synopsis.

Table 5.1
Sequential Policy Decisions
A Demand Shock in Germany

Germany		France	
Unemployment	2	Unemployment	0
Inflation	– 2	Inflation	0
Δ Government Purchases	2	Δ Government Purchases	0
Unemployment	0	Unemployment	0
Inflation	0	Inflation	0
Δ European Money Supply	0		
Unemployment	0	Unemployment	0
Inflation	0	Inflation	0

As a result, given a demand shock in Germany, sequential policy decisions produce zero unemployment and zero inflation in each of the member countries. There is an increase in German government purchases, no change in French government purchases, and no change in European money supply.

The loss functions of the European central bank, the German government, and the French government are respectively:

$$L = \pi_1^2 + \pi_2^2 \tag{1}$$

$$L_1 = u_1^2 \tag{2}$$

$$L_2 = u_2^2 \tag{3}$$

The initial loss of each policy maker is zero. The demand shock in Germany causes a loss to the European central bank of 4 units, a loss to the German government of equally 4 units, and a loss to the French government of zero units. Then sequential policy decisions reduce the loss of the European central bank from 4 to zero units. Correspondingly, they reduce the loss of the German government from 4 to zero units. And they keep the loss of the French government at zero units.

2) A supply shock in Germany. In each of the member countries, let initial unemployment be zero, and let initial inflation be zero as well. Step one refers to the supply shock in Germany. In terms of the model there is an increase in B_1 of 2 units and an increase in A_1 of equally 2 units. Step two refers to the time lag. Inflation in Germany goes from zero to 2 percent. Inflation in France stays at zero percent. Hence inflation in Europe goes from zero to 1 percent. Unemployment in Germany goes from zero to 2 percent. Unemployment in France stays at zero percent. Hence unemployment in Europe goes from zero to 1 percent.

Step three refers to fiscal policies in Germany and France. First consider fiscal policy in Germany. Current unemployment in Germany is 2 percent, and target unemployment in Germany is zero percent. So what is needed is an increase in German government purchases of 2 units. Second consider fiscal policy in France. Current unemployment in France is zero percent, and target unemployment in France is the same. So what is needed is no change in French government purchases. Step four refers to the time lag. Unemployment in Germany goes from 2 to zero percent. Unemployment in France stays at zero percent. Hence unemployment in Europe goes from 1 to zero percent. Inflation in Germany goes from 2 to 4 percent. Inflation in France stays at zero percent. Hence inflation in Europe goes from 1 to 2 percent.

Step five refers to monetary policy in Europe. Current inflation in Europe is 2 percent, and target inflation in Europe is zero percent. So what is needed is a reduction in European money supply of 2 units. Step six refers to the time lag. Unemployment in Germany goes from zero to 2 percent, as does unemployment in France. Hence unemployment in Europe goes from zero to 2 percent as well. Inflation in Germany goes from 4 to 2 percent. Inflation in France goes from zero to – 2 percent. Hence inflation in Europe goes from 2 to zero percent.

Step seven refers to fiscal policies in Germany and France. First consider fiscal policy in Germany. Current unemployment in Germany is 2 percent, and target unemployment in Germany is zero percent. So what is needed is an increase in German government purchases of 2 units. Second consider fiscal policy in France. Current unemployment in France is 2 percent, and target unemployment in France is zero percent. So what is needed is an increase in French government purchases of 2 units. Step eight refers to the time lag. Unemployment in Germany goes from 2 to zero percent, as does unemployment in France. Hence unemployment in Europe goes from 2 to zero percent as well. Inflation in Germany goes from 2 to 4 percent. Inflation in France goes from – 2 to zero percent. Hence inflation in Europe goes from zero to 2 percent.

Step nine refers to monetary policy in Europe. Current inflation in Europe is 2 percent, and target inflation in Europe is zero percent. So what is needed is a reduction in European money supply of 2 units. Step ten refers to the time lag. Unemployment in Germany goes from zero to 2 percent, as does unemployment in France. Hence unemployment in Europe goes from zero to 2 percent as well. Inflation in Germany goes from 4 to 2 percent. Inflation in France goes from zero to – 2 percent. Hence inflation in Europe goes from 2 to zero percent. And so on. Table 5.2 gives an overview.

As a result, given a supply shock in Germany, sequential policy decisions cause uniform oscillations in unemployment and inflation. And what is more, there is an explosion of government purchases and an implosion of money supply.

Table 5.2
Sequential Policy Decisions
A Supply Shock in Germany

Germany		France	
Unemployment	2	Unemployment	0
Inflation	2	Inflation	0
Δ Government Purchases	2	Δ Government Purchases	0
Unemployment	0	Unemployment	0
Inflation	4	Inflation	0
Δ European Money Supply	– 2		
Unemployment	2	Unemployment	2
Inflation	2	Inflation	– 2
Δ Government Purchases	2	Δ Government Purchases	2
Unemployment	0	Unemployment	0
Inflation	4	Inflation	0
Δ European Money Supply	– 2		
Unemployment	2	Unemployment	2
Inflation	2	Inflation	– 2
and so on			

3) A mixed shock in Germany. In each of the member countries, let initial unemployment be zero, and let initial inflation be zero as well. Step one refers to the mixed shock in Germany. In terms of the model there is an increase in B_1 of 4 units. Step two refers to the time lag. Inflation in Germany goes from zero to 4 percent. Inflation in France stays at zero percent. Thus inflation in Europe goes from zero to 2 percent. Unemployment in Germany stays at zero percent, as does unemployment in France. Thus unemployment in Europe stays at zero percent too.

Step three refers to fiscal policies in Germany and France. First consider fiscal policy in Germany. Current unemployment in Germany is zero percent, and target unemployment in Germany is the same. So what is needed is no change in German government purchases. Second consider fiscal policy in France. Current unemployment in France is zero percent, and target unemployment in France is the same. So what is needed is no change in French government purchases. Step four refers to the time lag. Unemployment in Germany stays at zero percent, as does unemployment in France. Thus unemployment in Europe stays at zero percent as well. Inflation in Germany stays at 4 percent, and inflation in France stays at zero percent. Thus inflation in Europe stays at 2 percent.

Step five refers to monetary policy in Europe. Current inflation in Europe is 2 percent, and target inflation in Europe is zero percent. So what is needed is a reduction in European money supply of 2 units. Step six refers to the time lag. Unemployment in Germany goes from zero to 2 percent, as does unemployment in France. Thus unemployment in Europe goes from zero to 2 percent as well. Inflation in Germany goes from 4 to 2 percent. Inflation in France goes from zero to – 2 percent. Thus inflation in Europe goes from 2 to zero percent.

Step seven refers to fiscal policies in Germany and France. First consider fiscal policy in Germany. Current unemployment in Germany is 2 percent, and target unemployment in Germany is zero percent. So what is needed is an increase in German government purchases of 2 units. Second consider fiscal policy in France. Current unemployment in France is 2 percent, and target unemployment in France is zero percent. So what is needed is an increase in French government purchases of 2 units. Step eight refers to the time lag. Unemployment in Germany goes from 2 to zero percent, as does unemployment in France. Thus unemployment in Europe goes from 2 to zero percent as well. Inflation in Germany goes from 2 to 4 percent. Inflation in France goes from – 2 to zero percent. Thus inflation in Europe goes from zero to 2 percent.

Step nine refers to monetary policy in Europe. Current inflation in Europe is 2 percent, and target inflation in Europe is zero percent. So what is needed is a reduction in European money supply of 2 units. Step ten refers to the time lag. Unemployment in Germany goes from zero to 2 percent, as does unemployment in France. Thus unemployment in Europe goes from zero to 2 percent as well. Inflation in Germany goes from 4 to 2 percent. Inflation in France goes from zero to – 2 percent. Thus inflation in Europe goes from 2 to zero percent. And so on. For a synopsis see Table 5.3.

Table 5.3
Sequential Policy Decisions
A Mixed Shock in Germany

Germany		France	
Unemployment	0	Unemployment	0
Inflation	4	Inflation	0
Δ Government Purchases	0	Δ Government Purchases	0
Unemployment	0	Unemployment	0
Inflation	4	Inflation	0
Δ European Money Supply	– 2		
Unemployment	2	Unemployment	2
Inflation	2	Inflation	– 2
Δ Government Purchases	2	Δ Government Purchases	2
Unemployment	0	Unemployment	0
Inflation	4	Inflation	0
Δ European Money Supply	– 2		
Unemployment	2	Unemployment	2
Inflation	2	Inflation	– 2
and so on			

As a result, given a mixed shock in Germany, sequential policy decisions cause uniform oscillations in unemployment and inflation. And what is more, there is an explosion of government purchases and an implosion of money supply.

4) Summary. Given a demand shock in Germany, sequential policy decisions produce zero unemployment and zero inflation in each of the member countries. There is an increase in German government purchases, no change in French government purchases, and no change in European money supply. Given a supply shock in Germany, sequential policy decisions cause uniform oscillations in unemployment and inflation. What is more, there is an explosion of government purchases and an implosion of money supply. And much the same applies to a mixed shock in Germany.

Chapter 2
Target System B

1. The Model

1) The static model. This chapter is based on target system B. The targets of the European central bank are zero inflation and zero unemployment in each of the member countries. The target of the German government is zero unemployment in Germany. And the target of the French government is zero unemployment in France.

The model of unemployment and inflation can be characterized by a system of four equations:

$$u_1 = A_1 - M - G_1 \quad (1)$$

$$u_2 = A_2 - M - G_2 \quad (2)$$

$$\pi_1 = B_1 + M + G_1 \quad (3)$$

$$\pi_2 = B_2 + M + G_2 \quad (4)$$

An increase in European money supply lowers unemployment in Germany and France. On the other hand, it raises inflation there. An increase in German government purchases lowers unemployment in Germany. On the other hand, it raises inflation there. Correspondingly, an increase in French government purchases lowers unemployment in France. On the other hand, it raises inflation there.

The targets of the European central bank are zero inflation and zero unemployment in each of the member countries. The instrument of the European central bank is European money supply. There are four targets but only one instrument, so what is needed is a loss function. We assume that the European central bank has a quadratic loss function:

$$L = \pi_1^2 + \pi_2^2 + u_1^2 + u_2^2 \quad (5)$$

M. Carlberg, *Dynamic Policy Interactions in a Monetary Union*,
DOI 10.1007/978-3-642-18228-0_15, © Springer-Verlag Berlin Heidelberg 2011

L is the loss to the European central bank caused by inflation and unemployment in each of the member countries. We assume equal weights in the loss function. The specific target of the European central bank is to minimize the loss, given the inflation functions and the unemployment functions. Taking account of equations (1), (2), (3) and (4), the loss function of the European central bank can be written as follows:

$$\begin{aligned} L &= (B_1 + M + G_1)^2 + (B_2 + M + G_2)^2 \\ &\quad + (A_1 - M - G_1)^2 + (A_2 - M - G_2)^2 \end{aligned} \tag{6}$$

Then the first-order condition for a minimum loss gives the reaction function of the European central bank:

$$4M = A_1 + A_2 - B_1 - B_2 - 2G_1 - 2G_2 \tag{7}$$

An increase in A_1 or A_2 requires an increase in European money supply. An increase in B_1 or B_2 requires a cut in European money supply. And an increase in German or French government purchases requires a cut in European money supply too.

The target of the German government is zero unemployment in Germany. The instrument of the German government is German government purchases. By equation (1), the reaction function of the German government is:

$$G_1 = A_1 - M \tag{8}$$

An increase in A_1 requires an increase in German government purchases. And a cut in European money supply requires an increase in German government purchases as well.

The target of the French government is zero unemployment in France. The instrument of the French government is French government purchases. By equation (2), the reaction function of the French government is:

$$G_2 = A_2 - M \tag{9}$$

An increase in A_2 requires an increase in French government purchases. And a cut in European money supply requires an increase in French government purchases as well.

The Nash equilibrium is determined by the reaction functions of the European central bank, the German government, and the French government. From the reaction functions follows:

$$A_1 + A_2 + B_1 + B_2 = 0 \tag{10}$$

Evidently, this is in contradiction to the assumption that A_1, A_2, B_1 and B_2 are given exogenously. As a result there is no Nash equilibrium.

2) The dynamic model. We assume that the governments and the central bank decide sequentially. First the governments decide, then the central bank decides. Step 1 refers to a specific shock. Step 2 refers to the time lag. Step 3 refers to fiscal policies in Germany and France. Step 4 refers to the time lag. Step 5 refers to monetary policy in Europe. Step 6 refers to the time lag. Step 7 refers to fiscal policies in Germany and France. Step 8 refers to the time lag. Step 9 refers to monetary policy in Europe. Step 10 refers to the time lag. And so on.

Now take a closer look at the dynamic model. Step 1 refers to a specific shock. Step 2 refers to the time lag. Step 3 refers to fiscal policies in Germany and France. The German government sets its purchases of German goods so as to achieve zero unemployment in Germany. The reaction function of the German government is:

$$G_1 = A_1 - M \tag{11}$$

The French government sets its purchases of French goods so as to achieve zero unemployment in France. The reaction function of the French government is:

$$G_2 = A_2 - M \tag{12}$$

Step 4 refers to the time lag. Step 5 refers to monetary policy in Europe. The European central bank sets European money supply so as to reduce its loss. The reaction function of the European central bank is:

$$4M = A_1 + A_2 - B_1 - B_2 - 2G_1 - 2G_2 \tag{13}$$

Step 6 refers to the time lag. Step 7 refers to fiscal policies in Germany and France. The German government sets its purchases of German goods so as to achieve zero unemployment in Germany. The reaction function of the German government is:

$$G_1 = A_1 - M \tag{14}$$

The French government sets its purchases of French goods so as to achieve zero unemployment in France. The reaction function of the French government is:

$$G_2 = A_2 - M \tag{15}$$

Step 8 refers to the time lag. Step 9 refers to monetary policy in Europe. The European central bank sets European money supply so as to reduce its loss. The reaction function of the European central bank is:

$$4M = A_1 + A_2 - B_1 - B_2 - 2G_1 - 2G_2 \tag{16}$$

Step 10 refers to the time lag. And so on. Then what are the dynamic characteristics of this process?

2. Some Numerical Examples

Here are three distinct cases:

- a demand shock in Germany
- a supply shock in Germany
- a mixed shock in Germany.

The targets of the European central bank are zero inflation and zero unemployment in each of the member countries. The target of the German government is zero unemployment in Germany. And the target of the French government is zero unemployment in France.

1) A demand shock in Germany. In each of the member countries, let initial unemployment be zero, and let initial inflation be zero as well. Step one refers to a decline in the demand for German goods. In terms of the model there is an increase in A_1 of 2 units and a decline in B_1 of equally 2 units. Step two refers to the time lag. Unemployment in Germany goes from zero to 2 percent. Unemployment in France stays at zero percent. Thus unemployment in Europe goes from zero to 1 percent. Inflation in Germany goes from zero to – 2 percent. Inflation in France stays at zero percent. Thus inflation in Europe goes from zero to – 1 percent.

Step three refers to fiscal policies in Germany and France. First consider fiscal policy in Germany. Current unemployment in Germany is 2 percent, and target unemployment in Germany is zero percent. So what is needed is an increase in German government purchases of 2 units. Second consider fiscal policy in France. Current unemployment in France is zero percent, and target unemployment in France is the same. So what is needed is no change in French government purchases. Step four refers to the time lag. Unemployment in Germany goes from 2 to zero percent. Unemployment in France stays at zero percent. Thus unemployment in Europe goes from 1 to zero percent. Inflation in Germany goes from – 2 to zero percent. Inflation in France stays at zero percent. Thus inflation in Europe goes from – 1 to zero percent.

Step five refers to monetary policy in Europe. Current unemployment in Europe and current inflation in Europe are zero percent each. Accordingly, target unemployment in Europe and target inflation in Europe are zero percent each. So what is needed is no change in European money supply. Step six refers to the time lag. Unemployment in Germany stays at zero percent, as does unemployment in France. Thus unemployment in Europe stays at zero percent as well. Inflation in Germany stays at zero percent, as does inflation in France. Thus inflation in Europe stays at zero percent as well. Table 5.4 presents a synopsis.

Table 5.4
Sequential Policy Decisions
A Demand Shock in Germany

Germany		France	
Unemployment	2	Unemployment	0
Inflation	– 2	Inflation	0
Δ Government Purchases	2	Δ Government Purchases	0
Unemployment	0	Unemployment	0
Inflation	0	Inflation	0
Δ European Money Supply	0		
Unemployment	0	Unemployment	0
Inflation	0	Inflation	0

As a result, given a demand shock in Germany, sequential policy decisions produce zero unemployment and zero inflation in each of the member countries. There is an increase in German government purchases, no change in French government purchases, and no change in European money supply.

The loss functions of the European central bank, the German government, and the French government are respectively:

$$L = \pi_1^2 + \pi_2^2 + u_1^2 + u_2^2 \tag{1}$$

$$L_1 = u_1^2 \tag{2}$$

$$L_2 = u_2^2 \tag{3}$$

The initial loss of each policy maker is zero. The demand shock in Germany causes a loss to the European central bank of 8 units, a loss to the German government of 4 units, and a loss to the French government of zero units. Then sequential policy decisions reduce the loss of the European central bank from 8 to zero units. Correspondingly, they reduce the loss of the German government from 4 to zero units. And they keep the loss of the French government at zero units.

2) A supply shock in Germany. In each of the member countries, let initial unemployment be zero, and let initial inflation be zero as well. Step one refers to the supply shock in Germany. In terms of the model there is an increase in B_1 of 2 units and an increase in A_1 of equally 2 units. Step two refers to the time lag. Inflation in Germany goes from zero to 2 percent. Inflation in France stays at zero percent. Hence inflation in Europe goes from zero to 1 percent. Unemployment in Germany goes from zero to 2 percent. Unemployment in France stays at zero percent. Hence unemployment in Europe goes from zero to 1 percent.

Step three refers to fiscal policies in Germany and France. First consider fiscal policy in Germany. Current unemployment in Germany is 2 percent, and target unemployment in Germany is zero percent. So what is needed is an increase in German government purchases of 2 units. Second consider fiscal policy in France. Current unemployment in France is zero percent, and target unemployment in France is the same. So what is needed is no change in French government purchases. Step four refers to the time lag. Unemployment in Germany goes from 2 to zero percent. Unemployment in France stays at zero percent. Hence unemployment in Europe goes from 1 to zero percent. Inflation in Germany goes from 2 to 4 percent. Inflation in France stays at zero percent. Hence inflation in Europe goes from 1 to 2 percent.

Step five refers to monetary policy in Europe. Current unemployment in Europe is zero percent, and current inflation in Europe is 2 percent. Accordingly, target unemployment in Europe and target inflation in Europe are 1 percent each.

So what is needed is a reduction in European money supply of 1 unit. Step six refers to the time lag. Unemployment in Germany goes from zero to 1 percent, as does unemployment in France. Hence unemployment in Europe goes from zero to 1 percent as well. Inflation in Germany goes from 4 to 3 percent. Inflation in France goes from zero to – 1 percent. Hence inflation in Europe goes from 2 to 1 percent.

Step seven refers to fiscal policies in Germany and France. First consider fiscal policy in Germany. Current unemployment in Germany is 1 percent, and target unemployment in Germany is zero percent. So what is needed is an increase in German government purchases of 1 unit. Second consider fiscal policy in France. Current unemployment in France is 1 percent, and target unemployment in France is zero percent. So what is needed is an increase in French government purchases of 1 unit. Step eight refers to the time lag. Unemployment in Germany goes from 1 to zero percent, as does unemployment in France. Hence unemployment in Europe goes from 1 to zero percent as well. Inflation in Germany goes from 3 to 4 percent. Inflation in France goes from – 1 to zero percent. Hence inflation in Europe goes from 1 to 2 percent.

Step nine refers to monetary policy in Europe. Current unemployment in Europe is zero percent, and current inflation in Europe is 2 percent. Accordingly, target unemployment in Europe and target inflation in Europe are 1 percent each. So what is needed is a reduction in European money supply of 1 unit. Step ten refers to the time lag. Unemployment in Germany goes from zero to 1 percent, as does unemployment in France. Hence unemployment in Europe goes from zero to 1 percent as well. Inflation in Germany goes from 4 to 3 percent. Inflation in France goes from zero to – 1 percent. Hence inflation in Europe goes from 2 to 1 percent. And so on. Table 5.5 gives an overview.

As a result, given a supply shock in Germany, sequential policy decisions cause uniform oscillations in unemployment and inflation. And what is more, there is an explosion of government purchases and an implosion of money supply.

Table 5.5
Sequential Policy Decisions
A Supply Shock in Germany

Germany		France	
Unemployment	2	Unemployment	0
Inflation	2	Inflation	0
Δ Government Purchases	2	Δ Government Purchases	0
Unemployment	0	Unemployment	0
Inflation	4	Inflation	0
Δ European Money Supply	– 1		
Unemployment	1	Unemployment	1
Inflation	3	Inflation	– 1
Δ Government Purchases	1	Δ Government Purchases	1
Unemployment	0	Unemployment	0
Inflation	4	Inflation	0
Δ European Money Supply	– 1		
Unemployment	1	Unemployment	1
Inflation	3	Inflation	– 1
and so on			

3) A mixed shock in Germany. In each of the member countries, let initial unemployment be zero, and let initial inflation be zero as well. Step one refers to the mixed shock in Germany. In terms of the model there is an increase in B_1 of 4 units. Step two refers to the time lag. Inflation in Germany goes from zero to 4 percent. Inflation in France stays at zero percent. Thus inflation in Europe goes from zero to 2 percent. Unemployment in Germany stays at zero percent, as does unemployment in France. Thus unemployment in Europe stays at zero percent too.

Step three refers to fiscal policies in Germany and France. First consider fiscal policy in Germany. Current unemployment in Germany is zero percent, and target unemployment in Germany is the same. So what is needed is no change in German government purchases. Second consider fiscal policy in France. Current unemployment in France is zero percent, and target unemployment in France is the same. So what is needed is no change in French government purchases. Step four refers to the time lag. Unemployment in Germany stays at zero percent, as does unemployment in France. Thus unemployment in Europe stays at zero percent as well. Inflation in Germany stays at 4 percent, and inflation in France stays at zero percent. Thus inflation in Europe stays at 2 percent.

Step five refers to monetary policy in Europe. Current unemployment in Europe is zero percent, and current inflation in Europe is 2 percent. Accordingly, target unemployment in Europe and target inflation in Europe are 1 percent each. So what is needed is a reduction in European money supply of 1 unit. Step six refers to the time lag. Unemployment in Germany goes from zero to 1 percent, as does unemployment in France. Thus unemployment in Europe goes from zero to 1 percent as well. Inflation in Germany goes from 4 to 3 percent. Inflation in France goes from zero to – 1 percent. Thus inflation in Europe goes from 2 to 1 percent.

Step seven refers to fiscal policies in Germany and France. First consider fiscal policy in Germany. Current unemployment in Germany is 1 percent, and target unemployment in Germany is zero percent. So what is needed is an increase in German government purchases of 1 unit. Second consider fiscal policy in France. Current unemployment in France is 1 percent, and target unemployment in France is zero percent. So what is needed is an increase in French government purchases of 1 unit. Step eight refers to the time lag. Unemployment in Germany goes from 1 to zero percent, as does unemployment in France. Thus unemployment in Europe goes from 1 to zero percent as well. Inflation in Germany goes from 3 to 4 percent. Inflation in France goes from – 1 to zero percent. Thus inflation in Europe goes from 1 to 2 percent.

Step nine refers to monetary policy in Europe. Current unemployment in Europe is zero percent, and current inflation in Europe is 2 percent. Accordingly, target unemployment in Europe and target inflation in Europe are 1 percent each. So what is needed is a reduction in European money supply of 1 unit. Step ten refers to the time lag. Unemployment in Germany goes from zero to 1 percent, as does unemployment in France. Thus unemployment in Europe goes from zero to 1 percent as well. Inflation in Germany goes from 4 to 3 percent. Inflation in France goes from zero to – 1 percent. Thus inflation in Europe goes from 2 to 1 percent. And so on. For a synopsis see Table 5.6.

Table 5.6
Sequential Policy Decisions
A Mixed Shock in Germany

Germany		France	
Unemployment	0	Unemployment	0
Inflation	4	Inflation	0
Δ Government Purchases	0	Δ Government Purchases	0
Unemployment	0	Unemployment	0
Inflation	4	Inflation	0
Δ European Money Supply	– 1		
Unemployment	1	Unemployment	1
Inflation	3	Inflation	– 1
Δ Government Purchases	1	Δ Government Purchases	1
Unemployment	0	Unemployment	0
Inflation	4	Inflation	0
Δ European Money Supply	– 1		
Unemployment	1	Unemployment	1
Inflation	3	Inflation	– 1
and so on			

As a result, given a mixed shock in Germany, sequential policy decisions cause uniform oscillations in unemployment and inflation. And what is more, there is an explosion of government purchases and an implosion of money supply.

4) Summary. Given a demand shock in Germany, sequential policy decisions produce zero unemployment and zero inflation in each of the member countries. There is an increase in German government purchases, no change in French government purchases, and no change in European money supply. Given a supply shock in Germany, sequential policy decisions cause uniform oscillations in unemployment and inflation. What is more, there is an explosion of government purchases and an implosion of money supply. And much the same applies to a mixed shock in Germany.

Chapter 3
Target System C

1. The Model

1) The static model. This chapter is based on target system C. The targets of the European central bank are zero inflation and zero unemployment in each of the member countries. The targets of the German government are zero unemployment and zero inflation in Germany. And the targets of the French government are zero unemployment and zero inflation in France.

The model of unemployment and inflation can be represented by a system of four equations:

$$u_1 = A_1 - M - G_1 \tag{1}$$

$$u_2 = A_2 - M - G_2 \tag{2}$$

$$\pi_1 = B_1 + M + G_1 \tag{3}$$

$$\pi_2 = B_2 + M + G_2 \tag{4}$$

An increase in European money supply lowers unemployment in Germany and France. On the other hand, it raises inflation there. An increase in German government purchases lowers unemployment in Germany. On the other hand, it raises inflation there. Correspondingly, an increase in French government purchases lowers unemployment in France. On the other hand, it raises inflation there.

The targets of the European central bank are zero inflation and zero unemployment in each of the member countries. The instrument of the European central bank is European money supply. There are four targets but only one instrument, so what is needed is a loss function. We assume that the European central bank has a quadratic loss function:

$$L = \pi_1^2 + \pi_2^2 + u_1^2 + u_2^2 \tag{5}$$

M. Carlberg, *Dynamic Policy Interactions in a Monetary Union*,
DOI 10.1007/978-3-642-18228-0_16, © Springer-Verlag Berlin Heidelberg 2011

L is the loss to the European central bank caused by inflation and unemployment in each of the member countries. We assume equal weights in the loss function. The specific target of the European central bank is to minimize the loss, given the inflation functions and the unemployment functions. Taking account of equations (1), (2), (3) and (4), the loss function of the European central bank can be written as follows:

$$\begin{aligned} L &= (B_1 + M + G_1)^2 + (B_2 + M + G_2)^2 \\ &+ (A_1 - M - G_1)^2 + (A_2 - M - G_2)^2 \end{aligned} \tag{6}$$

Then the first-order condition for a minimum loss gives the reaction function of the European central bank:

$$4M = A_1 + A_2 - B_1 - B_2 - 2G_1 - 2G_2 \tag{7}$$

An increase in A_1 or A_2 requires an increase in European money supply. An increase in B_1 or B_2 requires a cut in European money supply. And an increase in German or French government purchases requires a cut in European money supply too.

The targets of the German government are zero unemployment and zero inflation in Germany. The instrument of the German government is German government purchases. There are two targets but only one instrument, so what is needed is a loss function. We assume that the German government has a quadratic loss function:

$$L_1 = \pi_1^2 + u_1^2 \tag{8}$$

L_1 is the loss to the German government caused by inflation and unemployment in Germany. We assume equal weights in the loss function. The specific target of the German government is to minimize the loss, given the inflation function and the unemployment function. Taking account of equations (1) and (3), the loss function of the German government can be written as follows:

$$L_1 = (B_1 + M + G_1)^2 + (A_1 - M - G_1)^2 \tag{9}$$

Then the first-order condition for a minimum loss gives the reaction function of the German government:

$$2G_1 = A_1 - B_1 - 2M \tag{10}$$

An increase in A_1 requires an increase in German government purchases. An increase in B_1 requires a cut in German government purchases. And a cut in European money supply requires an increase in German government purchases.

The targets of the French government are zero unemployment and zero inflation in France. The instrument of the French government is French government purchases. There are two targets but only one instrument, so what is needed is a loss function. We assume that the French government has a quadratic loss function:

$$L_2 = \pi_2^2 + u_2^2 \tag{11}$$

L_2 is the loss to the French government caused by inflation and unemployment in France. We assume equal weights in the loss function. The specific target of the French government is to minimize the loss, given the inflation function and the unemployment function. Taking account of equations (2) and (4), the loss function of the French government can be written as follows:

$$L_2 = (B_2 + M + G_2)^2 + (A_2 - M - G_2)^2 \tag{12}$$

Then the first-order condition for a minimum loss gives the reaction function of the French government:

$$2G_2 = A_2 - B_2 - 2M \tag{13}$$

An increase in A_2 requires an increase in French government purchases. An increase in B_2 requires a cut in French government purchases. And a cut in European money supply requires an increase in French government purchases.

The Nash equilibrium is determined by the reaction functions of the European central bank, the German government, and the French government:

$$4M = A_1 + A_2 - B_1 - B_2 - 2G_1 - 2G_2 \tag{14}$$

$$2G_1 = A_1 - B_1 - 2M \tag{15}$$

$$2G_2 = A_2 - B_2 - 2M \tag{16}$$

Now take the sum of equations (15) and (16) to find out:

$$4M = A_1 + A_2 - B_1 - B_2 - 2G_1 - 2G_2 \tag{17}$$

Clearly, equations (14) and (17) are identical. There are three endogenous variables (M, G_1, G_2). On the other hand, there are only two independent equations. As a result there are multiple Nash equilibria.

Finally compare the target systems A, B and C. Under target system A there is no Nash equilibrium. Under target system B there is no Nash equilibrium either. And under target system C there are multiple Nash equilibria.

2) The dynamic model. We assume that the governments and the central bank decide sequentially. First the governments decide, then the central bank decides. Step 1 refers to a specific shock. Step 2 refers to the time lag. Step 3 refers to fiscal policies in Germany and France. Step 4 refers to the time lag. Step 5 refers to monetary policy in Europe. Step 6 refers to the time lag. Step 7 refers to fiscal policies in Germany and France. Step 8 refers to the time lag. Step 9 refers to monetary policy in Europe. Step 10 refers to the time lag. And so on.

Now have a closer look at the dynamic model. Step 1 refers to a specific shock. Step 2 refers to the time lag. Step 3 refers to fiscal policies in Germany and France. The German government sets its purchases of German goods so as to reduce its loss. The reaction function of the German government is:

$$2G_1 = A_1 - B_1 - 2M \tag{18}$$

The French government sets its purchases of French goods so as to reduce its loss. The reaction function of the French government is:

$$2G_2 = A_2 - B_2 - 2M \tag{19}$$

Step 4 refers to the time lag. Step 5 refers to monetary policy in Europe. The European central bank sets European money supply so as to reduce its loss. The reaction function of the European central bank is:

$$4M = A_1 + A_2 - B_1 - B_2 - 2G_1 - 2G_2 \tag{20}$$

Step 6 refers to the time lag. Step 7 refers to fiscal policies in Germany and France. The German government sets its purchases of German goods so as to reduce its loss. The reaction function of the German government is:

$$2G_1 = A_1 - B_1 - 2M \tag{21}$$

The French government sets its purchases of French goods so as to reduce its loss. The reaction function of the French government is:

$$2G_2 = A_2 - B_2 - 2M \tag{22}$$

Step 8 refers to the time lag. Step 9 refers to monetary policy in Europe. The European central bank sets European money supply so as to reduce its loss. The reaction function of the European central bank is:

$$4M = A_1 + A_2 - B_1 - B_2 - 2G_1 - 2G_2 \tag{23}$$

Step 10 refers to the time lag. And so on. Then what are the dynamic characteristics of this process?

2. Some Numerical Examples

Here are three distinct cases:

- a demand shock in Germany
- a supply shock in Germany
- a mixed shock in Germany.

The targets of the European central bank are zero inflation and zero unemployment in each of the member countries. The targets of the German government are zero unemployment and zero inflation in Germany. And the targets of the French government are zero unemployment and zero inflation in France.

1) A demand shock in Germany. In each of the member countries, let initial unemployment be zero, and let initial inflation be zero as well. Step one refers to a decline in the demand for German goods. In terms of the model there is an increase in A_1 of 2 units and a decline in B_1 of equally 2 units. Step two refers to the time lag. Unemployment in Germany goes from zero to 2 percent. Unemployment in France stays at zero percent. Thus unemployment in Europe goes from zero to 1 percent. Inflation in Germany goes from zero to – 2 percent. Inflation in France stays at zero percent. Thus inflation in Europe goes from zero to – 1 percent.

Step three refers to fiscal policies in Germany and France. First consider fiscal policy in Germany. Current unemployment in Germany is 2 percent, and current inflation in Germany is – 2 percent. Accordingly, target unemployment in Germany and target inflation in Germany are zero percent each. So what is needed is an increase in German government purchases of 2 units. Second consider fiscal policy in France. Current unemployment in France and current inflation in France are zero percent each. Accordingly, target unemployment in France and target inflation in France are zero percent each. So what is needed is no change in French government purchases.

Step four refers to the time lag. Unemployment in Germany goes from 2 to zero percent. Unemployment in France stays at zero percent. Thus unemployment in Europe goes from 1 to zero percent. Inflation in Germany goes from – 2 to zero percent. Inflation in France stays at zero percent. Thus inflation in Europe goes from – 1 to zero percent.

Step five refers to monetary policy in Europe. Current unemployment in Europe and current inflation in Europe are zero percent each. Accordingly, target unemployment in Europe and target inflation in Europe are zero percent each. So what is needed is no change in European money supply. Step six refers to the time lag. Unemployment in Germany stays at zero percent, as does unemployment in France. Thus unemployment in Europe stays at zero percent as well. Inflation in Germany stays at zero percent, as does inflation in France. Thus inflation in Europe stays at zero percent as well. Table 5.7 presents a synopsis.

Table 5.7
Sequential Policy Decisions
A Demand Shock in Germany

Germany		France	
Unemployment	2	Unemployment	0
Inflation	– 2	Inflation	0
Δ Government Purchases	2	Δ Government Purchases	0
Unemployment	0	Unemployment	0
Inflation	0	Inflation	0
Δ European Money Supply	0		
Unemployment	0	Unemployment	0
Inflation	0	Inflation	0

As a result, given a demand shock in Germany, sequential policy decisions produce zero unemployment and zero inflation in each of the member countries. There is an increase in German government purchases, no change in French government purchases, and no change in European money supply.

The loss functions of the European central bank, the German government, and the French government are respectively:

$$L = \pi_1^2 + \pi_2^2 + u_1^2 + u_2^2 \quad (1)$$

$$L_1 = u_1^2 + \pi_1^2 \quad (2)$$

$$L_2 = u_2^2 + \pi_2^2 \quad (3)$$

The initial loss of each policy maker is zero. The demand shock in Germany causes a loss to the European central bank of 8 units, a loss to the German government of equally 8 units, and a loss to the French government of zero units. Then sequential policy decisions reduce the loss of the European central bank from 8 to zero units. Correspondingly, they reduce the loss of the German government from 8 to zero units. And they keep the loss of the French government at zero units.

2) A supply shock in Germany. In each of the member countries, let initial unemployment be zero, and let initial inflation be zero as well. Step one refers to the supply shock in Germany. In terms of the model there is an increase in B_1 of 2 units and an increase in A_1 of equally 2 units. Step two refers to the time lag. Inflation in Germany goes from zero to 2 percent. Inflation in France stays at zero percent. Hence inflation in Europe goes from zero to 1 percent. Unemployment in Germany goes from zero to 2 percent. Unemployment in France stays at zero percent. Hence unemployment in Europe goes from zero to 1 percent.

Step three refers to fiscal policies in Germany and France. First consider fiscal policy in Germany. Current unemployment in Germany and current inflation in Germany are 2 percent each. Accordingly, target unemployment in Germany and target inflation in Germany are 2 percent each. So what is needed is no change in German government purchases. Second consider fiscal policy in France. Current unemployment in France and current inflation in France are zero percent each. Accordingly, target unemployment in France and target inflation in France are zero percent each. So what is needed is no change in French government purchases.

Step four refers to the time lag. Unemployment in Germany stays at 2 percent, and unemployment in France stays at zero percent. Hence unemployment in Europe stays at 1 percent. Inflation in Germany stays at 2 percent, and inflation in France stays at zero percent. Hence inflation in Europe stays at 1 percent.

Step five refers to monetary policy in Europe. Current unemployment in Europe and current inflation in Europe are 1 percent each. Accordingly, target unemployment in Europe and target inflation Europe are 1 percent each. So what is needed is no change in European money supply. Step six refers to the time lag. Unemployment in Germany stays at 2 percent, and unemployment in France stays at zero percent. Hence unemployment in Europe stays at 1 percent. Inflation in Germany stays at 2 percent, and inflation in France stays at zero percent. Hence inflation in Europe stays at 1 percent. Table 5.8 gives an overview.

Table 5.8
Sequential Policy Decisions
A Supply Shock in Germany

Germany		France	
Unemployment	2	Unemployment	0
Inflation	2	Inflation	0
Δ Government Purchases	0	Δ Government Purchases	0
Unemployment	2	Unemployment	0
Inflation	2	Inflation	0
Δ European Money Supply	0		
Unemployment	2	Unemployment	0
Inflation	2	Inflation	0

As a result, given a supply shock in Germany, sequential policy decisions are ineffective. There is no change in money supply and government purchases. Correspondingly, there is no change in unemployment and inflation. The initial loss of each policy maker is zero. The supply shock in Germany causes a loss to the European central bank of 8 units, a loss to the German government of equally 8 units, and a loss to the French government of zero units. Then sequential policy decisions keep the loss of the European central bank at 8 units. Similarly, they keep the loss of the German government at 8 units. And they keep the loss of the French government at zero units.

3) A mixed shock in Germany. In each of the member countries, let initial unemployment be zero, and let initial inflation be zero as well. Step one refers to the mixed shock in Germany. In terms of the model there is an increase in B_1 of 4 units. Step two refers to the time lag. Inflation in Germany goes from zero to 4 percent. Inflation in France stays at zero percent. Thus inflation in Europe goes from zero to 2 percent. Unemployment in Germany stays at zero percent, as does unemployment in France. Thus unemployment in Europe stays at zero percent too.

Step three refers to fiscal policies in Germany and France. First consider fiscal policy in Germany. Current unemployment in Germany is zero percent, and current inflation in Germany is 4 percent. Accordingly, target unemployment in Germany and target inflation in Germany are 2 percent each. So what is needed is a reduction in German government purchases of 2 units. Second consider fiscal policy in France. Current unemployment in France and current inflation in France are zero percent each. Accordingly, target unemployment in France and target inflation in France are zero percent each. So what is needed is no change in French government purchases.

Step four refers to the time lag. Unemployment in Germany goes from zero to 2 percent. Unemployment in France stays at zero percent. Thus unemployment in Europe goes from zero to 1 percent. Inflation in Germany goes from 4 to 2 percent. Inflation in France stays at zero percent. Thus inflation in Europe goes from 2 to 1 percent.

Step five refers to monetary policy in Europe. Current unemployment in Europe and current inflation in Europe are 1 percent each. Accordingly, target unemployment in Europe and target inflation Europe are 1 percent each. So what is needed is no change in European money supply. Step six refers to the time lag. Unemployment in Germany stays at 2 percent, and unemployment in France stays at zero percent. Thus unemployment in Europe stays at 1 percent. Inflation in Germany stays at 2 percent, and inflation in France stays at zero percent. Thus inflation in Europe stays at 1 percent. For a synopsis see Table 5.9.

Table 5.9
Sequential Policy Decisions
A Mixed Shock in Germany

Germany		France	
Unemployment	0	Unemployment	0
Inflation	4	Inflation	0
Δ Government Purchases	– 2	Δ Government Purchases	0
Unemployment	2	Unemployment	0
Inflation	2	Inflation	0
Δ European Money Supply	0		
Unemployment	2	Unemployment	0
Inflation	2	Inflation	0

As a result, given a mixed shock in Germany, sequential policy decisions lower German inflation. On the other hand, they raise German unemployment. And what is more, sequential policy decisions keep up zero unemployment and zero inflation in France. There is a reduction in German government purchases, no change in French government purchases, and no change in European money supply.

The initial loss of each policy maker is zero. The mixed shock in Germany causes a loss to the European central bank of 16 units, a loss to the German government of equally 16 units, and a loss to the French government of zero units. Then sequential policy decisions reduce the loss of the European central bank from 16 to 8 units. Similarly, they reduce the loss of the German government from 16 to 8 units. And they keep the loss of the French government at zero units.

4) Summary. Given a demand shock in Germany, sequential policy decisions produce zero unemployment and zero inflation in each of the member countries. There is an increase in German government purchases, no change in French government purchases, and no change in European money supply. Given a supply shock in Germany, sequential policy decisions are ineffective. There is no change in government purchases and money supply. Correspondingly, there is no change in unemployment and inflation. Given a mixed shock in Germany, sequential policy decisions lower German inflation. On the other hand, they raise German unemployment. And what is more, sequential policy decisions keep up zero unemployment and zero inflation in France. There is a reduction in German government purchases, no change in French government purchases, and no change in European money supply.

Part Six

Central Bank and Governments Decide Simultaneously and Independently

Cold-Turkey Policies

Chapter 1
Target System A

1. The Model

1) The static model. The monetary union consists of two countries, say Germany and France. The member countries are the same size and have the same behavioural functions. This chapter is based on target system A. The targets of the European central bank are zero inflation in Germany and France respectively. The target of the German government is zero unemployment in Germany. And the target of the French government is zero unemployment in France.

The model of unemployment and inflation can be represented by a system of four equations:

$$u_1 = A_1 - M - G_1 \tag{1}$$

$$u_2 = A_2 - M - G_2 \tag{2}$$

$$\pi_1 = B_1 + M + G_1 \tag{3}$$

$$\pi_2 = B_2 + M + G_2 \tag{4}$$

Here u_1 denotes the rate of unemployment in Germany, u_2 is the rate of unemployment in France, π_1 is the rate of inflation in Germany, π_2 is the rate of inflation in France, M is European money supply, G_1 is German government purchases, G_2 is French government purchases, A_1 is some other factors bearing on the rate of unemployment in Germany, A_2 is some other factors bearing on the rate of unemployment in France, B_1 is some other factors bearing on the rate of inflation in Germany, and B_2 is some other factors bearing on the rate of inflation in France. The endogenous variables are the rate of unemployment in Germany, the rate of unemployment in France, the rate of inflation in Germany, and the rate of inflation in France.

An increase in European money supply lowers unemployment in Germany and France. On the other hand, it raises inflation there. An increase in German

M. Carlberg, *Dynamic Policy Interactions in a Monetary Union*,
DOI 10.1007/978-3-642-18228-0_17,

government purchases lowers unemployment in Germany. On the other hand, it raises inflation there. Correspondingly, an increase in French government purchases lowers unemployment in France. On the other hand, it raises inflation there. Fiscal policy in one of the member countries has no effect on unemployment or inflation in the other country.

The targets of the European central bank are zero inflation in Germany and France respectively. The instrument of the European central bank is European money supply. There are two targets but only one instrument, so what is needed is a loss function. We assume that the European central bank has a quadratic loss function:

$$L = \pi_1^2 + \pi_2^2 \tag{5}$$

L is the loss to the European central bank caused by inflation in Germany and France. We assume equal weights in the loss function. The specific target of the European central bank is to minimize the loss, given the inflation functions. Taking account of equations (3) and (4), the loss function of the European central bank can be written as follows:

$$L = (B_1 + M + G_1)^2 + (B_2 + M + G_2)^2 \tag{6}$$

Then the first-order condition for a minimum loss gives the reaction function of the European central bank:

$$2M = -B_1 - B_2 - G_1 - G_2 \tag{7}$$

An increase in B_1 or B_2 requires a cut in European money supply. And an increase in German or French government purchases requires a cut in European money supply too.

The target of the German government is zero unemployment in Germany. The instrument of the German government is German government purchases. By equation (1), the reaction function of the German government is:

$$G_1 = A_1 - M \tag{8}$$

An increase in A_1 requires an increase in German government purchases. And a cut in European money supply requires an increase in German government purchases as well.

The target of the French government is zero unemployment in France. The instrument of the French government is French government purchases. By equation (2), the reaction function of the French government is:

$$G_2 = A_2 - M \tag{9}$$

An increase in A_2 requires an increase in French government purchases. And a cut in European money supply requires an increase in French government purchases as well.

The Nash equilibrium is determined by the reaction functions of the European central bank, the German government, and the French government. From the reaction functions follows:

$$A_1 + A_2 + B_1 + B_2 = 0 \tag{10}$$

Evidently, this is in contradiction to the assumption that A_1, A_2, B_1 and B_2 are given exogenously. As a result there is no Nash equilibrium.

2) The dynamic model. We assume that the central bank and the governments decide simultaneously and independently. Step 1 refers to a specific shock. Step 2 refers to the time lag. Step 3 refers to monetary and fiscal policies. Step 4 refers to the time lag. Step 5 refers to monetary and fiscal policies. Step 6 refers to the time lag. And so on.

Now have a closer look at the dynamic model. Step 1 refers to a specific shock. This could be a demand shock, a supply shock or a mixed shock, in Germany or France. Step 2 refers to the time lag. This includes both the inside lag and the outside lag. In step 3, the central bank and the governments decide simultaneously and independently. The European central bank sets European money supply so as to achieve zero inflation in Europe. The reaction function of the European central bank is:

$$2M = -B_1 - B_2 - G_1 - G_2 \tag{11}$$

The German government sets its purchases of German goods so as to achieve zero unemployment in Germany. The reaction function of the German government is:

$$G_1 = A_1 - M \tag{12}$$

The French government sets its purchases of French goods so as to achieve zero unemployment in France. The reaction function of the French government is:

$$G_2 = A_2 - M \tag{13}$$

Step 4 refers to the time lag. In step 5, the central bank and the governments decide simultaneously and independently. The European central bank sets European money supply so as to achieve zero inflation in Europe. The reaction function of the European central bank is:

$$2M = -B_1 - B_2 - G_1 - G_2 \tag{14}$$

The German government sets its purchases of German goods so as to achieve zero unemployment in Germany. The reaction function of the German government is:

$$G_1 = A_1 - M \tag{15}$$

The French government sets its purchases of French goods so as to achieve zero unemployment in France. The reaction function of the French government is:

$$G_2 = A_2 - M \tag{16}$$

Step 6 refers to the time lag. And so on. Then what are the dynamic characteristics of this process?

2. Some Numerical Examples

It proves useful to study three distinct cases:

- a demand shock in Germany
- a supply shock in Germany
- a mixed shock in Germany.

The targets of the European central bank are zero inflation in Germany and France respectively. The target of the German government is zero unemployment in Germany. And the target of the French government is zero unemployment in France.

1) A demand shock in Germany. In each of the member countries, let initial unemployment be zero, and let initial inflation be zero as well. Step one refers to a decline in the demand for German goods. In terms of the model there is an increase in A_1 of 4 units and a decline in B_1 of equally 4 units. Step two refers to the time lag. Unemployment in Germany goes from zero to 4 percent. Unemployment in France stays at zero percent. Thus unemployment in Europe goes from zero to 2 percent. Inflation in Germany goes from zero to – 4 percent. Inflation in France stays at zero percent. Thus inflation in Europe goes from zero to – 2 percent.

In step three, the central bank and the governments decide simultaneously and independently. First consider monetary policy in Europe. Current inflation in Europe is – 2 percent, and target inflation in Europe is zero percent. So what is needed is an increase in European money supply of 2 units. Second consider fiscal policy in Germany. Current unemployment in Germany is 4 percent, and target unemployment in Germany is zero percent. So what is needed is an increase in German government purchases of 4 units. Third consider fiscal policy in France. Current unemployment in France is zero percent, and target unemployment in France is the same. So what is needed is no change in French government purchases.

Step four refers to the time lag. Unemployment in Germany goes from 4 to – 2 percent. Unemployment in France goes from zero to – 2 percent. Thus unemployment in Europe goes from 2 to – 2 percent. Inflation in Germany goes from – 4 to 2 percent. Inflation in France goes from zero to 2 percent. Thus inflation in Europe goes from – 2 to 2 percent.

In step five, the central bank and the governments decide simultaneously and independently. First consider monetary policy in Europe. Current inflation in Europe is 2 percent, and target inflation in Europe is zero percent. So what is needed is a reduction in European money supply of 2 units. Second consider fiscal policy in Germany. Current unemployment in Germany is – 2 percent, and target unemployment in Germany is zero percent. So what is needed is a reduction in German government purchases of 2 units. Third consider fiscal policy in France. Current unemployment in France is – 2 percent, and target unemployment in France is zero percent. So what is needed is a reduction in French government purchases of 2 units.

Step six refers to the time lag. Unemployment in Germany goes from – 2 to 2 percent, as does unemployment in France. Thus unemployment in Europe goes from – 2 to 2 percent as well. Inflation in Germany goes from 2 to – 2 percent, as does inflation in France. Thus inflation in Europe goes from 2 to – 2 percent as well. And so on. Table 6.1 presents a synopsis.

As a result, given a demand shock in Germany, simultaneous and independent policy decisions cause uniform oscillations in unemployment and inflation. The economy oscillates between underemployment and overemployment. Accordingly, the economy oscillates between deflation and inflation. And what is more, there are uniform oscillations in money supply and government purchases.

2) A supply shock in Germany. In each of the member countries, let initial unemployment be zero, and let initial inflation be zero as well. Step one refers to the supply shock in Germany. In terms of the model there is an increase in B_1 of 4 units and an increase in A_1 of equally 4 units. Step two refers to the time lag. Inflation in Germany goes from zero to 4 percent. Inflation in France stays at zero percent. Hence inflation in Europe goes from zero to 2 percent. Unemployment in Germany goes from zero to 4 percent. Unemployment in France stays at zero percent. Hence unemployment in Europe goes from zero to 2 percent.

Table 6.1
Simultaneous and Independent Policy Decisions
A Demand Shock in Germany

Germany		France	
Unemployment	4	Unemployment	0
Inflation	– 4	Inflation	0
Δ European Money Supply	2		
Δ Government Purchases	4	Δ Government Purchases	0
Unemployment	– 2	Unemployment	– 2
Inflation	2	Inflation	2
Δ European Money Supply	– 2		
Δ Government Purchases	– 2	Δ Government Purchases	– 2
Unemployment	2	Unemployment	2
Inflation	– 2	Inflation	– 2
and so on			

In step three, the central bank and the governments decide simultaneously and independently. First consider monetary policy in Europe. Current inflation in Europe is 2 percent, and target inflation in Europe is zero percent. So what is needed is a reduction in European money supply of 2 units. Second consider fiscal policy in Germany. Current unemployment in Germany is 4 percent, and target unemployment in Germany is zero percent. So what is needed is an increase in German government purchases of 4 units. Third consider fiscal policy in France. Current unemployment in France is zero percent, and target unemployment in France is the same. So what is needed is no change in French government purchases.

Step four refers to the time lag. Unemployment in Germany goes from 4 to 2 percent. Unemployment in France goes from zero to 2 percent. Hence unemployment in Europe stays at 2 percent. Inflation in Germany goes from 4 to 6 percent. Inflation in France goes from zero to – 2 percent. Hence inflation in Europe stays at 2 percent.

In step five, the central bank and the governments decide simultaneously and independently. First consider monetary policy in Europe. Current inflation in Europe is 2 percent, and target inflation in Europe is zero percent. So what is needed is a reduction in European money supply of 2 units. Second consider fiscal policy in Germany. Current unemployment in Germany is 2 percent, and target unemployment in Germany is zero percent. So what is needed is an increase in German government purchases of 2 units. Third consider fiscal policy in France. Current unemployment in France is 2 percent, and target unemployment in France is zero percent. So what is needed is an increase in French government purchases of 2 units.

Step six refers to the time lag. Unemployment in Germany stays at 2 percent, as does unemployment in France. Hence unemployment in Europe stays at 2 percent too. Inflation in Germany stays at 6 percent, and inflation in France stays at – 2 percent. Hence inflation in Europe stays at 2 percent. And so on. Table 6.2 gives an overview.

As a result, given a supply shock in Germany, simultaneous and independent policy decisions lower German unemployment and raise German inflation. On the other hand, they raise French unemployment and lower French inflation. And what is more, there is an explosion of government purchases and an implosion of money supply.

3) A mixed shock in Germany. In each of the member countries, let initial unemployment be zero, and let initial inflation be zero as well. Step one refers to the mixed shock in Germany. In terms of the model there is an increase in B_1 of 4 units. Step two refers to the time lag. Inflation in Germany goes from zero to 4 percent. Inflation in France stays at zero percent. Thus inflation in Europe goes from zero to 2 percent. Unemployment in Germany stays at zero percent, as does unemployment in France. Thus unemployment in Europe stays at zero percent too.

Table 6.2
Simultaneous and Independent Policy Decisions
A Supply Shock in Germany

Germany		France	
Unemployment	4	Unemployment	0
Inflation	4	Inflation	0
Δ European Money Supply	– 2		
Δ Government Purchases	4	Δ Government Purchases	0
Unemployment	2	Unemployment	2
Inflation	6	Inflation	– 2
Δ European Money Supply	– 2		
Δ Government Purchases	2	Δ Government Purchases	2
Unemployment	2	Unemployment	2
Inflation	6	Inflation	– 2
and so on			

In step three, the central bank and the governments decide simultaneously and independently. First consider monetary policy in Europe. Current inflation in Europe is 2 percent, and target inflation in Europe is zero percent. So what is needed is a reduction in European money supply of 2 units. Second consider fiscal policy in Germany. Current unemployment in Germany is zero percent, and target unemployment in Germany is the same. So what is needed is no change in German government purchases. Third consider fiscal policy in France. Current unemployment in France is zero percent, and target unemployment in France is the same. So what is needed is no change in French government purchases.

Step four refers to the time lag. Unemployment in Germany goes from zero to 2 percent, as does unemployment in France. Thus unemployment in Europe goes from zero to 2 percent as well. Inflation in Germany goes from 4 to 2 percent. Inflation in France goes from zero to – 2 percent. Thus inflation in Europe goes from 2 to zero percent.

In step five, the central bank and the governments decide simultaneously and independently. First consider monetary policy in Europe. Current inflation in Europe is zero percent, and target inflation in Europe is the same. So what is needed is no change in European money supply. Second consider fiscal policy in Germany. Current unemployment in Germany is 2 percent, and target unemployment in Germany is zero percent. So what is needed is an increase in German government purchases of 2 units. Third consider fiscal policy in France. Current unemployment in France is 2 percent, and target unemployment in France is zero percent. So what is needed is an increase in French government purchases of 2 units.

Step six refers to the time lag. Unemployment in Germany goes from 2 to zero percent, as does unemployment in France. Thus unemployment in Europe goes from 2 to zero percent too. Inflation in Germany goes from 2 to 4 percent. Inflation in France goes from – 2 to zero percent. Thus inflation in Europe goes from zero to 2 percent. And so on. For a synopsis see Table 6.3.

As a result, given a mixed shock in Germany, simultaneous and independent policy decisions cause uniform oscillations in unemployment and inflation. And what is more, there is an explosion of government purchases and an implosion of money supply.

4) Summary. Given a demand shock in Germany, simultaneous and independent policy decisions cause uniform oscillations in unemployment and inflation. In addition, there are uniform oscillations in money supply and government purchases. Given a supply shock in Germany, simultaneous and independent policy decisions lower German unemployment and raise German inflation. On the other hand, they raise French unemployment and lower French inflation. And what is more, there is an explosion of government purchases and an implosion of money supply. Given a mixed shock in Germany, simultaneous and independent policy decisions cause uniform oscillations in unemployment and inflation. And what is more, there is an explosion of government purchases and an implosion of money supply.

Table 6.3
Simultaneous and Independent Policy Decisions
A Mixed Shock in Germany

Germany		France	
Unemployment	0	Unemployment	0
Inflation	4	Inflation	0
Δ European Money Supply	− 2		
Δ Government Purchases	0	Δ Government Purchases	0
Unemployment	2	Unemployment	2
Inflation	2	Inflation	− 2
Δ European Money Supply	0		
Δ Government Purchases	2	Δ Government Purchases	2
Unemployment	0	Unemployment	0
Inflation	4	Inflation	0
and so on			

Chapter 2
Target System B

1. The Model

1) The static model. This chapter is based on target system B. The targets of the European central bank are zero inflation and zero unemployment in each of the member countries. The target of the German government is zero unemployment in Germany. And the target of the French government is zero unemployment in France.

The model of unemployment and inflation can be characterized by a system of four equations:

$$u_1 = A_1 - M - G_1 \tag{1}$$

$$u_2 = A_2 - M - G_2 \tag{2}$$

$$\pi_1 = B_1 + M + G_1 \tag{3}$$

$$\pi_2 = B_2 + M + G_2 \tag{4}$$

An increase in European money supply lowers unemployment in Germany and France. On the other hand, it raises inflation there. An increase in German government purchases lowers unemployment in Germany. On the other hand, it raises inflation there. Correspondingly, an increase in French government purchases lowers unemployment in France. On the other hand, it raises inflation there.

The targets of the European central bank are zero inflation and zero unemployment in each of the member countries. The instrument of the European central bank is European money supply. There are four targets but only one instrument, so what is needed is a loss function. We assume that the European central bank has a quadratic loss function:

$$L = \pi_1^2 + \pi_2^2 + u_1^2 + u_2^2 \tag{5}$$

M. Carlberg, *Dynamic Policy Interactions in a Monetary Union*,
DOI 10.1007/978-3-642-18228-0_18, © Springer-Verlag Berlin Heidelberg 2011

L is the loss to the European central bank caused by inflation and unemployment in each of the member countries. We assume equal weights in the loss function. The specific target of the European central bank is to minimize the loss, given the inflation functions and the unemployment functions. Taking account of equations (1), (2), (3) and (4), the loss function of the European central bank can be written as follows:

$$L = (B_1 + M + G_1)^2 + (B_2 + M + G_2)^2 + (A_1 - M - G_1)^2 + (A_2 - M - G_2)^2 \quad (6)$$

Then the first-order condition for a minimum loss gives the reaction function of the European central bank:

$$4M = A_1 + A_2 - B_1 - B_2 - 2G_1 - 2G_2 \quad (7)$$

An increase in A_1 or A_2 requires an increase in European money supply. An increase in B_1 or B_2 requires a cut in European money supply. And an increase in German or French government purchases requires a cut in European money supply too.

The target of the German government is zero unemployment in Germany. The instrument of the German government is German government purchases. By equation (1), the reaction function of the German government is:

$$G_1 = A_1 - M \quad (8)$$

An increase in A_1 requires an increase in German government purchases. And a cut in European money supply requires an increase in German government purchases as well.

The target of the French government is zero unemployment in France. The instrument of the French government is French government purchases. By equation (2), the reaction function of the French government is:

$$G_2 = A_2 - M \quad (9)$$

An increase in A_2 requires an increase in French government purchases. And a cut in European money supply requires an increase in French government purchases as well.

The Nash equilibrium is determined by the reaction functions of the European central bank, the German government, and the French government. From the reaction functions follows:

$$A_1 + A_2 + B_1 + B_2 = 0 \tag{10}$$

Evidently, this is in contradiction to the assumption that A_1, A_2, B_1 and B_2 are given exogenously. As a result there is no Nash equilibrium.

2) The dynamic model. We assume that the central bank and the governments decide simultaneously and independently. Step 1 refers to a specific shock. Step 2 refers to the time lag. Step 3 refers to monetary and fiscal policies. Step 4 refers to the time lag. Step 5 refers to monetary and fiscal policies. Step 6 refers to the time lag. And so on.

Now take a closer look at the dynamic model. Step 1 refers to a specific shock. Step 2 refers to the time lag. In step 3, the central bank and the governments decide simultaneously and independently. The European central bank sets European money supply so as to reduce its loss. The reaction function of the European central bank is:

$$4M = A_1 + A_2 - B_1 - B_2 - 2G_1 - 2G_2 \tag{11}$$

The German government sets its purchases of German goods so as to achieve zero unemployment in Germany. The reaction function of the German government is:

$$G_1 = A_1 - M \tag{12}$$

The French government sets its purchases of French goods so as to achieve zero unemployment in France. The reaction function of the French government is:

$$G_2 = A_2 - M \tag{13}$$

Step 4 refers to the time lag. In step 5, the central bank and the governments decide simultaneously and independently. The European central bank sets European money supply so as to reduce its loss. The reaction function of the European central bank is:

$$4M = A_1 + A_2 - B_1 - B_2 - 2G_1 - 2G_2 \tag{14}$$

The German government sets its purchases of German goods so as to achieve zero unemployment in Germany. The reaction function of the German government is:

$$G_1 = A_1 - M \tag{15}$$

The French government sets its purchases of French goods so as to achieve zero unemployment in France. The reaction function of the French government is:

$$G_2 = A_2 - M \tag{16}$$

Step 6 refers to the time lag. And so on. Then what are the dynamic characteristics of this process?

2. Some Numerical Examples

Here are three distinct cases:

- a demand shock in Germany
- a supply shock in Germany
- a mixed shock in Germany.

The targets of the European central bank are zero inflation and zero unemployment in each of the member countries. The target of the German government is zero unemployment in Germany. And the target of the French government is zero unemployment in France.

1) A demand shock in Germany. In each of the member countries, let initial unemployment be zero, and let initial inflation be zero as well. Step one refers to a decline in the demand for German goods. In terms of the model there is an increase in A_1 of 4 units and a decline in B_1 of equally 4 units. Step two refers to the time lag. Unemployment in Germany goes from zero to 4 percent. Unemployment in France stays at zero percent. Thus unemployment in Europe goes from zero to 2 percent. Inflation in Germany goes from zero to – 4 percent. Inflation in France stays at zero percent. Thus inflation in Europe goes from zero to – 2 percent.

In step three, the central bank and the governments decide simultaneously and independently. First consider monetary policy in Europe. Current unemployment in Europe is 2 percent, and current inflation in Europe is – 2 percent. Accordingly, target unemployment in Europe and target inflation in Europe are zero percent each. So what is needed is an increase in European money supply of 2 units. Second consider fiscal policy in Germany. Current unemployment in Germany is 4 percent, and target unemployment in Germany is zero percent. So what is needed is an increase in German government purchases of 4 units. Third consider fiscal policy in France. Current unemployment in France is zero percent, and target unemployment in France is the same. So what is needed is no change in French government purchases.

Step four refers to the time lag. Unemployment in Germany goes from 4 to – 2 percent. Unemployment in France goes from zero to – 2 percent. Thus unemployment in Europe goes from 2 to – 2 percent. Inflation in Germany goes from – 4 to 2 percent. Inflation in France goes from zero to 2 percent. Thus inflation in Europe goes from – 2 to 2 percent.

In step five, the central bank and the governments decide simultaneously and independently. First consider monetary policy in Europe. Current unemployment in Europe is – 2 percent, and current inflation in Europe is 2 percent. Accordingly, target unemployment in Europe and target inflation in Europe are zero percent each. So what is needed is a reduction in European money supply of 2 units. Second consider fiscal policy in Germany. Current unemployment in Germany is – 2 percent, and target unemployment in Germany is zero percent. So what is needed is a reduction in German government purchases of 2 units. Third consider fiscal policy in France. Current unemployment in France is – 2 percent, and target unemployment in France is zero percent. So what is needed is a reduction in French government purchases of 2 units.

Step six refers to the time lag. Unemployment in Germany goes from – 2 to 2 percent, as does unemployment in France. Thus unemployment in Europe goes from – 2 to 2 percent as well. Inflation in Germany goes from 2 to – 2 percent, as does inflation in France. Thus inflation in Europe goes from 2 to – 2 percent as well. And so on. Table 6.4 presents a synopsis.

As a result, given a demand shock in Germany, simultaneous and independent policy decisions cause uniform oscillations in unemployment and inflation. The economy oscillates between underemployment and overemployment. Accordingly, the economy oscillates between deflation and inflation. And what is more, there are uniform oscillations in money supply and government purchases.

2) A supply shock in Germany. In each of the member countries, let initial unemployment be zero, and let initial inflation be zero as well. Step one refers to the supply shock in Germany. In terms of the model there is an increase in B_1 of 4 units and an increase in A_1 of equally 4 units. Step two refers to the time lag. Inflation in Germany goes from zero to 4 percent. Inflation in France stays at zero percent. Hence inflation in Europe goes from zero to 2 percent. Unemployment in Germany goes from zero to 4 percent. Unemployment in

France stays at zero percent. Hence unemployment in Europe goes from zero to 2 percent.

Table 6.4
Simultaneous and Independent Policy Decisions
A Demand Shock in Germany

Germany		France	
Unemployment	4	Unemployment	0
Inflation	– 4	Inflation	0
Δ European Money Supply	2		
Δ Government Purchases	4	Δ Government Purchases	0
Unemployment	– 2	Unemployment	– 2
Inflation	2	Inflation	2
Δ European Money Supply	– 2		
Δ Government Purchases	– 2	Δ Government Purchases	– 2
Unemployment	2	Unemployment	2
Inflation	– 2	Inflation	– 2
and so on			

In step three, the central bank and the governments decide simultaneously and independently. First consider monetary policy in Europe. Current unemployment in Europe is 2 percent, and current inflation in Europe is 2 percent as well. Accordingly, target unemployment in Europe and target inflation in Europe are 2 percent each. So what is needed is no change in European money supply. Second consider fiscal policy in Germany. Current unemployment in Germany is 4 percent, and target unemployment in Germany is zero percent. So what is needed is an increase in German government purchases of 4 units. Third consider fiscal policy in France. Current unemployment in France is zero percent, and target unemployment in France is the same. So what is needed is no change in French government purchases.

Step four refers to the time lag. Unemployment in Germany goes from 4 to zero percent. Unemployment in France stays at zero percent. Hence unemployment in Europe goes from 2 to zero percent. Inflation in Germany goes from 4 to 8 percent. Inflation in France stays at zero percent. Hence inflation in Europe goes from 2 to 4 percent.

In step five, the central bank and the governments decide simultaneously and independently. First consider monetary policy in Europe. Current unemployment in Europe is zero percent, and current inflation is Europe is 4 percent. Accordingly, target unemployment in Europe and target inflation in Europe are 2 percent each. So what is needed is a reduction in European money supply of 2 units. Second consider fiscal policy in Germany. Current unemployment in Germany is zero percent, and target unemployment in Germany is the same. So what is needed is no change in German government purchases. Third consider fiscal policy in France. Current unemployment in France is zero percent, and target unemployment in France is the same. So what is needed is no change in French government purchases.

Step six refers to the time lag. Unemployment in Germany goes from zero to 2 percent, as does unemployment in France. Hence unemployment in Europe goes from zero to 2 percent too. Inflation in Germany goes from 8 to 6 percent. Inflation in France goes from zero to – 2 percent. Hence inflation in Europe goes from 4 to 2 percent.

In step seven, the central bank and the governments decide simultaneously and independently. First consider monetary policy in Europe. Current unemployment in Europe is 2 percent, and current inflation in Europe is 2 percent as well. Accordingly, target unemployment in Europe and target inflation in Europe are 2 percent each. So what is needed is no change in European money supply. Second consider fiscal policy in Germany. Current unemployment in Germany is 2 percent, and target unemployment in Germany is zero percent. So what is needed is an increase in German government purchases of 2 units. Third consider fiscal policy in France. Current unemployment in France is 2 percent, and target unemployment in France is zero percent. So what is needed is an increase in French government purchases of 2 units.

Step eight refers to the time lag. Unemployment in Germany goes from 2 to zero percent, as does unemployment in France. Hence unemployment in Europe goes from 2 to zero percent too. Inflation in Germany goes from 6 to 8 percent. Inflation in France goes from – 2 to zero percent. Hence inflation in Europe goes from 2 to 4 percent. And so on. Table 6.5 gives an overview.

Table 6.5
Simultaneous and Independent Policy Decisions
A Supply Shock in Germany

Germany		France	
Unemployment	4	Unemployment	0
Inflation	4	Inflation	0
Δ European Money Supply	0		
Δ Government Purchases	4	Δ Government Purchases	0
Unemployment	0	Unemployment	0
Inflation	8	Inflation	0
Δ European Money Supply	– 2		
Δ Government Purchases	0	Δ Government Purchases	0
Unemployment	2	Unemployment	2
Inflation	6	Inflation	– 2
Δ European Money Supply	0		
Δ Government Purchases	2	Δ Government Purchases	2
Unemployment	0	Unemployment	0
Inflation	8	Inflation	0
and so on			

As a result, given a supply shock in Germany, simultaneous and independent policy decisions cause uniform oscillations in unemployment and inflation. And what is more, there is an explosion of government purchases and an implosion of money supply.

3) A mixed shock in Germany. In each of the member countries, let initial unemployment be zero, and let initial inflation be zero as well. Step one refers to the mixed shock in Germany. In terms of the model there is an increase in B_1 of 4 units. Step two refers to the time lag. Inflation in Germany goes from zero to 4 percent. Inflation in France stays at zero percent. Thus inflation in Europe goes from zero to 2 percent. Unemployment in Germany stays at zero percent, as does unemployment in France. Thus unemployment in Europe stays at zero percent too.

In step three, the central bank and the governments decide simultaneously and independently. First consider monetary policy in Europe. Current unemployment in Europe is zero percent, and current inflation in Europe is 2 percent. Accordingly, target unemployment in Europe and target inflation in Europe are 1 percent each. So what is needed is a reduction in European money supply of 1 unit. Second consider fiscal policy in Germany. Current unemployment in Germany is zero percent, and target unemployment in Germany is the same. So what is needed is no change in German government purchases. Third consider fiscal policy in France. Current unemployment in France is zero percent, and target unemployment in France is the same. So what is needed is no change in French government purchases.

Step four refers to the time lag. Unemployment in Germany goes from zero to 1 percent, as does unemployment in France. Thus unemployment in Europe goes from zero to 1 percent as well. Inflation in Germany goes from 4 to 3 percent. Inflation in France goes from zero to – 1 percent. Thus inflation in Europe goes from 2 to 1 percent.

In step five, the central bank and the governments decide simultaneously and independently. First consider monetary policy in Europe. Current unemployment in Europe is 1 percent, and current inflation in Europe is 1 percent too. Accordingly, target unemployment in Europe and target inflation in Europe are 1 percent each. So what is needed is no change in European money supply. Second consider fiscal policy in Germany. Current unemployment in Germany is 1 percent, and target unemployment in Germany is zero percent. So what is needed is an increase in German government purchases of 1 unit. Third consider fiscal policy in France. Current unemployment in France is 1 percent, and target unemployment in France is zero percent. So what is needed is an increase in French government purchases of 1 unit.

Step six refers to the time lag. Unemployment in Germany goes from 1 to zero percent, as does unemployment in France. Thus unemployment in Europe goes from 1 to zero percent too. Inflation in Germany goes from 3 to 4 percent. Inflation in France goes from – 1 to zero percent. Thus inflation in Europe goes from 1 to 2 percent. And so on. For a synopsis see Table 6.6.

Table 6.6
Simultaneous and Independent Policy Decisions
A Mixed Shock in Germany

Germany		France	
Unemployment	0	Unemployment	0
Inflation	4	Inflation	0
Δ European Money Supply	– 1		
Δ Government Purchases	0	Δ Government Purchases	0
Unemployment	1	Unemployment	1
Inflation	3	Inflation	– 1
Δ European Money Supply	0		
Δ Government Purchases	1	Δ Government Purchases	1
Unemployment	0	Unemployment	0
Inflation	4	Inflation	0
and so on			

As a result, given a mixed shock in Germany, simultaneous and independent policy decisions cause uniform oscillations in unemployment and inflation. And what is more, there is an explosion of government purchases and an implosion of money supply.

4) Summary. Given a demand shock in Germany, simultaneous and independent policy decisions cause uniform oscillations in unemployment and inflation. In addition, there are uniform oscillations in money supply and government purchases. Given a supply shock in Germany, simultaneous and independent policy decisions cause uniform oscillations in unemployment and inflation. What is more, there is an explosion of government purchases and an implosion of money supply. And much the same applies to a mixed shock in Germany.

Chapter 3
Target System C

1. The Model

1) The static model. This chapter is based on target system C. The targets of the European central bank are zero inflation and zero unemployment in each of the member countries. The targets of the German government are zero unemployment and zero inflation in Germany. And the targets of the French government are zero unemployment and zero inflation in France.

The model of unemployment and inflation can be represented by a system of four equations:

$$u_1 = A_1 - M - G_1 \tag{1}$$

$$u_2 = A_2 - M - G_2 \tag{2}$$

$$\pi_1 = B_1 + M + G_1 \tag{3}$$

$$\pi_2 = B_2 + M + G_2 \tag{4}$$

An increase in European money supply lowers unemployment in Germany and France. On the other hand, it raises inflation there. An increase in German government purchases lowers unemployment in Germany. On the other hand, it raises inflation there. Correspondingly, an increase in French government purchases lowers unemployment in France. On the other hand, it raises inflation there.

The targets of the European central bank are zero inflation and zero unemployment in each of the member countries. The instrument of the European central bank is European money supply. There are four targets but only one instrument, so what is needed is a loss function. We assume that the European central bank has a quadratic loss function:

$$L = \pi_1^2 + \pi_2^2 + u_1^2 + u_2^2 \tag{5}$$

M. Carlberg, *Dynamic Policy Interactions in a Monetary Union*,
DOI 10.1007/978-3-642-18228-0_19, © Springer-Verlag Berlin Heidelberg 2011

L is the loss to the European central bank caused by inflation and unemployment in each of the member countries. We assume equal weights in the loss function. The specific target of the European central bank is to minimize the loss, given the inflation functions and the unemployment functions. Taking account of equations (1), (2), (3) and (4), the loss function of the European central bank can be written as follows:

$$\begin{aligned} L = {} & (B_1 + M + G_1)^2 + (B_2 + M + G_2)^2 \\ & + (A_1 - M - G_1)^2 + (A_2 - M - G_2)^2 \end{aligned} \tag{6}$$

Then the first-order condition for a minimum loss gives the reaction function of the European central bank:

$$4M = A_1 + A_2 - B_1 - B_2 - 2G_1 - 2G_2 \tag{7}$$

An increase in A_1 or A_2 requires an increase in European money supply. An increase in B_1 or B_2 requires a cut in European money supply. And an increase in German or French government purchases requires a cut in European money supply too.

The targets of the German government are zero unemployment and zero inflation in Germany. The instrument of the German government is German government purchases. There are two targets but only one instrument, so what is needed is a loss function. We assume that the German government has a quadratic loss function:

$$L_1 = \pi_1^2 + u_1^2 \tag{8}$$

L_1 is the loss to the German government caused by inflation and unemployment in Germany. We assume equal weights in the loss function. The specific target of the German government is to minimize the loss, given the inflation function and the unemployment function. Taking account of equations (1) and (3), the loss function of the German government can be written as follows:

$$L_1 = (B_1 + M + G_1)^2 + (A_1 - M - G_1)^2 \tag{9}$$

Then the first-order condition for a minimum loss gives the reaction function of the German government:

$$2G_1 = A_1 - B_1 - 2M \tag{10}$$

An increase in A_1 requires an increase in German government purchases. An increase in B_1 requires a cut in German government purchases. And a cut in European money supply requires an increase in German government purchases.

The targets of the French government are zero unemployment and zero inflation in France. The instrument of the French government is French government purchases. There are two targets but only one instrument, so what is needed is a loss function. We assume that the French government has a quadratic loss function:

$$L_2 = \pi_2^2 + u_2^2 \tag{11}$$

L_2 is the loss to the French government caused by inflation and unemployment in France. We assume equal weights in the loss function. The specific target of the French government is to minimize the loss, given the inflation function and the unemployment function. Taking account of equations (2) and (4), the loss function of the French government can be written as follows:

$$L_2 = (B_2 + M + G_2)^2 + (A_2 - M - G_2)^2 \tag{12}$$

Then the first-order condition for a minimum loss gives the reaction function of the French government:

$$2G_2 = A_2 - B_2 - 2M \tag{13}$$

An increase in A_2 requires an increase in French government purchases. An increase in B_2 requires a cut in French government purchases. And a cut in European money supply requires an increase in French government purchases.

The Nash equilibrium is determined by the reaction functions of the European central bank, the German government, and the French government:

$$4M = A_1 + A_2 - B_1 - B_2 - 2G_1 - 2G_2 \tag{14}$$

$$2G_1 = A_1 - B_1 - 2M \tag{15}$$

$$2G_2 = A_2 - B_2 - 2M \tag{16}$$

Now take the sum of equations (15) and (16) to find out:

$$4M = A_1 + A_2 - B_1 - B_2 - 2G_1 - 2G_2 \tag{17}$$

Clearly, equations (14) and (17) are identical. There are three endogenous variables (M, G_1, G_2). On the other hand, there are only two independent equations. As a result there are multiple Nash equilibria.

Finally compare the target systems A, B and C. Under target system A there is no Nash equilibrium. Under target system B there is no Nash equilibrium either. And under target system C there are multiple Nash equilibria.

2) The dynamic model. We assume that the central bank and the governments decide simultaneously and independently. Step 1 refers to a specific shock. Step 2 refers to the time lag. Step 3 refers to monetary and fiscal policies. Step 4 refers to the time lag. Step 5 refers to monetary and fiscal policies. Step 6 refers to the time lag. And so on.

Now have a closer look at the dynamic model. Step 1 refers to a specific shock. Step 2 refers to the time lag. In step 3, the central bank and the governments decide simultaneously and independently. The European central bank sets European money supply so as to reduce its loss. The reaction function of the European central bank is:

$$4M = A_1 + A_2 - B_1 - B_2 - 2G_1 - 2G_2 \tag{18}$$

The German government sets its purchases of German goods so as to reduce its loss. The reaction function of the German government is:

$$2G_1 = A_1 - B_1 - 2M \tag{19}$$

The French government sets its purchases of French goods so as to reduce its loss. The reaction function of the French government is:

$$2G_2 = A_2 - B_2 - 2M \tag{20}$$

Step 4 refers to the time lag. In step 5, the central bank and the governments decide simultaneously and independently. The European central bank sets European money supply so as to reduce its loss. The reaction function of the European central bank is:

$$4M = A_1 + A_2 - B_1 - B_2 - 2G_1 - 2G_2 \tag{21}$$

The German government sets its purchases of German goods so as to reduce its loss. The reaction function of the German government is:

$$2G_1 = A_1 - B_1 - 2M \tag{22}$$

The French government sets its purchases of French goods so as to reduce its loss. The reaction function of the French government is:

$$2G_2 = A_2 - B_2 - 2M \tag{23}$$

Step 6 refers to the time lag. And so on. Then what are the dynamic characteristics of this process?

2. Some Numerical Examples

Here are three distinct cases:

- a demand shock in Germany
- a supply shock in Germany
- a mixed shock in Germany.

The targets of the European central bank are zero inflation and zero unemployment in each of the member countries. The targets of the German government are zero unemployment and zero inflation in Germany. And the targets of the French government are zero unemployment and zero inflation in France.

1) A demand shock in Germany. In each of the member countries, let initial unemployment be zero, and let initial inflation be zero as well. Step one refers to a decline in the demand for German goods. In terms of the model there is an increase in A_1 of 4 units and a decline in B_1 of equally 4 units. Step two refers to the time lag. Unemployment in Germany goes from zero to 4 percent. Unemployment in France stays at zero percent. Thus unemployment in Europe goes from zero to 2 percent. Inflation in Germany goes from zero to – 4 percent. Inflation in France stays at zero percent. Thus inflation in Europe goes from zero to – 2 percent.

In step three, the central bank and the governments decide simultaneously and independently. First consider monetary policy in Europe. Current unemployment in Europe is 2 percent, and current inflation in Europe is – 2 percent. Accordingly, target unemployment in Europe and target inflation in Europe are zero percent each. So what is needed is an increase in European money supply of 2 units. Second consider fiscal policy in Germany. Current unemployment in Germany is 4 percent, and current inflation in Germany is – 4 percent. Accordingly, target unemployment in Germany and target inflation in Germany are zero percent each. So what is needed is an increase in German government purchases of 4 units. Third consider fiscal policy in France. Current unemployment in France is zero percent, and current inflation in France is zero percent too. Accordingly, target unemployment in France and target inflation in

France are zero percent each. So what is needed is no change in French government purchases.

Step four refers to the time lag. Unemployment in Germany goes from 4 to – 2 percent. Unemployment in France goes from zero to – 2 percent. Thus unemployment in Europe goes from 2 to – 2 percent. Inflation in Germany goes from – 4 to 2 percent. Inflation in France goes from zero to 2 percent. Thus inflation in Europe goes from – 2 to 2 percent.

In step five, the central bank and the governments decide simultaneously and independently. First consider monetary policy in Europe. Current unemployment in Europe is – 2 percent, and current inflation in Europe is 2 percent. Accordingly, target unemployment in Europe and target inflation in Europe are zero percent each. So what is needed is a reduction in European money supply of 2 units. Second consider fiscal policy in Germany. Current unemployment in Germany is – 2 percent, and current inflation in Germany is 2 percent. Accordingly, target unemployment in Germany and target inflation in Germany are zero percent each. So what is needed is a reduction in German government purchases of 2 units. Third consider fiscal policy in France. Current unemployment in France is – 2 percent, and current inflation in France is 2 percent. Accordingly, target unemployment in France and target inflation in France are zero percent each. So what is needed is a reduction in French government purchases of 2 units.

Step six refers to the time lag. Unemployment in Germany goes from – 2 to 2 percent, as does unemployment in France. Thus unemployment in Europe goes from – 2 to 2 percent as well. Inflation in Germany goes from 2 to – 2 percent, as does inflation in France. Thus inflation in Europe goes from 2 to – 2 percent as well. And so on. Table 6.7 presents a synopsis.

As a result, given a demand shock in Germany, simultaneous and independent policy decisions cause uniform oscillations in unemployment and inflation. The economy oscillates between underemployment and overemployment. Accordingly, the economy oscillates between deflation and inflation. And what is more, there are uniform oscillations in money supply and government purchases.

Table 6.7
Simultaneous and Independent Policy Decisions
A Demand Shock in Germany

Germany		France	
Unemployment	4	Unemployment	0
Inflation	– 4	Inflation	0
Δ European Money Supply	2		
Δ Government Purchases	4	Δ Government Purchases	0
Unemployment	– 2	Unemployment	– 2
Inflation	2	Inflation	2
Δ European Money Supply	– 2		
Δ Government Purchases	– 2	Δ Government Purchases	– 2
Unemployment	2	Unemployment	2
Inflation	– 2	Inflation	– 2
and so on			

2) A supply shock in Germany. In each of the member countries, let initial unemployment be zero, and let initial inflation be zero as well. Step one refers to the supply shock in Germany. In terms of the model there is an increase in B_1 of 4 units and an increase in A_1 of equally 4 units. Step two refers to the time lag. Inflation in Germany goes from zero to 4 percent. Inflation in France stays at zero percent. Hence inflation in Europe goes from zero to 2 percent. Unemployment in Germany goes from zero to 4 percent. Unemployment in France stays at zero percent. Hence unemployment in Europe goes from zero to 2 percent.

In step three, the central bank and the governments decide simultaneously and independently. First consider monetary policy in Europe. Current unemployment in Europe is 2 percent, and current inflation in Europe is 2 percent as well. Accordingly, target unemployment in Europe and target inflation in Europe are 2 percent each. So what is needed is no change in European money supply. Second consider fiscal policy in Germany. Current unemployment in Germany is 4 percent, and current inflation in Germany is 4 percent too. Accordingly, target unemployment in Germany and target inflation in Germany are 4 percent each. So what is needed is no change in German government purchases. Third consider fiscal policy in France. Current unemployment in France is zero percent, and current inflation in France is zero percent too. Accordingly, target unemployment in France and target inflation in France are zero percent each. So what is needed is no change in French government purchases.

Step four refers to the time lag. Unemployment in Germany stays at 4 percent, and unemployment in France stays at zero percent. Hence unemployment in Europe stays at 2 percent. Inflation in Germany stays at 4 percent, and inflation in France stays at zero percent. Hence inflation in Europe stays at 2 percent. Table 6.8 gives an overview.

Table 6.8
Simultaneous and Independent Policy Decisions
A Supply Shock in Germany

Germany		France	
Unemployment	4	Unemployment	0
Inflation	4	Inflation	0
Δ European Money Supply	0		
Δ Government Purchases	0	Δ Government Purchases	0
Unemployment	4	Unemployment	0
Inflation	4	Inflation	0

As a result, given a supply shock in Germany, simultaneous and independent policy decisions are ineffective. There is no change in European money supply, no change in German government purchases, and no change in French government purchases. Correspondingly, there is no change in unemployment and inflation.

3) A mixed shock in Germany. In each of the member countries, let initial unemployment be zero, and let initial inflation be zero as well. Step one refers to the mixed shock in Germany. In terms of the model there is an increase in B_1 of 4 units. Step two refers to the time lag. Inflation in Germany goes from zero to 4 percent. Inflation in France stays at zero percent. Thus inflation in Europe goes from zero to 2 percent. Unemployment in Germany stays at zero percent, as does unemployment in France. Thus unemployment in Europe stays at zero percent too.

In step three, the central bank and the governments decide simultaneously and independently. First consider monetary policy in Europe. Current unemployment in Europe is zero percent, and current inflation in Europe is 2 percent. Accordingly, target unemployment in Europe and target inflation in Europe are 1 percent each. So what is needed is a reduction in European money supply of 1 unit. Second consider fiscal policy in Germany. Current unemployment in Germany is zero percent, and current inflation in Germany is 4 percent. Accordingly, target unemployment in Germany and target inflation in Germany are 2 percent each. So what is needed is a reduction in German government purchases of 2 units. Third consider fiscal policy in France. Current unemployment in France is zero percent, and current inflation in France is zero percent too. Accordingly, target unemployment in France and target inflation in France are zero percent each. So what is needed is no change in French government purchases.

Step four refers to the time lag. Unemployment in Germany goes from zero to 3 percent. Unemployment in France goes from zero to 1 percent. Thus unemployment in Europe goes from zero to 2 percent. Inflation in Germany goes from 4 to 1 percent. Inflation in France goes from zero to – 1 percent. Thus inflation in Europe goes from 2 to zero percent.

In step five, the central bank and the governments decide simultaneously and independently. First consider monetary policy in Europe. Current unemployment in Europe is 2 percent, and current inflation in Europe is zero percent. Accordingly, target unemployment in Europe and target inflation in Europe are 1 percent each. So what is needed is an increase in European money supply of 1 unit. Second consider fiscal policy in Germany. Current unemployment in Germany is 3 percent, and current inflation in Germany is 1 percent. Accordingly, target unemployment in Germany and target inflation in Germany are 2 percent each. So what is needed is an increase in German government purchases of 1 unit. Third consider fiscal policy in France. Current unemployment in France is 1 percent, and current inflation in France is – 1 percent. Accordingly, target unemployment in France and target inflation in France are zero percent each. So what is needed is an increase in French government purchases of 1 unit.

Step six refers to the time lag. Unemployment in Germany goes from 3 to 1 percent. Unemployment in France goes from 1 to – 1 percent. Thus unemployment in Europe goes from 2 to zero percent. Inflation in Germany goes from 1 to 3 percent. Inflation in France goes from – 1 to 1 percent. Thus inflation in Europe goes from zero to 2 percent. And so on. For a synopsis see Table 6.9.

As a result, given a mixed shock in Germany, simultaneous and independent policy decisions cause uniform oscillations in unemployment and inflation. And what is more, there are uniform oscillations in money supply and government purchases.

4) Summary. Given a demand shock in Germany, simultaneous and independent policy decisions cause uniform oscillations in unemployment and inflation. And what is more, there are uniform oscillations in money supply and government purchases. Given a supply shock in Germany, policy decisions are ineffective. There is no change in European money supply, no change in German government purchases, and no change in French government purchases. Correspondingly, there is no change in unemployment and inflation. Given a mixed shock in Germany, policy decisions cause uniform oscillations in unemployment and inflation. And what is more, there are uniform oscillations in money supply and government purchases.

Table 6.9
Simultaneous and Independent Policy Decisions
A Mixed Shock in Germany

Germany		France	
Unemployment	0	Unemployment	0
Inflation	4	Inflation	0
Δ European Money Supply	– 1		
Δ Government Purchases	– 2	Δ Government Purchases	0
Unemployment	3	Unemployment	1
Inflation	1	Inflation	– 1
Δ European Money Supply	1		
Δ Government Purchases	1	Δ Government Purchases	1
Unemployment	1	Unemployment	– 1
Inflation	3	Inflation	1
and so on			

Part Seven

Central Bank and Governments Decide Simultaneously and Independently

Gradualist Policies

Chapter 1
The Model

1) The static model. The monetary union consists of two countries, say Germany and France. The member countries are the same size and have the same behavioural functions. This chapter is based on target system A. The targets of the European central bank are zero inflation in Germany and France respectively. The target of the German government is zero unemployment in Germany. And the target of the French government is zero unemployment in France.

The model of unemployment and inflation can be represented by a system of four equations:

$$u_1 = A_1 - M - G_1 \tag{1}$$

$$u_2 = A_2 - M - G_2 \tag{2}$$

$$\pi_1 = B_1 + M + G_1 \tag{3}$$

$$\pi_2 = B_2 + M + G_2 \tag{4}$$

An increase in European money supply lowers unemployment in Germany and France. On the other hand, it raises inflation there. An increase in German government purchases lowers unemployment in Germany. On the other hand, it raises inflation there. Correspondingly, an increase in French government purchases lowers unemployment in France. On the other hand, it raises inflation there. Fiscal policy in one of the member countries has no effect on unemployment or inflation in the other country.

The targets of the European central bank are zero inflation in Germany and France respectively. The instrument of the European central bank is European money supply. There are two targets but only one instrument, so what is needed is a loss function. We assume that the European central bank has a quadratic loss function:

$$L = \pi_1^2 + \pi_2^2 \tag{5}$$

M. Carlberg, *Dynamic Policy Interactions in a Monetary Union*,
DOI 10.1007/978-3-642-18228-0_20, © Springer-Verlag Berlin Heidelberg 2011

L is the loss to the European central bank caused by inflation in Germany and France. We assume equal weights in the loss function. The specific target of the European central bank is to minimize the loss, given the inflation functions. Taking account of equations (3) and (4), the loss function of the European central bank can be written as follows:

$$L = (B_1 + M + G_1)^2 + (B_2 + M + G_2)^2 \tag{6}$$

Then the first-order condition for a minimum loss gives the reaction function of the European central bank:

$$2M = -B_1 - B_2 - G_1 - G_2 \tag{7}$$

An increase in B_1 or B_2 requires a cut in European money supply. And an increase in German or French government purchases requires a cut in European money supply too.

The target of the German government is zero unemployment in Germany. The instrument of the German government is German government purchases. By equation (1), the reaction function of the German government is:

$$G_1 = A_1 - M \tag{8}$$

An increase in A_1 requires an increase in German government purchases. And a cut in European money supply requires an increase in German government purchases as well.

The target of the French government is zero unemployment in France. The instrument of the French government is French government purchases. By equation (2), the reaction function of the French government is:

$$G_2 = A_2 - M \tag{9}$$

An increase in A_2 requires an increase in French government purchases. And a cut in European money supply requires an increase in French government purchases as well.

The Nash equilibrium is determined by the reaction functions of the European central bank, the German government, and the French government. From the reaction functions follows:

$$A_1 + A_2 + B_1 + B_2 = 0 \tag{10}$$

Evidently, this is in contradiction to the assumption that A_1, A_2, B_1 and B_2 are given exogenously. As a result there is no Nash equilibrium.

2) The dynamic model. The target of the European central bank is to cut European inflation by half. The target of the German government is to cut German unemployment by half. And the target of the French government is to cut French unemployment by half. We assume that the central bank and the governments decide simultaneously and independently. Step 1 refers to a specific shock. Step 2 refers to the time lag. Step 3 refers to monetary and fiscal policies. Step 4 refers to the time lag. Step 5 refers to monetary and fiscal policies. Step 6 refers to the time lag. And so on.

Now have a closer look at the dynamic model. Step 1 refers to a specific shock. This could be a demand shock, a supply shock or a mixed shock, in Germany or France. Step 2 refers to the time lag. This includes both the inside lag and the outside lag. In step 3, the central bank and the governments decide simultaneously and independently. The European central bank sets European money supply so as to cut European inflation by half. The reaction function of the European central bank is:

$$4M = -B_1 - B_2 - G_1 - G_2 \tag{11}$$

The German government sets its purchases of German goods so as to cut German unemployment by half. The reaction function of the German government is:

$$2G_1 = A_1 - M \tag{12}$$

The French government sets its purchases of French goods so as to cut French unemployment by half. The reaction function of the French government is:

$$2G_2 = A_2 - M \tag{13}$$

Step 4 refers to the time lag. In step 5, the central bank and the governments decide simultaneously and independently. The European central bank sets European money supply so as to cut European inflation by half. The reaction function of the European central bank is:

$$4M = -B_1 - B_2 - G_1 - G_2 \tag{14}$$

The German government sets its purchases of German goods so as to cut German unemployment by half. The reaction function of the German government is:

$$2G_1 = A_1 - M \tag{15}$$

The French government sets its purchases of French goods so as to cut French unemployment by half. The reaction function of the French government is:

$$2G_2 = A_2 - M \tag{16}$$

Step 6 refers to the time lag. And so on. Then what are the dynamic characteristics of this process?

Chapter 2
Some Numerical Examples

It proves useful to study two distinct cases:

- a demand shock in Germany
- a supply shock in Germany.

The target of the European central bank is to cut European inflation by half. The target of the German government is to cut German unemployment by half. And the target of the French government is to cut French unemployment by half.

1) A demand shock in Germany. In each of the member countries, let initial unemployment be zero, and let initial inflation be zero as well. Step one refers to a decline in the demand for German goods. In terms of the model there is an increase in A_1 of 8 units and a decline in B_1 of equally 8 units. Step two refers to the time lag. Unemployment in Germany goes from zero to 8 percent. Unemployment in France stays at zero percent. Thus unemployment in Europe goes from zero to 4 percent. Inflation in Germany goes from zero to – 8 percent. Inflation in France stays at zero percent. Thus inflation in Europe goes from zero to – 4 percent.

In step three, the central bank and the governments decide simultaneously and independently. First consider monetary policy in Europe. The European central bank sets European money supply so as to cut European inflation by half. Current inflation in Europe is – 4 percent, and target inflation in Europe is – 2 percent. So what is needed is an increase in European money supply of 2 units. Second consider fiscal policy in Germany. The German government sets its purchases so as to cut German unemployment by half. Current unemployment in Germany is 8 percent, and target unemployment in Germany is 4 percent. So what is needed is an increase in German government purchases of 4 units. Third consider fiscal policy in France. The French government sets its purchases so as to cut French unemployment by half. Current unemployment in France is zero percent, and target unemployment in France is the same. So what is needed is no change in French government purchases.

M. Carlberg, *Dynamic Policy Interactions in a Monetary Union*,
DOI 10.1007/978-3-642-18228-0_21, © Springer-Verlag Berlin Heidelberg 2011

Step four refers to the time lag. Unemployment in Germany goes from 8 to 2 percent. Unemployment in France goes from zero to – 2 percent. Thus unemployment in Europe goes from 4 to zero percent. Inflation in Germany goes from – 8 to – 2 percent. Inflation in France goes from zero to 2 percent. Thus inflation in Europe goes from – 4 to zero percent.

In step five, the central bank and the governments decide simultaneously and independently. First consider monetary policy in Europe. The European central bank sets European money supply so as to cut European inflation by half. Current inflation in Europe is zero percent, and target inflation in Europe is the same. So what is needed is no change in European money supply. Second consider fiscal policy in Germany. The German government sets its purchases so as to cut German unemployment by half. Current unemployment in Germany is 2 percent, and target unemployment in Germany is 1 percent. So what is needed is an increase in German government purchases of 1 unit. Third consider fiscal policy in France. The French government sets its purchases so as to cut French unemployment by half. Current unemployment in France is – 2 percent, and target unemployment in France is – 1 percent. So what is needed is a reduction in French government purchases of 1 unit.

Step six refers to the time lag. Unemployment in Germany goes from 2 to 1 percent. Unemployment in France goes from – 2 to – 1 percent. Thus unemployment in Europe stays at zero percent. Inflation in Germany goes from – 2 to – 1 percent. Inflation in France goes from 2 to 1 percent. Thus inflation in Europe stays at zero percent. And so on. Table 7.1 presents a synopsis.

As a result, given a demand shock in Germany, simultaneous and independent policy decisions produce zero unemployment and zero inflation in each of the member countries. There is an increase in European money supply, an increase in German government purchases, a reduction in French government purchases, and an increase in European government purchases.

Table 7.1
Gradualist Policies
A Demand Shock in Germany

Germany		France	
Unemployment	8	Unemployment	0
Inflation	– 8	Inflation	0
Δ European Money Supply	2		
Δ Government Purchases	4	Δ Government Purchases	0
Unemployment	2	Unemployment	– 2
Inflation	– 2	Inflation	2
Δ European Money Supply	0		
Δ Government Purchases	2	Δ Government Purchases	– 2
Unemployment	1	Unemployment	– 1
Inflation	– 1	Inflation	1
and so on			

2) A supply shock in Germany. In each of the member countries, let initial unemployment be zero, and let initial inflation be zero as well. Step one refers to the supply shock in Germany. In terms of the model there is an increase in B_1 of 8 units and an increase in A_1 of equally 8 units. Step two refers to the time lag. Inflation in Germany goes from zero to 8 percent. Inflation in France stays at zero percent. Hence inflation in Europe goes from zero to 4 percent. Unemployment in Germany goes from zero to 8 percent. Unemployment in France stays at zero percent. Hence unemployment in Europe goes from zero to 4 percent.

In step three, the central bank and the governments decide simultaneously and independently. First consider monetary policy in Europe. The European central bank sets European money supply so as to cut European inflation by half.

Current inflation in Europe is 4 percent, and target inflation in Europe is 2 percent. So what is needed is a reduction in European money supply of 2 units. Second consider fiscal policy in Germany. The German government sets its purchases so as to cut German unemployment by half. Current unemployment in Germany is 8 percent, and target unemployment in Germany is 4 percent. So what is needed is an increase in German government purchases of 4 units. Third consider fiscal policy in France. The French government sets its purchases so as to cut French unemployment by half. Current unemployment in France is zero percent, and target unemployment in France is the same. So what is needed is no change in French government purchases.

Step four refers to the time lag. Unemployment in Germany goes from 8 to 6 percent. Unemployment in France goes from zero to 2 percent. Hence unemployment in Europe stays at 4 percent. Inflation in Germany goes from 8 to 10 percent. Inflation in France goes from zero to – 2 percent. Hence inflation in Europe stays at 4 percent.

In step five, the central bank and the governments decide simultaneously and independently. First consider monetary policy in Europe. The European central bank sets European money supply so as to cut European inflation by half. Current inflation in Europe is 4 percent, and target inflation in Europe is 2 percent. So what is needed is a reduction in European money supply of 2 units. Second consider fiscal policy in Germany. The German government sets its purchases so as to cut German unemployment by half. Current unemployment in Germany is 6 percent, and target unemployment in Germany is 3 percent. So what is needed is an increase in German government purchases of 3 units. Third consider fiscal policy in France. The French government sets its purchases so as to cut French unemployment by half. Current unemployment in France is 2 percent, and target unemployment in France is 1 percent. So what is needed is an increase in French government purchases of 1 unit.

Step six refers to the time lag. Unemployment in Germany goes from 6 to 5 percent. Unemployment in France goes from 2 to 3 percent. Hence unemployment in Europe stays at 4 percent. Inflation in Germany goes from 10 to 11 percent. Inflation in France goes from – 2 to – 3 percent. Hence inflation in Europe stays at 4 percent. And so on. Table 7.2 gives an overview.

In the long-run equilibrium, in each period, there is a reduction in European money supply of 2 units, there is an increase in German government purchases of 2 units, and there is an increase in French government purchases of equally 2 units. Unemployment in Germany stays at 4 percent, as does unemployment in France. Thus unemployment in Europe stays at 4 percent too. Inflation in Germany stays at 12 percent, and inflation in France stays at – 4 percent. Thus inflation in Europe stays at 4 percent.

As a result, given a supply shock in Germany, simultaneous and independent policy decisions lower German unemployment and raise German inflation. On the other hand, they raise French unemployment and lower French inflation. And what is more, there is an explosion of government purchases and an implosion of money supply.

Table 7.2
Gradualist Policies
A Supply Shock in Germany

Germany		France	
Unemployment	8	Unemployment	0
Inflation	8	Inflation	0
Δ European Money Supply	– 2		
Δ Government Purchases	4	Δ Government Purchases	0
Unemployment	6	Unemployment	2
Inflation	10	Inflation	– 2
Δ European Money Supply	– 2		
Δ Government Purchases	3	Δ Government Purchases	1
Unemployment	5	Unemployment	3
Inflation	11	Inflation	– 3
and so on			

3) Summary. Given a demand shock in Germany, simultaneous and independent policy decisions produce zero unemployment and zero inflation in each of the member countries. There is an increase in European money supply, an increase in German government purchases, a reduction in French government purchases, and an increase in European government purchases. Given a supply shock in Germany, simultaneous and independent policy decisions lower German unemployment and raise German inflation. Conversely, they raise French unemployment and lower French inflation. And what is more, there is an explosion of government purchases and an implosion of money supply.

Part Eight

Central Bank and Governments Cooperate

Chapter 1
The Model

The monetary union consists of two countries, say Germany and France. The member countries are the same size and have the same behavioural functions. The model of unemployment and inflation can be represented by a system of four equations:

$$u_1 = A_1 - M - G_1 \quad (1)$$

$$u_2 = A_2 - M - G_2 \quad (2)$$

$$\pi_1 = B_1 + M + G_1 \quad (3)$$

$$\pi_2 = B_2 + M + G_2 \quad (4)$$

Here u_1 denotes the rate of unemployment in Germany, u_2 is the rate of unemployment in France, π_1 is the rate of inflation in Germany, π_2 is the rate of inflation in France, M is European money supply, G_1 is German government purchases, G_2 is French government purchases, A_1 is some other factors bearing on the rate of unemployment in Germany, A_2 is some other factors bearing on the rate of unemployment in France, B_1 is some other factors bearing on the rate of inflation in Germany, and B_2 is some other factors bearing on the rate of inflation in France. The endogenous variables are the rate of unemployment in Germany, the rate of unemployment in France, the rate of inflation in Germany, and the rate of inflation in France.

An increase in European money supply lowers unemployment in Germany and France. On the other hand, it raises inflation there. An increase in German government purchases lowers unemployment in Germany. On the other hand, it raises inflation there. Correspondingly, an increase in French government purchases lowers unemployment in France. On the other hand, it raises inflation there. Fiscal policy in one of the member countries has no effect on unemployment or inflation in the other country.

M. Carlberg, *Dynamic Policy Interactions in a Monetary Union*,
DOI 10.1007/978-3-642-18228-0_22, © Springer-Verlag Berlin Heidelberg 2011

The policy makers are the European central bank, the German government, and the French government. The targets of policy cooperation are zero inflation and zero unemployment in each of the member countries. The instruments of policy cooperation are European money supply, German government purchases, and French government purchases. There are four targets but only three instruments, so what is needed is a loss function. We assume that the policy makers agree on a common loss function:

$$L = \pi_1^2 + \pi_2^2 + u_1^2 + u_2^2 \tag{5}$$

L is the loss caused by inflation and unemployment in each of the member countries. For ease of exposition we assume equal weights in the loss function. Of course this is a plausible assumption. Another plausible assumption could be:

$$L = 1.5(\pi_1^2 + \pi_2^2) + 0.5(u_1^2 + u_2^2) \tag{6}$$

The specific target of policy cooperation is to minimize the loss, given the inflation functions and the unemployment functions. Taking account of equations (1), (2), (3) and (4), the loss function under policy cooperation can be written as follows:

$$\begin{aligned} L = {} & (B_1 + M + G_1)^2 + (B_2 + M + G_2)^2 \\ & + (A_1 - M - G_1)^2 + (A_2 - M - G_2)^2 \end{aligned} \tag{7}$$

Then the first-order conditions for a minimum loss are:

$$4M = A_1 + A_2 - B_1 - B_2 - 2G_1 - 2G_2 \tag{8}$$

$$2G_1 = A_1 - B_1 - 2M \tag{9}$$

$$2G_2 = A_2 - B_2 - 2M \tag{10}$$

Equation (8) shows the first-order condition with respect to European money supply. Equation (9) shows the first-order condition with respect to German government purchases. And equation (10) shows the first-order condition with respect to French government purchases. Adding up equations (9) and (10) gives:

$$4M = A_1 + A_2 - B_1 - B_2 - 2G_1 - 2G_2 \tag{11}$$

Obviously, equations (8) and (11) are identical.

The cooperative equilibrium is determined by the first-order conditions for a minimum loss:

$$2M + 2G_1 = A_1 - B_1 \tag{12}$$

$$2M + 2G_2 = A_2 - B_2 \tag{13}$$

Equations (12) and (13) yield the optimum combinations of European money supply, German government purchases, and French government purchases. There are three endogenous variables. On the other hand, there are only two independent equations. Thus there is an infinite number of solutions. As a result, monetary and fiscal cooperation can reduce the loss caused by inflation and unemployment.

Chapter 2
Some Numerical Examples

Here are eight distinct cases:

- a demand shock in Germany
- a supply shock in Germany
- a mixed shock in Germany
- another mixed shock in Germany
- a common demand shock in Europe
- a common supply shock in Europe
- a common mixed shock in Europe
- another common mixed shock in Europe.

The targets of policy cooperation are zero inflation and zero unemployment in each of the member countries.

1) A demand shock in Germany. In each of the member countries, let initial unemployment be zero, and let initial inflation be zero as well. Step one refers to a decline in the demand for German goods. In terms of the model there is an increase in A_1 of 2 units and a decline in B_1 of equally 2 units. Step two refers to the time lag. Unemployment in Germany goes from zero to 2 percent. Unemployment in France stays at zero percent. Inflation in Germany goes from zero to – 2 percent. And inflation in France stays at zero percent.

Step three refers to the policy response. According to the model, a first solution is an increase in European money supply of 1 unit, an increase in German government purchases of 1 unit, and a reduction in French government purchases of equally 1 unit. Step four refers to the time lag. Unemployment in Germany goes from 2 to zero percent. Unemployment in France stays at zero percent. Inflation in Germany goes from – 2 to zero percent. And inflation in France stays at zero percent. Table 8.1 presents a synopsis.

As a result, given a demand shock in Germany, policy cooperation achieves zero unemployment and zero inflation in each of the member countries. There is an increase in European money supply, an increase in German government

M. Carlberg, *Dynamic Policy Interactions in a Monetary Union*,
DOI 10.1007/978-3-642-18228-0_23, © Springer-Verlag Berlin Heidelberg 2011

purchases, a reduction in French government purchases, and no change in European government purchases.

A second solution is an increase in European money supply of 2 units, no change in German government purchases, and a reduction in French government purchases of 2 units. A third solution is no change in European money supply, an increase in German government purchases of 2 units, and no change in French government purchases. And so on. The loss function under policy cooperation is:

$$L = \pi_1^2 + \pi_2^2 + u_1^2 + u_2^2 \qquad (1)$$

The initial loss is zero. The demand shock in Germany causes a loss of 8 units. Then policy cooperation brings the loss down to zero again.

Table 8.1
Policy Cooperation
A Demand Shock in Germany

Germany		France	
Unemployment	2	Unemployment	0
Inflation	– 2	Inflation	0
Δ European Money Supply	1		
Δ Government Purchases	1	Δ Government Purchases	– 1
Unemployment	0	Unemployment	0
Inflation	0	Inflation	0

2) A supply shock in Germany. In each of the member countries, let initial unemployment be zero, and let initial inflation be zero as well. Step one refers to the supply shock in Germany. In terms of the model there is an increase in B_1 of 2 units and an increase in A_1 of equally 2 units. Step two refers to the time lag. Inflation in Germany goes from zero to 2 percent. Inflation in France stays at

zero percent. Unemployment in Germany goes from zero to 2 percent. And unemployment in France stays at zero percent.

Step three refers to the policy response. According to the model, a first solution is no change in European money supply, no change in German government purchases, and no change in French government purchases. Step four refers to the time lag. Inflation in Germany stays at 2 percent, and inflation in France stays at zero percent. Thus inflation in Europe stays at 1 percent. Unemployment in Germany stays at 2 percent, and unemployment in France stays at zero percent. Thus unemployment in Europe stays at 1 percent. Table 8.2 gives an overview.

Table 8.2
Policy Cooperation
A Supply Shock in Germany

Germany		France	
Unemployment	2	Unemployment	0
Inflation	2	Inflation	0
Δ European Money Supply	0		
Δ Government Purchases	0	Δ Government Purchases	0
Unemployment	2	Unemployment	0
Inflation	2	Inflation	0

As a result, given a supply shock in Germany, policy cooperation is ineffective. There is no change in money supply and government purchases. Correspondingly, there is no change in unemployment and inflation. A second solution is an increase in European money supply of 1 unit, a reduction in German government purchases of 1 unit, and a reduction in French government purchases of equally 1 unit. A third solution is a reduction in European money supply of 1 unit, an increase in German government purchases of 1 unit, and an increase in French government purchases of equally 1 unit. And so on. The initial loss is zero. The supply shock in Germany causes a loss of 8 units. However, policy cooperation cannot reduce the loss.

3) A mixed shock in Germany. In each of the member countries, let initial unemployment be zero, and let initial inflation be zero as well. Step one refers to the mixed shock in Germany. In terms of the model there is an increase in B_1 of 4 units. Step two refers to the time lag. Inflation in Germany goes from zero to 4 percent. Inflation in France stays at zero percent. Unemployment in Germany stays at zero percent, as does unemployment in France.

Step three refers to the policy response. According to the model, a first solution is a reduction in European money supply of 1 unit, a reduction in German government purchases of 1 unit, and an increase in French government purchases of equally 1 unit. Step four refers to the time lag. Unemployment in Germany goes from zero to 2 percent. Unemployment in France stays at zero percent. Hence unemployment in Europe goes from zero to 1 percent. Inflation in Germany goes from 4 to 2 percent. Inflation in France stays at zero percent. Hence inflation in Europe goes from 2 to 1 percent. For a synopsis see Table 8.3.

As a result, given a mixed shock in Germany, policy cooperation lowers German inflation. On the other hand, it raises German unemployment. And what is more, it keeps up zero unemployment and zero inflation in France. There is a reduction in European money supply, a reduction in German government purchases, an increase in French government purchases, and no change in European government purchases.

A second solution is a reduction in European money supply of 2 units, no change in German government purchases, and an increase in French government purchases of 2 units. A third solution is no change in European money supply, a reduction in German government purchases of 2 units, and no change in French government purchases. And so on. The initial loss is zero. The mixed shock in Germany causes a loss of 16 units. Then policy cooperation brings the loss down to 8 units.

Table 8.3
Policy Cooperation
A Mixed Shock in Germany

Germany		France	
Unemployment	0	Unemployment	0
Inflation	4	Inflation	0
Δ European Money Supply	– 1		
Δ Government Purchases	– 1	Δ Government Purchases	1
Unemployment	2	Unemployment	0
Inflation	2	Inflation	0

4) Another type of a mixed shock in Germany. In each of the member countries, let initial unemployment be zero, and let initial inflation be zero as well. Step one refers to the mixed shock in Germany. In terms of the model there is an increase in A_1 of 4 units. Step two refers to the time lag. Unemployment in Germany goes from zero to 4 percent. Unemployment in France stays at zero percent. Inflation in Germany stays at zero percent, as does inflation in France.

Step three refers to the policy response. According to the model, a first solution is an increase in European money supply of 1 unit, an increase in German government purchases of 1 unit, and a reduction in French government purchases of equally 1 unit. Step four refers to the time lag. Unemployment in Germany goes from 4 to 2 percent. Unemployment in France stays at zero percent. Thus unemployment in Europe goes from 2 to 1 percent. Inflation in Germany goes from zero to 2 percent. Inflation in France stays at zero percent. Thus inflation in Europe goes from zero to 1 percent. For an overview see Table 8.4.

As a result, given another type of a mixed shock in Germany, policy cooperation lowers German unemployment. On the other hand, it raises German inflation. And what is more, it keeps up zero unemployment and zero inflation in

France. There is an increase in European money supply, an increase in German government purchases, a reduction in French government purchases, and no change in European government purchases.

A second solution is an increase in European money supply of 2 units, no change in German government purchases, and a reduction in French government purchases of 2 units. A third solution is no change in European money supply, an increase in German government purchases of 2 units, and no change in French government purchases. And so on. The initial loss is zero. The mixed shock in Germany causes a loss of 16 units. Then policy cooperation brings the loss down to 8 units.

Table 8.4
Policy Cooperation
Another Mixed Shock in Germany

Germany		France	
Unemployment	4	Unemployment	0
Inflation	0	Inflation	0
Δ European Money Supply	1		
Δ Government Purchases	1	Δ Government Purchases	– 1
Unemployment	2	Unemployment	0
Inflation	2	Inflation	0

5) A common demand shock in Europe. In each of the member countries, let initial unemployment be zero, and let initial inflation be zero as well. Step one refers to a decline in the demand for European goods. In terms of the model there is an increase in A_1 of 2 units, an increase in A_2 of 2 units, a decline in B_1 of 2 units, and a decline in B_2 of 2 units. Step two refers to the time lag. Unemployment in Germany goes from zero to 2 percent, as does unemployment

in France. Inflation in Germany goes from zero to – 2 percent, as does inflation in France.

Step three refers to the policy response. According to the model, a first solution is an increase in European money supply of 2 units, no change in German government purchases, and no change in French government purchases. Step four refers to the time lag. Unemployment in Germany goes from 2 to zero percent, as does unemployment in France. Inflation in Germany goes from – 2 to zero percent, as does inflation in France. Table 8.5 presents a synopsis.

Table 8.5
Policy Cooperation
A Common Demand Shock

Germany		France	
Unemployment	2	Unemployment	2
Inflation	– 2	Inflation	– 2
Δ European Money Supply	2		
Δ Government Purchases	0	Δ Government Purchases	0
Unemployment	0	Unemployment	0
Inflation	0	Inflation	0

As a result, given a common demand shock, policy cooperation achieves zero unemployment and zero inflation in each of the member countries. There is an increase in European money supply, no change in German government purchases, and no change in French government purchases.

A second solution is an increase in European money supply of 1 unit, an increase in German government purchases of 1 unit, and an increase in French government purchases of equally 1 unit. A third solution is no change in European money supply, an increase in German government purchases of 2 units, and an increase in French government purchases of equally 2 units. And so on. The initial loss is zero. The common demand shock causes a loss of 16 units. Then policy cooperation brings the loss down to zero again.

6) A common supply shock in Europe. In each of the member countries, let initial unemployment be zero, and let initial inflation be zero as well. Step one refers to the common supply shock in Europe. In terms of the model there is an increase in B_1 of 2 units, an increase in B_2 of 2 units, an increase in A_1 of 2 units, and an increase in A_2 of equally 2 units. Step two refers to the time lag. Inflation in Germany goes from zero to 2 percent, as does inflation in France. Unemployment in Germany goes from zero to 2 percent, as does unemployment in France.

Step three refers to the policy response. According to the model, a first solution is no change in European money supply, no change in German government purchases, and no change in French government purchases. Step four refers to the time lag. Inflation in Germany stays at 2 percent, as does inflation in France. Unemployment in Germany stays at 2 percent, as does unemployment in France. Table 8.6 gives an overview.

Table 8.6
Policy Cooperation
A Common Supply Shock

Germany		France	
Unemployment	2	Unemployment	2
Inflation	2	Inflation	2
Δ European Money Supply	0		
Δ Government Purchases	0	Δ Government Purchases	0
Unemployment	2	Unemployment	2
Inflation	2	Inflation	2

As a result, given a common supply shock, policy cooperation is ineffective. There is no change in money supply and government purchases. Correspondingly, there is no change in unemployment and inflation. A second solution is an increase in European money supply of 1 unit, a reduction in German government purchases of 1 unit, and a reduction in French government purchases of equally 1 unit. A third solution is a reduction in European money supply of 1 unit, an increase in German government purchases of 1 unit, and an increase in French government purchases of equally 1 unit. And so on. The initial loss is zero. Then the common supply shock causes a loss of 16 units. However, policy cooperation cannot reduce the loss.

7) A common mixed shock in Europe. In each of the member countries, let initial unemployment be zero, and let initial inflation be zero as well. Step one refers to the common mixed shock in Europe. In terms of the model there is an increase in B_1 of 4 units and an increase in B_2 of equally 4 units. Step two refers to the time lag. Inflation in Germany goes from zero to 4 percent, as does inflation in France. Unemployment in Germany stays at zero percent, as does unemployment in France.

Step three refers to the policy response. According to the model, a first solution is a reduction in European money supply of 2 units, no change in German government purchases, and no change in French government purchases. Step four refers to the time lag. Unemployment in Germany goes from zero to 2 percent, as does unemployment in France. Inflation in Germany goes from 4 to 2 percent, as does inflation in France. For a synopsis see Table 8.7.

As a result, given a common mixed shock, policy cooperation lowers inflation in Germany and France. On the other hand, it raises unemployment there. There is a reduction in European money supply, no change in German government purchases, and no change in French government purchases.

A second solution is a reduction in European money supply of 1 unit, a reduction in German government purchases of 1 unit, and a reduction in French government purchases of equally 1 unit. A third solution is no change in European money supply, a reduction in German government purchases of 2 units, and a reduction in French government purchases of equally 2 units. And so on.

The initial loss is zero. The common mixed shock causes a loss of 32 units. Then policy cooperation brings the loss down to 16 units.

Table 8.7
Policy Cooperation
A Common Mixed Shock

Germany		France	
Unemployment	0	Unemployment	0
Inflation	4	Inflation	4
Δ European Money Supply	– 2		
Δ Government Purchases	0	Δ Government Purchases	0
Unemployment	2	Unemployment	2
Inflation	2	Inflation	2

8) Another type of a common mixed shock in Europe. In each of the member countries, let initial unemployment be zero, and let initial inflation be zero as well. Step one refers to the common mixed shock in Europe. In terms of the model there is an increase in A_1 of 4 units and an increase in A_2 of equally 4 units. Step two refers to the time lag. Unemployment in Germany goes from zero to 4 percent, as does unemployment in France. Inflation in Germany stays at zero percent, as does inflation in France.

Step three refers to the policy response. According to the model, a first solution is an increase in European money supply of 2 units, no change in German government purchases, and no change in French government purchases. Step four refers to the time lag. Unemployment in Germany goes from 4 to 2 percent, as does unemployment in France. Inflation in Germany goes from zero to 2 percent, as does inflation in France. For an overview see Table 8.8.

As a result, given another type of a common mixed shock, policy cooperation lowers unemployment in Germany and France. On the other hand, it raises inflation there. There is an increase in European money supply, no change in German government purchases, and no change in French government purchases.

A second solution is an increase in European money supply of 1 unit, an increase in German government purchases of 1 unit, and an increase in French government purchases of equally 1 unit. A third solution is no change in European money supply, an increase in German government purchases of 2 units, and an increase in French government purchases of equally 2 units. And so on. The initial loss is zero. The common mixed shock causes a loss of 32 units. Then policy cooperation brings the loss down to 16 units.

Table 8.8
Policy Cooperation
Another Common Mixed Shock

Germany		France	
Unemployment	4	Unemployment	4
Inflation	0	Inflation	0
Δ European Money Supply	2		
Δ Government Purchases	0	Δ Government Purchases	0
Unemployment	2	Unemployment	2
Inflation	2	Inflation	2

9) Summary. Given a demand shock in Germany, policy cooperation achieves zero unemployment and zero inflation in each of the member countries. Given a supply shock in Germany, policy cooperation is ineffective. There is no change in money supply and government purchases. Correspondingly, there is no change in unemployment and inflation. Given a mixed shock in Germany, policy

cooperation lowers German inflation. On the other hand, it raises German unemployment. And what is more, it keeps up zero unemployment and zero inflation in France. Given another type of a mixed shock in Germany, policy cooperation lowers German unemployment. On the other hand, it raises German inflation. And what is more, it keeps up zero unemployment and zero inflation in France.

Given a common demand shock in Europe, policy cooperation achieves zero unemployment and zero inflation in each of the member countries. Given a common supply shock in Europe, policy cooperation is ineffective. There is no change in money supply and government purchases. Correspondingly, there is no change in unemployment and inflation. Given a common mixed shock in Europe, policy cooperation lowers inflation in Germany and France. On the other hand, it raises unemployment there. Given another type of a common mixed shock in Europe, policy cooperation lowers unemployment in Germany and France. On the other hand, it raises inflation there.

10) Comparing policy cooperation with policy interaction. Policy interaction, as a rule, causes uniform oscillations in unemployment and inflation. And what is more, it causes an explosion of government purchases and an implosion of money supply. Policy cooperation, as a rule, reduces the loss caused by unemployment and inflation. There is a one-time change in unemployment and inflation. Correspondingly, there is a one-time change in money supply and government purchases. Judging from this point of view, policy cooperation seems to be superior to policy interaction.

Appendix
Nonexistence of a Nash Equilibrium

The appendix deals with a closed economy. An increase in money supply lowers unemployment. On the other hand, it raises inflation. Correspondingly, an increase in government purchases lowers unemployment. On the other hand, it raises inflation. The target of the central bank is zero inflation. By contrast, the target of the government is zero unemployment.

The model of unemployment and inflation can be represented by a system of two equations:

$$u = A - \alpha M - \beta G \tag{1}$$

$$\pi = B + \alpha\varepsilon M + \beta\varepsilon G \tag{2}$$

Of course this is a reduced form. Here u denotes the rate of unemployment, π is the rate of inflation, M is money supply, G is government purchases, α is the monetary policy multiplier with respect to unemployment, $\alpha\varepsilon$ is the monetary policy multiplier with respect to inflation, β is the fiscal policy multiplier with respect to unemployment, $\beta\varepsilon$ is the fiscal policy multiplier with respect to inflation, A is some other factors bearing on the rate of unemployment, and B is some other factors bearing on the rate of inflation. The endogenous variables are the rate of unemployment and the rate of inflation.

According to equation (1), the rate of unemployment is a positive function of A, a negative function of money supply, and a negative function of government purchases. According to equation (2), the rate of inflation is a positive function of B, a positive function of money supply, and a positive function of government purchases. A unit increase in A raises the rate of unemployment by 1 percentage point. A unit increase in B raises the rate of inflation by 1 percentage point. A unit increase in money supply lowers the rate of unemployment by α percentage points. On the other hand, it raises the rate of inflation by $\alpha\varepsilon$ percentage points. A unit increase in government purchases lowers the rate of unemployment by β

M. Carlberg, *Dynamic Policy Interactions in a Monetary Union*,
DOI 10.1007/978-3-642-18228-0, © Springer-Verlag Berlin Heidelberg 2011

percentage points. On the other hand, it raises the rate of inflation by $\beta\varepsilon$ percentage points.

The target of the central bank is zero inflation. The instrument of the central bank is money supply. By equation (2), the reaction function of the central bank is:

$$\alpha\varepsilon M = - B - \beta\varepsilon G \tag{3}$$

Suppose the government raises its purchases. Then, as a response, the central bank lowers money supply.

The target of the government is zero unemployment. The instrument of the government is government purchases. By equation (1), the reaction function of the government is:

$$\beta G = A - \alpha M \tag{4}$$

Suppose the central bank lowers money supply. Then, as a response, the government raises its purchases.

The Nash equilibrium is determined by the reaction functions of the central bank and the government. From the reaction function of the central bank follows:

$$\frac{dM}{dG} = -\frac{\beta}{\alpha} \tag{5}$$

And from the reaction function of the government follows:

$$\frac{dG}{dM} = -\frac{\alpha}{\beta} \tag{6}$$

That is to say, the reaction curves do not intersect. As a result, there is no Nash equilibrium.

Conclusion

1. First the Central Bank Decides, then the Governments Decide

1.1. Target System A

1) The static model. The monetary union consists of two countries, say Germany and France. The member countries are the same size and have the same behavioural functions. This section is based on target system A. The targets of the European central bank are zero inflation in Germany and France respectively. The target of the German government is zero unemployment in Germany. And the target of the French government is zero unemployment in France.

An increase in European money supply lowers unemployment in Germany and France. On the other hand, it raises inflation there. An increase in German government purchases lowers unemployment in Germany. On the other hand, it raises inflation there. Correspondingly, an increase in French government purchases lowers unemployment in France. On the other hand, it raises inflation there. Fiscal policy in one of the member countries has no effect on unemployment or inflation in the other country.

The targets of the European central bank are zero inflation in Germany and France. The instrument of the European central bank is European money supply. There are two targets but only one instrument, so what is needed is a loss function. We assume that the European central bank has a quadratic loss function. The amount of loss depends on inflation in Germany and France. The European central bank sets European money supply so as to minimize its loss. The first-order condition for a minimum loss gives the reaction function of the European central bank. Suppose the German government raises its purchases of German goods. Then, as a response, the European central bank lowers its money supply.

The target of the German government is zero unemployment in Germany. The instrument of the German government is its purchases of German goods. From this follows the reaction function of the German government. Suppose the European central bank lowers its money supply. Then, as a response, the German government raises its purchases of German goods. Correspondingly, the target of the French government is zero unemployment in France. The instrument of the French government is its purchases of French goods. From this follows the reaction function of the French government. Suppose the European central bank lowers its money supply. Then, as a response, the French government raises its purchases of French goods.

The Nash equilibrium is determined by the reaction functions of the European central bank, the German government, and the French government. As a result there is no Nash equilibrium.

2) The dynamic model. We assume that the central bank and the governments decide sequentially. First the central bank decides, then the governments decide. Step 1 refers to a specific shock. Step 2 refers to the time lag. Step 3 refers to monetary policy in Europe. Step 4 refers to the time lag. Step 5 refers to fiscal policies in Germany and France. Step 6 refers to the time lag. Step 7 refers to monetary policy in Europe. Step 8 refers to the time lag. Step 9 refers to fiscal policies in Germany and France. Step 10 refers to the time lag. And so on.

Now have a closer look at the process of sequential policy decisions. Step 1 refers to a specific shock. This could be a demand shock, a supply shock or a mixed shock, in Germany or France. Step 2 refers to the time lag. This includes both the inside lag and the outside lag. Step 3 refers to monetary policy in Europe. The European central bank sets European money supply so as to achieve zero inflation in Europe. Step 4 refers to the time lag. Step 5 refers to fiscal policies in Germany and France. The German government sets its purchases of German goods so as to achieve zero unemployment in Germany. And the French government sets its purchases of French goods so as to achieve zero unemployment in France. Step 6 refers to the time lag.

Step 7 refers to monetary policy in Europe. The European central bank sets European money supply so as to achieve zero inflation in Europe. Step 8 refers to the time lag. Step 9 refers to fiscal policies in Germany and France. The German government sets its purchases of German goods so as to achieve zero unemployment in Germany. And the French government sets its purchases of French goods so as to achieve zero unemployment in France. Step 10 refers to the time lag. And so on.

3) Some specific shocks. Given a demand shock in Germany, sequential policy decisions produce zero unemployment and zero inflation in each of the member countries. There is an increase in European money supply, an increase in German government purchases, a reduction in French government purchases, and no change in European government purchases as a whole. The initial loss of each policy maker is zero. The demand shock in Germany causes a loss to the European central bank of 4 units, a loss to the German government of equally 4 units, and a loss to the French government of zero units. Then sequential policy decisions reduce the loss of the European central bank from 4 to zero units. Correspondingly, they reduce the loss of the German government from 4 to zero units. And they keep the loss of the French government at zero units.

Given a supply shock in Germany, sequential policy decisions cause uniform oscillations in unemployment and inflation. What is more, there is an explosion of government purchases and an implosion of money supply. And much the same applies to a mixed shock in Germany.

1.2. Target System B

1) The static model. This section is based on target system B. The targets of the European central bank are zero inflation and zero unemployment in each of the member countries. The target of the German government is zero unemployment in Germany. And the target of the French government is zero unemployment in France. An increase in European money supply lowers unemployment in Germany and France. On the other hand, it raises inflation there. An increase in German government purchases lowers unemployment in

Germany. On the other hand, it raises inflation there. Correspondingly, an increase in French government purchases lowers unemployment in France. On the other hand, it raises inflation there.

The targets of the European central bank are zero inflation and zero unemployment in each of the member countries. The instrument of the European central bank is European money supply. There are four targets but only one instrument, so what is needed is a loss function. We assume that the European central bank has a quadratic loss function. The amount of loss depends on inflation and unemployment in each of the member countries. The European central bank sets European money supply so as to minimize its loss. The first-order condition for a minimum loss gives the reaction function of the European central bank. Suppose the German government raises its purchases of German goods. Then, as a response, the European central bank lowers its money supply.

The target of the German government is zero unemployment in Germany. The instrument of the German government is its purchases of German goods. From this follows the reaction function of the German government. Suppose the European central bank lowers its money supply. Then, as a response, the German government raises its purchases of German goods. Correspondingly, the target of the French government is zero unemployment in France. The instrument of the French government is its purchases of French goods. From this follows the reaction function of the French government. Suppose the European central bank lowers its money supply. Then, as a response, the French government raises its purchases of French goods.

The Nash equilibrium is determined by the reaction functions of the European central bank, the German government, and the French government. As a result there is no Nash equilibrium.

2) The dynamic model. We assume that the central bank and the governments decide sequentially. First the central bank decides, then the governments decide. Step 1 refers to a specific shock. Step 2 refers to the time lag. Step 3 refers to monetary policy in Europe. Step 4 refers to the time lag. Step 5 refers to fiscal policies in Germany and France. Step 6 refers to the time lag. Step 7 refers to monetary policy in Europe. Step 8 refers to the time lag. Step 9

refers to fiscal policies in Germany and France. Step 10 refers to the time lag. And so on.

Now take a closer look at the process of sequential policy decisions. Step 1 refers to a specific shock. Step 2 refers to the time lag. Step 3 refers to monetary policy in Europe. The European central bank sets European money supply so as to reduce its own loss. Step 4 refers to the time lag. Step 5 refers to fiscal policies in Germany and France. The German government sets its purchases of German goods so as to achieve zero unemployment in Germany. And the French government sets its purchases of French goods so as to achieve zero unemployment in France. Step 6 refers to the time lag.

Step 7 refers to monetary policy in Europe. The European central bank sets European money supply so as to reduce its own loss. Step 8 refers to the time lag. Step 9 refers to fiscal policies in Germany and France. The German government sets its purchases of German goods so as to achieve zero unemployment in Germany. And the French government sets its purchases of French goods so as to achieve zero unemployment in France. Step 10 refers to the time lag. And so on.

3) Some specific shocks. Given a demand shock in Germany, sequential policy decisions produce zero unemployment and zero inflation in each of the member countries. There is an increase in European money supply, an increase in German government purchases, a reduction in French government purchases, and no change in European government purchases as a whole. The initial loss of each policy maker is zero. The demand shock in Germany causes a loss to the European central bank of 8 units, a loss to the German government of 4 units, and a loss to the French government of zero units. Then sequential policy decisions reduce the loss of the European central bank from 8 to zero units. Correspondingly, they reduce the loss of the German government from 4 to zero units. And they keep the loss of the French government at zero units.

Given a supply shock in Germany, sequential policy decisions cause uniform oscillations in unemployment and inflation. What is more, there is an explosion of government purchases and an implosion of money supply. And much the same applies to a mixed shock in Germany.

1.3. Target System C

1) The static model. This section is based on target system C. The targets of the European central bank are zero inflation and zero unemployment in each of the member countries. The targets of the German government are zero unemployment and zero inflation in Germany. And the targets of the French government are zero unemployment and zero inflation in France. An increase in European money supply lowers unemployment in Germany and France. On the other hand, it raises inflation there. An increase in German government purchases lowers unemployment in Germany. On the other hand, it raises inflation there. Correspondingly, an increase in French government purchases lowers unemployment in France. On the other hand, it raises inflation there.

The targets of the European central bank are zero inflation and zero unemployment in each of the member countries. The instrument of the European central bank is European money supply. There are four targets but only one instrument, so what is needed is a loss function. We assume that the European central bank has a quadratic loss function. The amount of loss depends on inflation and unemployment in each of the member countries. The European central bank sets European money supply so as to minimize its own loss. The first-order condition for a minimum loss gives the reaction function of the European central bank. Suppose the German government raises its purchases of German goods. Then, as a response, the European central bank lowers its money supply.

The targets of the German government are zero unemployment and zero inflation in Germany. The instrument of the German government is its purchases of German goods. There are two targets but only one instrument, so what is needed is a loss function. We assume that the German government has a quadratic loss function. The amount of loss depends on unemployment and inflation in Germany. The German government sets its purchases of German goods so as to minimize its own loss. The first-order condition for a minimum loss gives the reaction function of the German government. Suppose the European central bank lowers its money supply. Then, as a response, the German government raises its purchases of German goods.

Correspondingly, the targets of the French government are zero unemployment and zero inflation in France. The instrument of the French government is its purchases of French goods. There are two targets but only one instrument, so what is needed is a loss function. We assume that the French government has a quadratic loss function. The amount of loss depends on unemployment and inflation in France. The French government sets its purchases of French goods so as to minimize its own loss. The first-order condition for a minimum loss gives the reaction function of the French government. Suppose the European central bank lowers its money supply. Then, as a response, the French government raises its purchases of French goods.

The Nash equilibrium is determined by the reaction functions of the European central bank, the German government, and the French government. As a result there are multiple Nash equilibria.

2) The dynamic model. We assume that the central bank and the governments decide sequentially. First the central bank decides, then the governments decide. Step 1 refers to a specific shock. Step 2 refers to the time lag. Step 3 refers to monetary policy in Europe. Step 4 refers to the time lag. Step 5 refers to fiscal policies in Germany and France. Step 6 refers to the time lag. Step 7 refers to monetary policy in Europe. Step 8 refers to the time lag. Step 9 refers to fiscal policies in Germany and France. Step 10 refers to the time lag. And so on.

Now have a closer look at the process of sequential policy decisions. Step 1 refers to a specific shock. Step 2 refers to the time lag. Step 3 refers to monetary policy in Europe. The European central bank sets European money supply so as to reduce its own loss. Step 4 refers to the time lag. Step 5 refers to fiscal policies in Germany and France. The German government sets its purchases of German goods so as to reduce its own loss. And the French government sets its purchases of French goods so as to reduce its own loss. Step 6 refers to the time lag.

Step 7 refers to monetary policy in Europe. The European central bank sets European money supply so as to reduce its own loss. Step 8 refers to the time lag. Step 9 refers to fiscal policies in Germany and France. The German government sets its purchases of German goods so as to reduce its own loss. And the French government sets its purchases of French goods so as to reduce its own loss. Step 10 refers to the time lag. And so on.

3) Some specific shocks. Given a demand shock in Germany, sequential policy decisions produce zero unemployment and zero inflation in each of the member countries. There is an increase in European money supply, an increase in German government purchases, a reduction in French government purchases, and no change in European government purchases as a whole. The initial loss of each policy maker is zero. The demand shock in Germany causes a loss to the European central bank of 8 units, a loss to the German government of equally 8 units, and a loss to the French government of zero units. Then sequential policy decisions reduce the loss of the European central bank from 8 to zero units. Correspondingly, they reduce the loss of the German government from 8 to zero units. And they keep the loss of the French government at zero units.

Given a supply shock in Germany, sequential policy decisions are ineffective. There is no change in money supply and government purchases. Correspondingly, there is no change in unemployment and inflation. The initial loss of each policy maker is zero. The supply shock in Germany causes a loss to the European central bank of 8 units, a loss to the German government of equally 8 units, and a loss to the French government of zero units. Then sequential policy decisions keep the loss of the European central bank at 8 units. Similarly, they keep the loss of the German government at 8 units. And they keep the loss of the French government at zero units.

Given a mixed shock in Germany, sequential policy decisions lower German inflation. On the other hand, they raise German unemployment. And what is more, sequential policy decisions keep up zero unemployment and zero inflation in France. There is a reduction in European money supply, a reduction in German government purchases, an increase in French government purchases, and no change in European government purchases as a whole. The initial loss of each policy maker is zero. The mixed shock in Germany causes a loss to the European central bank of 16 units, a loss to the German government of equally 16 units, and a loss to the French government of zero units. Then sequential policy decisions reduce the loss of the European central bank from 16 to 8 units. Similarly, they reduce the loss of the German government from 16 to 8 units. And they keep the loss of the French government at zero units.

2. First the Governments Decide, then the Central Bank Decides

2.1. Target System A

1) The static model. The monetary union consists of two countries, say Germany and France. The member countries are the same size and have the same behavioural functions. This section is based on target system A. The targets of the European central bank are zero inflation in Germany and France respectively. The target of the German government is zero unemployment in Germany. And the target of the French government is zero unemployment in France.

An increase in European money supply lowers unemployment in Germany and France. On the other hand, it raises inflation there. An increase in German government purchases lowers unemployment in Germany. On the other hand, it raises inflation there. Correspondingly, an increase in French government purchases lowers unemployment in France. On the other hand, it raises inflation there. Fiscal policy in one of the member countries has no effect on unemployment or inflation in the other country.

The targets of the European central bank are zero inflation in Germany and France. The instrument of the European central bank is European money supply. There are two targets but only one instrument, so what is needed is a loss function. We assume that the European central bank has a quadratic loss function. The amount of loss depends on inflation in Germany and France. The European central bank sets European money supply so as to minimize its loss. The first-order condition for a minimum loss gives the reaction function of the European central bank. Suppose the German government raises its purchases of German goods. Then, as a response, the European central bank lowers its money supply.

The target of the German government is zero unemployment in Germany. The instrument of the German government is its purchases of German goods. From this follows the reaction function of the German government. Suppose the

European central bank lowers its money supply. Then, as a response, the German government raises its purchases of German goods. Correspondingly, the target of the French government is zero unemployment in France. The instrument of the French government is its purchases of French goods. From this follows the reaction function of the French government. Suppose the European central bank lowers its money supply. Then, as a response, the French government raises its purchases of French goods.

The Nash equilibrium is determined by the reaction functions of the European central bank, the German government, and the French government. As a result there is no Nash equilibrium.

2) The dynamic model. We assume that the governments and the central bank decide sequentially. First the governments decide, then the central bank decides. Step 1 refers to a specific shock. Step 2 refers to the time lag. Step 3 refers to fiscal policies in Germany and France. Step 4 refers to the time lag. Step 5 refers to monetary policy in Europe. Step 6 refers to the time lag. Step 7 refers to fiscal policies in Germany and France. Step 8 refers to the time lag. Step 9 refers to monetary policy in Europe. Step 10 refers to the time lag. And so on.

Now have a closer look at the process of inverse sequential policy decisions. Step 1 refers to a specific shock. Step 2 refers to the time lag. Step 3 refers to fiscal policies in Germany and France. The German government sets its purchases of German goods so as to achieve zero unemployment in Germany. And the French government sets its purchases of French goods so as to achieve zero unemployment in France. Step 4 refers to the time lag. Step 5 refers to monetary policy in Europe. The European central bank sets European money supply so as to achieve zero inflation in Europe. Step 6 refers to the time lag.

Step 7 refers to fiscal policies in Germany and France. The German government sets its purchases of German goods so as to achieve zero unemployment in Germany. And the French government sets its purchases of French goods so as to achieve zero unemployment in France. Step 8 refers to the time lag. Step 9 refers to monetary policy in Europe. The European central bank sets European money supply so as to achieve zero inflation in Europe. Step 10 refers to the time lag. And so on.

3) Some specific shocks. Given a demand shock in Germany, sequential policy decisions produce zero unemployment and zero inflation in each of the member countries. There is an increase in German government purchases, no change in French government purchases, and no change in European money supply. The initial loss of each policy maker is zero. The demand shock in Germany causes a loss to the European central bank of 4 units, a loss to the German government of equally 4 units, and a loss to the French government of zero units. Then sequential policy decisions reduce the loss of the European central bank from 4 to zero units. Correspondingly, they reduce the loss of the German government from 4 to zero units. And they keep the loss of the French government at zero units.

Given a supply shock in Germany, sequential policy decisions cause uniform oscillations in unemployment and inflation. What is more, there is an explosion of government purchases and an implosion of money supply. And much the same applies to a mixed shock in Germany.

2.2. Target System B

1) The static model. This section is based on target system B. The targets of the European central bank are zero inflation and zero unemployment in each of the member countries. The target of the German government is zero unemployment in Germany. And the target of the French government is zero unemployment in France. An increase in European money supply lowers unemployment in Germany and France. On the other hand, it raises inflation there. An increase in German government purchases lowers unemployment in Germany. On the other hand, it raises inflation there. Correspondingly, an increase in French government purchases lowers unemployment in France. On the other hand, it raises inflation there.

The targets of the European central bank are zero inflation and zero unemployment in each of the member countries. The instrument of the European central bank is European money supply. There are four targets but only one instrument, so what is needed is a loss function. We assume that the European central bank has a quadratic loss function. The amount of loss depends on inflation and unemployment in each of the member countries. The European central bank sets European money supply so as to minimize its loss. The first-order condition for a minimum loss gives the reaction function of the European central bank. Suppose the German government raises its purchases of German goods. Then, as a response, the European central bank lowers its money supply.

The target of the German government is zero unemployment in Germany. The instrument of the German government is its purchases of German goods. From this follows the reaction function of the German government. Suppose the European central bank lowers its money supply. Then, as a response, the German government raises its purchases of German goods. Correspondingly, the target of the French government is zero unemployment in France. The instrument of the French government is its purchases of French goods. From this follows the reaction function of the French government. Suppose the European central bank lowers its money supply. Then, as a response, the French government raises its purchases of French goods.

The Nash equilibrium is determined by the reaction functions of the European central bank, the German government, and the French government. As a result there is no Nash equilibrium.

2) The dynamic model. We assume that the governments and the central bank decide sequentially. First the governments decide, then the central bank decides. Step 1 refers to a specific shock. Step 2 refers to the time lag. Step 3 refers to fiscal policies in Germany and France. Step 4 refers to the time lag. Step 5 refers to monetary policy in Europe. Step 6 refers to the time lag. Step 7 refers to fiscal policies in Germany and France. Step 8 refers to the time lag. Step 9 refers to monetary policy in Europe. Step 10 refers to the time lag. And so on.

Now take a closer look at the process of inverse sequential policy decisions. Step 1 refers to a specific shock. Step 2 refers to the time lag. Step 3 refers to fiscal policies in Germany and France. The German government sets its purchases of German goods so as to achieve zero unemployment in Germany. And the French government sets its purchases of French goods so as to achieve zero unemployment in France. Step 4 refers to the time lag. Step 5 refers to monetary policy in Europe. The European central bank sets European money supply so as to reduce its own loss. Step 6 refers to the time lag.

Step 7 refers to fiscal policies in Germany and France. The German government sets its purchases of German goods so as to achieve zero unemployment in Germany. And the French government sets its purchases of French goods so as to achieve zero unemployment in France. Step 8 refers to the time lag. Step 9 refers to monetary policy in Europe. The European central bank sets European money supply so as to reduce its own loss. Step 10 refers to the time lag. And so on.

3) Some specific shocks. Given a demand shock in Germany, sequential policy decisions produce zero unemployment and zero inflation in each of the member countries. There is an increase in German government purchases, no change in French government purchases, and no change in European money supply. The initial loss of each policy maker is zero. The demand shock in Germany causes a loss to the European central bank of 8 units, a loss to the German government of 4 units, and a loss to the French government of zero units. Then sequential policy decisions reduce the loss of the European central bank from 8 to zero units. Correspondingly, they reduce the loss of the German government from 4 to zero units. And they keep the loss of the French government at zero units.

Given a supply shock in Germany, sequential policy decisions cause uniform oscillations in unemployment and inflation. What is more, there is an explosion of government purchases and an implosion of money supply. And much the same applies to a mixed shock in Germany.

2.3. Target System C

1) The static model. This section is based on target system C. The targets of the European central bank are zero inflation and zero unemployment in each of the member countries. The targets of the German government are zero unemployment and zero inflation in Germany. And the targets of the French government are zero unemployment and zero inflation in France. An increase in European money supply lowers unemployment in Germany and France. On the other hand, it raises inflation there. An increase in German government purchases lowers unemployment in Germany. On the other hand, it raises inflation there. Correspondingly, an increase in French government purchases lowers unemployment in France. On the other hand, it raises inflation there.

The targets of the European central bank are zero inflation and zero unemployment in each of the member countries. The instrument of the European central bank is European money supply. There are four targets but only one instrument, so what is needed is a loss function. We assume that the European central bank has a quadratic loss function. The amount of loss depends on inflation and unemployment in each of the member countries. The European central bank sets European money supply so as to minimize its own loss. The first-order condition for a minimum loss gives the reaction function of the European central bank. Suppose the German government raises its purchases of German goods. Then, as a response, the European central bank lowers its money supply.

The targets of the German government are zero unemployment and zero inflation in Germany. The instrument of the German government is its purchases of German goods. There are two targets but only one instrument, so what is needed is a loss function. We assume that the German government has a quadratic loss function. The amount of loss depends on unemployment and inflation in Germany. The German government sets its purchases of German goods so as to minimize its own loss. The first-order condition for a minimum loss gives the reaction function of the German government. Suppose the European central bank lowers its money supply. Then, as a response, the German government raises its purchases of German goods.

Correspondingly, the targets of the French government are zero unemployment and zero inflation in France. The instrument of the French government is its purchases of French goods. There are two targets but only one instrument, so what is needed is a loss function. We assume that the French government has a quadratic loss function. The amount of loss depends on unemployment and inflation in France. The French government sets its purchases of French goods so as to minimize its own loss. The first-order condition for a minimum loss gives the reaction function of the French government. Suppose the European central bank lowers its money supply. Then, as a response, the French government raises its purchases of French goods.

The Nash equilibrium is determined by the reaction functions of the European central bank, the German government, and the French government. As a result there are multiple Nash equilibria.

2) The dynamic model. We assume that the governments and the central bank decide sequentially. First the governments decide, then the central bank decides. Step 1 refers to a specific shock. Step 2 refers to the time lag. Step 3 refers to fiscal policies in Germany and France. Step 4 refers to the time lag. Step 5 refers to monetary policy in Europe. Step 6 refers to the time lag. Step 7 refers to fiscal policies in Germany and France. Step 8 refers to the time lag. Step 9 refers to monetary policy in Europe. Step 10 refers to the time lag. And so on.

Now have a closer look at the process of inverse sequential policy decisions. Step 1 refers to a specific shock. Step 2 refers to the time lag. Step 3 refers to fiscal policies in Germany and France. The German government sets its purchases of German goods so as to reduce its own loss. And the French government sets its purchases of French goods so as to reduce its own loss. Step 4 refers to the time lag. Step 5 refers to monetary policy in Europe. The European central bank sets European money supply so as to reduce its own loss. Step 6 refers to the time lag.

Step 7 refers to fiscal policies in Germany and France. The German government sets its purchases of German goods so as to reduce its own loss. And the French government sets its purchases of French goods so as to reduce its own loss. Step 8 refers to the time lag. Step 9 refers to monetary policy in Europe. The

European central bank sets European money supply so as to reduce its own loss. Step 10 refers to the time lag. And so on.

3) Some specific shocks. Given a demand shock in Germany, sequential policy decisions produce zero unemployment and zero inflation in each of the member countries. There is an increase in German government purchases, no change in French government purchases, and no change in European money supply. The initial loss of each policy maker is zero. The demand shock in Germany causes a loss to the European central bank of 8 units, a loss to the German government of equally 8 units, and a loss to the French government of zero units. Then sequential policy decisions reduce the loss of the European central bank from 8 to zero units. Correspondingly, they reduce the loss of the German government from 8 to zero units. And they keep the loss of the French government at zero units.

Given a supply shock in Germany, sequential policy decisions are ineffective. There is no change in money supply and government purchases. Correspondingly, there is no change in unemployment and inflation. The initial loss of each policy maker is zero. The supply shock in Germany causes a loss to the European central bank of 8 units, a loss to the German government of equally 8 units, and a loss to the French government of zero units. Then sequential policy decisions keep the loss of the European central bank at 8 units. Similarly, they keep the loss of the German government at 8 units. And they keep the loss of the French government at zero units.

Given a mixed shock in Germany, sequential policy decisions lower German inflation. On the other hand, they raise German unemployment. And what is more, sequential policy decisions keep up zero unemployment and zero inflation in France. There is a reduction in German government purchases, no change in French government purchases, and no change in European money supply. The initial loss of each policy maker is zero. The mixed shock in Germany causes a loss to the European central bank of 16 units, a loss to the German government of equally 16 units, and a loss to the French government of zero units. Then sequential policy decisions reduce the loss of the European central bank from 16 to 8 units. Similarly, they reduce the loss of the German government from 16 to 8 units. And they keep the loss of the French government at zero units.

3. Central Bank and Governments Decide Simultaneously and Independently: Cold-Turkey Policies

3.1. Target System A

1) The static model. The monetary union consists of two countries, say Germany and France. The member countries are the same size and have the same behavioural functions. This section is based on target system A. The targets of the European central bank are zero inflation in Germany and France respectively. The target of the German government is zero unemployment in Germany. And the target of the French government is zero unemployment in France.

An increase in European money supply lowers unemployment in Germany and France. On the other hand, it raises inflation there. An increase in German government purchases lowers unemployment in Germany. On the other hand, it raises inflation there. Correspondingly, an increase in French government purchases lowers unemployment in France. On the other hand, it raises inflation there. Fiscal policy in one of the member countries has no effect on unemployment or inflation in the other country.

The targets of the European central bank are zero inflation in Germany and France. The instrument of the European central bank is European money supply. There are two targets but only one instrument, so what is needed is a loss function. We assume that the European central bank has a quadratic loss function. The amount of loss depends on inflation in Germany and France. The European central bank sets European money supply so as to minimize its loss. The first-order condition for a minimum loss gives the reaction function of the European central bank. Suppose the German government raises its purchases of German goods. Then, as a response, the European central bank lowers its money supply.

The target of the German government is zero unemployment in Germany. The instrument of the German government is its purchases of German goods.

From this follows the reaction function of the German government. Suppose the European central bank lowers its money supply. Then, as a response, the German government raises its purchases of German goods. Correspondingly, the target of the French government is zero unemployment in France. The instrument of the French government is its purchases of French goods. From this follows the reaction function of the French government. Suppose the European central bank lowers its money supply. Then, as a response, the French government raises its purchases of French goods.

The Nash equilibrium is determined by the reaction functions of the European central bank, the German government, and the French government. As a result there is no Nash equilibrium.

2) The dynamic model. We assume that the central bank and the governments decide simultaneously and independently. Step 1 refers to a specific shock. Step 2 refers to the time lag. Step 3 refers to monetary and fiscal policies. Step 4 refers to the time lag. Step 5 refers to monetary and fiscal policies. Step 6 refers to the time lag. And so on.

Now have a closer look at the process of simultaneous and independent policy decisions. Step 1 refers to a specific shock. Step 2 refers to the time lag. In step 3, the central bank and the governments decide simultaneously and independently. The European central bank sets European money supply so as to achieve zero inflation in Europe. The German government sets its purchases of German goods so as to achieve zero unemployment in Germany. And the French government sets its purchases of French goods so as to achieve zero unemployment in France. Step 4 refers to the time lag.

In step 5, the central bank and the governments decide simultaneously and independently. The European central bank sets European money supply so as to achieve zero inflation in Europe. The German government sets its purchases of German goods so as to achieve zero unemployment in Germany. And the French government sets its purchases of French goods so as to achieve zero unemployment in France. Step 6 refers to the time lag. And so on.

3) Some specific shocks. Given a demand shock in Germany, simultaneous and independent policy decisions cause uniform oscillations in unemployment

and inflation. The economy oscillates between underemployment and overemployment. Accordingly, the economy oscillates between deflation and inflation. In addition, there are uniform oscillations in money supply and government purchases.

Given a supply shock in Germany, simultaneous and independent policy decisions lower German unemployment and raise German inflation. On the other hand, they raise French unemployment and lower French inflation. And what is more, there is an explosion of government purchases and an implosion of money supply.

Given a mixed shock in Germany, simultaneous and independent policy decisions cause uniform oscillations in unemployment and inflation. And what is more, there is an explosion of government purchases and an implosion of money supply.

3.2. Target System B

1) The static model. This section is based on target system B. The targets of the European central bank are zero inflation and zero unemployment in each of the member countries. The target of the German government is zero unemployment in Germany. And the target of the French government is zero unemployment in France. An increase in European money supply lowers unemployment in Germany and France. On the other hand, it raises inflation there. An increase in German government purchases lowers unemployment in Germany. On the other hand, it raises inflation there. Correspondingly, an increase in French government purchases lowers unemployment in France. On the other hand, it raises inflation there.

The targets of the European central bank are zero inflation and zero unemployment in each of the member countries. The instrument of the European central bank is European money supply. There are four targets but only one instrument, so what is needed is a loss function. We assume that the European central bank has a quadratic loss function. The amount of loss depends on inflation and unemployment in each of the member countries. The European central bank sets European money supply so as to minimize its loss. The first-order condition for a minimum loss gives the reaction function of the European central bank. Suppose the German government raises its purchases of German goods. Then, as a response, the European central bank lowers its money supply.

The target of the German government is zero unemployment in Germany. The instrument of the German government is its purchases of German goods. From this follows the reaction function of the German government. Suppose the European central bank lowers its money supply. Then, as a response, the German government raises its purchases of German goods. Correspondingly, the target of the French government is zero unemployment in France. The instrument of the French government is its purchases of French goods. From this follows the reaction function of the French government. Suppose the European central bank lowers its money supply. Then, as a response, the French government raises its purchases of French goods.

The Nash equilibrium is determined by the reaction functions of the European central bank, the German government, and the French government. As a result there is no Nash equilibrium.

2) The dynamic model. We assume that the central bank and the governments decide simultaneously and independently. Step 1 refers to a specific shock. Step 2 refers to the time lag. Step 3 refers to monetary and fiscal policies. Step 4 refers to the time lag. Step 5 refers to monetary and fiscal policies. Step 6 refers to the time lag. And so on.

Now take a closer look at the process of simultaneous and independent policy decisions. Step 1 refers to a specific shock. Step 2 refers to the time lag. In step 3, the central bank and the governments decide simultaneously and independently. The European central bank sets European money supply so as to reduce its own loss. The German government sets its purchases of German goods so as to achieve zero unemployment in Germany. And the French government sets its purchases of French goods so as to achieve zero unemployment in France. Step 4 refers to the time lag.

In step 5, the central bank and the governments decide simultaneously and independently. The European central bank sets European money supply so as to reduce its own loss. The German government sets its purchases of German goods so as to achieve zero unemployment in Germany. And the French government sets its purchases of French goods so as to achieve zero unemployment in France. Step 6 refers to the time lag. And so on.

3) Some specific shocks. Given a demand shock in Germany, simultaneous and independent policy decisions cause uniform oscillations in unemployment and inflation. The economy oscillates between underemployment and overemployment. Accordingly, the economy oscillates between deflation and inflation. In addition, there are uniform oscillations in money supply and government purchases.

Given a supply shock in Germany, simultaneous and independent policy decisions cause uniform oscillations in unemployment and inflation. What is more, there is an explosion of government purchases and an implosion of money supply. And much the same applies to a mixed shock in Germany.

3.3. Target System C

1) The static model. This section is based on target system C. The targets of the European central bank are zero inflation and zero unemployment in each of the member countries. The targets of the German government are zero unemployment and zero inflation in Germany. And the targets of the French government are zero unemployment and zero inflation in France. An increase in European money supply lowers unemployment in Germany and France. On the other hand, it raises inflation there. An increase in German government purchases lowers unemployment in Germany. On the other hand, it raises inflation there. Correspondingly, an increase in French government purchases lowers unemployment in France. On the other hand, it raises inflation there.

The targets of the European central bank are zero inflation and zero unemployment in each of the member countries. The instrument of the European central bank is European money supply. There are four targets but only one instrument, so what is needed is a loss function. We assume that the European central bank has a quadratic loss function. The amount of loss depends on inflation and unemployment in each of the member countries. The European central bank sets European money supply so as to minimize its own loss. The first-order condition for a minimum loss gives the reaction function of the European central bank. Suppose the German government raises its purchases of German goods. Then, as a response, the European central bank lowers its money supply.

The targets of the German government are zero unemployment and zero inflation in Germany. The instrument of the German government is its purchases of German goods. There are two targets but only one instrument, so what is needed is a loss function. We assume that the German government has a quadratic loss function. The amount of loss depends on unemployment and inflation in Germany. The German government sets its purchases of German goods so as to minimize its own loss. The first-order condition for a minimum loss gives the reaction function of the German government. Suppose the European central bank lowers its money supply. Then, as a response, the German government raises its purchases of German goods.

Correspondingly, the targets of the French government are zero unemployment and zero inflation in France. The instrument of the French government is its purchases of French goods. There are two targets but only one instrument, so what is needed is a loss function. We assume that the French government has a quadratic loss function. The amount of loss depends on unemployment and inflation in France. The French government sets its purchases of French goods so as to minimize its own loss. The first-order condition for a minimum loss gives the reaction function of the French government. Suppose the European central bank lowers its money supply. Then, as a response, the French government raises its purchases of French goods.

The Nash equilibrium is determined by the reaction functions of the European central bank, the German government, and the French government. As a result there are multiple Nash equilibria.

2) The dynamic model. We assume that the central bank and the governments decide simultaneously and independently. Step 1 refers to a specific shock. Step 2 refers to the time lag. Step 3 refers to monetary and fiscal policies. Step 4 refers to the time lag. Step 5 refers to monetary and fiscal policies. Step 6 refers to the time lag. And so on.

Now have a closer look at the process of simultaneous and independent policy decisions. Step 1 refers to a specific shock. Step 2 refers to the time lag. In step 3, the central bank and the governments decide simultaneously and independently. The European central bank sets European money supply so as to reduce its own loss. The German government sets its purchases of German goods so as to reduce its own loss. And the French government sets its purchases of French goods so as to reduce its own loss. Step 4 refers to the time lag.

In step 5, the central bank and the governments decide simultaneously and independently. The European central bank sets European money supply so as to reduce its own loss. The German government sets its purchases of German goods so as to reduce its own loss. And the French government sets its purchases of French goods so as to reduce its own loss. Step 6 refers to the time lag. And so on.

3) Some specific shocks. Given a demand shock in Germany, simultaneous and independent policy decisions cause uniform oscillations in unemployment and inflation. The economy oscillates between underemployment and overemployment. Accordingly, the economy oscillates between deflation and inflation. And what is more, there are uniform oscillations in money supply and government purchases.

Given a supply shock in Germany, simultaneous and independent policy decisions are ineffective. There is no change in European money supply, no change in German government purchases, and no change in French government purchases. Correspondingly, there is no change in unemployment and inflation.

Given a mixed shock in Germany, simultaneous and independent policy decisions cause uniform oscillations in unemployment and inflation. And what is more, there are uniform oscillations in money supply and government purchases.

4. Central Bank and Governments Decide Simultaneously and Independently: Gradualist Policies

1) The static model. The monetary union consists of two countries, say Germany and France. The member countries are the same size and have the same behavioural functions. This section is based on target system A. The targets of the European central bank are zero inflation in Germany and France respectively. The target of the German government is zero unemployment in Germany. And the target of the French government is zero unemployment in France.

An increase in European money supply lowers unemployment in Germany and France. On the other hand, it raises inflation there. An increase in German government purchases lowers unemployment in Germany. On the other hand, it raises inflation there. Correspondingly, an increase in French government purchases lowers unemployment in France. On the other hand, it raises inflation there. Fiscal policy in one of the member countries has no effect on unemployment or inflation in the other country.

The targets of the European central bank are zero inflation in Germany and France. The instrument of the European central bank is European money supply. There are two targets but only one instrument, so what is needed is a loss function. We assume that the European central bank has a quadratic loss function. The amount of loss depends on inflation in Germany and France. The European central bank sets European money supply so as to minimize its loss. The first-order condition for a minimum loss gives the reaction function of the European central bank. Suppose the German government raises its purchases of

German goods. Then, as a response, the European central bank lowers its money supply.

The target of the German government is zero unemployment in Germany. The instrument of the German government is its purchases of German goods. From this follows the reaction function of the German government. Suppose the European central bank lowers its money supply. Then, as a response, the German government raises its purchases of German goods. Correspondingly, the target of the French government is zero unemployment in France. The instrument of the French government is its purchases of French goods. From this follows the reaction function of the French government. Suppose the European central bank lowers its money supply. Then, as a response, the French government raises its purchases of French goods.

The Nash equilibrium is determined by the reaction functions of the European central bank, the German government, and the French government. As a result there is no Nash equilibrium.

2) The dynamic model. The target of the European central bank is to cut European inflation by half. The target of the German government is to cut German unemployment by half. And the target of the French government is to cut French unemployment by half. We assume that the central bank and the governments decide simultaneously and independently. Step 1 refers to a specific shock. Step 2 refers to the time lag. Step 3 refers to monetary and fiscal policies. Step 4 refers to the time lag. Step 5 refers to monetary and fiscal policies. Step 6 refers to the time lag. And so on.

Now have a closer look at the process of simultaneous and independent policy decisions. Step 1 refers to a specific shock. Step 2 refers to the time lag. In step 3, the central bank and the governments decide simultaneously and independently. The European central bank sets European money supply so as to cut European inflation by half. The German government sets its purchases of German goods so as to cut German unemployment by half. And the French government sets its purchases of French goods so as to cut French unemployment by half. Step 4 refers to the time lag.

In step 5, the central bank and the governments decide simultaneously and independently. The European central bank sets European money supply so as to cut European inflation by half. The German government sets its purchases of German goods so as to cut German unemployment by half. And the French government sets its purchases of French goods so as to cut French unemployment by half. Step 6 refers to the time lag. And so on.

3) Some specific shocks. Given a demand shock in Germany, simultaneous and independent policy decisions produce zero unemployment and zero inflation in each of the member countries. There is an increase in European money supply, an increase in German government purchases, a reduction in French government purchases, and an increase in European government purchases. Given a supply shock in Germany, simultaneous and independent policy decisions lower German unemployment and raise German inflation. Conversely, they raise French unemployment and lower French inflation. And what is more, there is an explosion of government purchases and an implosion of money supply.

5. Central Bank and Governments Cooperate

1) The model. The monetary union consists of two countries, say Germany and France. The member countries are the same size and have the same behavioural functions. An increase in European money supply lowers unemployment in Germany and France. On the other hand, it raises inflation there. An increase in German government purchases lowers unemployment in Germany. On the other hand, it raises inflation there. Correspondingly, an increase in French government purchases lowers unemployment in France. On the other hand, it raises inflation there.

The policy makers are the European central bank, the German government, and the French government. The targets of policy cooperation are zero inflation and zero unemployment in each of the member countries. The instruments of policy cooperation are European money supply, German government purchases, and French government purchases. There are four targets but only three instruments, so what is needed is a loss function. We assume that the policy makers agree on a common loss function. The amount of loss depends on inflation and unemployment in each of the member countries. The policy makers set European money supply, German government purchases, and French government purchases so as to minimize the common loss.

The cooperative equilibrium is determined by the first-order conditions for a minimum loss. It yields the optimum combinations of European money supply, German government purchases, and French government purchases.

2) Some specific shocks. Given a demand shock in Germany, policy cooperation achieves zero unemployment and zero inflation in each of the member countries. A first solution is an increase in European money supply of 1 unit, an increase in German government purchases of 1 unit, and a reduction in French government purchases of equally 1 unit. A second solution is an increase in European money supply of 2 units, no change in German government purchases, and a reduction in French government purchases of 2 units. A third solution is no change in European money supply, an increase in German government purchases of 2 units, and no change in French government purchases. And so on. The initial loss is zero. The demand shock in Germany causes a loss of 8 units. Then policy cooperation brings the loss down to zero again.

Given a supply shock in Germany, policy cooperation is ineffective. A first solution is no change in European money supply, no change in German government purchases, and no change in French government purchases. A second solution is an increase in European money supply of 1 unit, a reduction in German government purchases of 1 unit, and a reduction in French government purchases of equally 1 unit. A third solution is a reduction in European money supply of 1 unit, an increase in German government purchases of 1 unit, and an increase in French government purchases of equally 1 unit. And so on. The initial loss is zero. The supply shock in Germany causes a loss of 8 units. However, policy cooperation cannot reduce the loss.

Given a mixed shock in Germany, policy cooperation lowers German inflation. On the other hand, it raises German unemployment. And what is more, it keeps up zero unemployment and zero inflation in France. A first solution is a reduction in European money supply of 1 unit, a reduction in German government purchases of 1 unit, and an increase in French government purchases of equally 1 unit. A second solution is a reduction in European money supply of 2 units, no change in German government purchases, and an increase in French government purchases of 2 units. A third solution is no change in European money supply, a reduction in German government purchases of 2 units, and no change in French government purchases. And so on. The initial loss is zero. The mixed shock in Germany causes a loss of 16 units. Then policy cooperation brings the loss down to 8 units.

3) Comparing policy cooperation with policy interaction. Policy interaction, as a rule, causes uniform oscillations in unemployment and inflation. And what is more, it causes an explosion of government purchases and an implosion of money supply. Policy cooperation, as a rule, reduces the loss caused by unemployment and inflation. There is a one-time change in unemployment and inflation. Correspondingly, there is a one-time change in money supply and government purchases. Judging from this point of view, policy cooperation seems to be superior to policy interaction.

Result

1. Sequential Policy Decisions

1) The static model. The monetary union consists of two countries, say Germany and France. The member countries are the same size and have the same behavioural functions. An increase in European money supply lowers unemployment in Germany and France. On the other hand, it raises inflation there. An increase in German government purchases lowers unemployment in Germany. On the other hand, it raises inflation there. Correspondingly, an increase in French government purchases lowers unemployment in France. On the other hand, it raises inflation there.

The targets of the European central bank are zero inflation in Germany and France. The instrument of the European central bank is European money supply. There are two targets but only one instrument, so what is needed is a loss function. We assume that the European central bank has a quadratic loss function. The amount of loss depends on inflation in Germany and France. The European central bank sets European money supply so as to minimize its loss. The first-order condition for a minimum loss gives the reaction function of the European central bank. Suppose the German government raises its purchases of German goods. Then, as a response, the European central bank lowers its money supply.

The target of the German government is zero unemployment in Germany. The instrument of the German government is its purchases of German goods. From this follows the reaction function of the German government. Suppose the European central bank lowers its money supply. Then, as a response, the German government raises its purchases of German goods. Correspondingly, the target of the French government is zero unemployment in France. The instrument of the French government is its purchases of French goods. From this follows the reaction function of the French government. Suppose the European central bank lowers its money supply. Then, as a response, the French government raises its purchases of French goods.

The Nash equilibrium is determined by the reaction functions of the European central bank, the German government, and the French government. As a result there is no Nash equilibrium.

2) The dynamic model. We assume that the central bank and the governments decide sequentially. First the central bank decides, then the governments decide. Step 1 refers to a specific shock. Step 2 refers to the time lag. Step 3 refers to monetary policy in Europe. Step 4 refers to the time lag. Step 5 refers to fiscal policies in Germany and France. Step 6 refers to the time lag. Step 7 refers to monetary policy in Europe. Step 8 refers to the time lag. Step 9 refers to fiscal policies in Germany and France. Step 10 refers to the time lag. And so on.

Now have a closer look at the process of sequential policy decisions. Step 1 refers to a specific shock. This could be a demand shock, a supply shock or a mixed shock, in Germany or France. Step 2 refers to the time lag. This includes both the inside lag and the outside lag. Step 3 refers to monetary policy in Europe. The European central bank sets European money supply so as to achieve zero inflation in Europe. Step 4 refers to the time lag. Step 5 refers to fiscal policies in Germany and France. The German government sets its purchases of German goods so as to achieve zero unemployment in Germany. And the French government sets its purchases of French goods so as to achieve zero unemployment in France. Step 6 refers to the time lag.

Step 7 refers to monetary policy in Europe. The European central bank sets European money supply so as to achieve zero inflation in Europe. Step 8 refers to the time lag. Step 9 refers to fiscal policies in Germany and France. The German government sets its purchases of German goods so as to achieve zero unemployment in Germany. And the French government sets its purchases of French goods so as to achieve zero unemployment in France. Step 10 refers to the time lag. And so on.

3) Some specific shocks. Given a demand shock in Germany, sequential policy decisions produce zero unemployment and zero inflation in each of the member countries. There is an increase in European money supply, an increase in German government purchases, a reduction in French government purchases, and

no change in European government purchases as a whole. Given a supply shock in Germany, sequential policy decisions cause uniform oscillations in unemployment and inflation. What is more, there is an explosion of government purchases and an implosion of money supply. And much the same applies to a mixed shock in Germany.

2. Simultaneous and Independent Policy Decisions

1) The static model is the same as before.

2) The dynamic model. We assume that the central bank and the governments decide simultaneously and independently. Step 1 refers to a specific shock. Step 2 refers to the time lag. Step 3 refers to monetary and fiscal policies. Step 4 refers to the time lag. Step 5 refers to monetary and fiscal policies. Step 6 refers to the time lag. And so on.

Now have a closer look at the process of simultaneous and independent policy decisions. Step 1 refers to a specific shock. Step 2 refers to the time lag. In step 3, the central bank and the governments decide simultaneously and independently. The European central bank sets European money supply so as to achieve zero inflation in Europe. The German government sets its purchases of German goods so as to achieve zero unemployment in Germany. And the French government sets its purchases of French goods so as to achieve zero unemployment in France. Step 4 refers to the time lag.

In step 5, the central bank and the governments decide simultaneously and independently. The European central bank sets European money supply so as to achieve zero inflation in Europe. The German government sets its purchases of German goods so as to achieve zero unemployment in Germany. And the French government sets its purchases of French goods so as to achieve zero unemployment in France. Step 6 refers to the time lag. And so on.

3) Some specific shocks. Given a demand shock in Germany, simultaneous and independent policy decisions cause uniform oscillations in unemployment and inflation. In addition, there are uniform oscillations in money supply and government purchases. Given a supply shock in Germany, simultaneous and independent policy decisions lower German unemployment and raise German inflation. On the other hand, they raise French unemployment and lower French inflation. And what is more, there is an explosion of government purchases and an implosion of money supply. Given a mixed shock in Germany, simultaneous and independent policy decisions cause uniform oscillations in unemployment and inflation. And what is more, there is an explosion of government purchases and an implosion of money supply.

3. Policy Cooperation

1) The model. The policy makers are the European central bank, the German government, and the French government. The targets of policy cooperation are zero inflation and zero unemployment in each of the member countries. The instruments of policy cooperation are European money supply, German government purchases, and French government purchases. There are four targets but only three instruments, so what is needed is a loss function. We assume that the policy makers agree on a common loss function. The amount of loss depends on inflation and unemployment in each of the member countries. The policy makers set European money supply, German government purchases, and French government purchases so as to minimize the common loss.

The cooperative equilibrium is determined by the first-order conditions for a minimum loss. It yields the optimum combinations of European money supply, German government purchases, and French government purchases.

2) Some specific shocks. Given a demand shock in Germany, policy cooperation achieves zero unemployment and zero inflation in each of the member countries. A first solution is an increase in European money supply, an

increase in German government purchases, a reduction in French government purchases, and no change in European government purchases as a whole. Given a supply shock in Germany, policy cooperation is ineffective. There is no change in money supply and government purchases. Accordingly, there is no change in unemployment and inflation. Given a mixed shock in Germany, policy cooperation lowers German inflation. On the other hand, it raises German unemployment. And what is more, it keeps up zero unemployment and zero inflation in France. A first solution is a reduction in European money supply, a reduction in German government purchases, an increase in French government purchases, and no change in European government purchases as a whole.

3) Comparing policy cooperation with policy interaction. Policy interaction, as a rule, causes uniform oscillations in unemployment and inflation. And what is more, it causes an explosion of government purchases and an implosion of money supply. Policy cooperation, as a rule, reduces the loss caused by unemployment and inflation. There is a one-time change in unemployment and inflation. Correspondingly, there is a one-time change in money supply and government purchases. Judging from this point of view, policy cooperation seems to be superior to policy interaction.

Symbols

A	autonomous term
A_1	autonomous term for Germany
A_2	autonomous term for France
B	autonomous term
B_1	autonomous term for Germany
B_2	autonomous term for France
G	government purchases
G_1	German government purchases
G_2	French government purchases
L	loss of European central bank
L_1	loss of German government
L_2	loss of French government
M	money supply, European money supply
u	rate of unemployment in Europe
u_1	rate of unemployment in Germany
u_2	rate of unemployment in France
α	monetary policy multiplier (unemployment)
$\alpha\varepsilon$	monetary policy multiplier (inflation)
β	fiscal policy multiplier (unemployment)
$\beta\varepsilon$	fiscal policy multiplier (inflation)
π	rate of inflation in Europe
π_1	rate of inflation in Germany
π_2	rate of inflation in France

The Current Research Project

The present book is part of a larger research project on monetary union, see Carlberg (1999 - 2010). Volume two (2000) deals with the scope and limits of macroeconomic policy in a monetary union. The leading protagonists are the union central bank, national governments, and national trade unions. Special emphasis is put on wage shocks and wage restraint. This book develops a series of basic, intermediate and more advanced models. A striking feature is the numerical estimation of policy multipliers. A lot of diagrams serve to illustrate the subject in hand. The monetary union is an open economy with high capital mobility. The exchange rate between the monetary union and the rest of the world is flexible. The world interest rate can be exogenous or endogenous. The union countries may differ in money demand, consumption, imports, openness, or size.

Volume three (2001) explores the new economics of monetary union. It discusses the effects of shocks and policies on output and prices. Shocks and policies are country-specific or common. They occur on the demand or supply side. Countries can differ in behavioural functions. Wages can be fixed, flexible, or slow. In addition, fixed wages and flexible wages can coexist. Take for instance fixed wages in Germany and flexible wages in France. Or take fixed wages in Europe and flexible wages in America. Throughout this book makes use of the rate-of-growth method. This method, together with suitable initial conditions, proves to be very powerful. Further topics are inflation and disinflation. Take for instance inflation in Germany and price stability in France. Then what policy is needed for disinflation in the union? And what will be the dynamic effects on Germany and France?

Volume four (2002) deals with the causes and cures of inflation in a monetary union. It studies the effects of money growth and output growth on inflation. The focus is on producer inflation, currency depreciation and consumer inflation. For instance, what determines the rate of consumer inflation in Europe, and what in America? Moreover, what determines the rate of consumer inflation in Germany, and what in France? Further issues are real depreciation, nominal and real interest rates, the growth of nominal wages, the growth of producer real wages, and the growth of consumer real wages. Here productivity growth and labour growth play significant roles. Another issue is target inflation and required money growth. A prominent feature of this book is microfoundations for a monetary union.

Volume five (2003) deals with the international coordination of economic policy in a monetary union. It discusses the process of policy competition and the structure of policy cooperation. As to policy competition, the focus is on competition between the union central bank, the German government, and the French government. Similarly, as to policy cooperation, the focus is on cooperation between the union central bank, the German government, and the French government. The key questions are: Does the process of policy competition lead to price stability and full employment? Can these targets be achieved through policy cooperation? And is policy cooperation superior to policy competition?

Volume six (2004) studies the interactions between monetary and fiscal policies in the euro area. The policy makers are the union central bank, the German government, the French government, and other governments. The policy targets are price stability in the union, full employment in Germany, full employment in France, etc. The policy instruments are union money supply, German government purchases, French government purchases, etc. As a rule, the spillovers of fiscal policy are negative. The policy makers follow either cold-turkey or gradualist strategies. The policy decisions are taken sequentially or simultaneously. Policy expectations are adaptive or rational. This book carefully discusses the case for central bank independence and fiscal cooperation.

Volume seven (2005) deals with the international coordination of monetary and fiscal policies in the world economy. It examines the process of policy competition and the structure of policy cooperation. As to policy competition, the focus is on monetary and fiscal competition between Europe and America. Similarly, as to policy cooperation, the focus is on monetary and fiscal cooperation between Europe and America. The spillover effects of monetary policy are negative while the spillover effects of fiscal policy are positive. The policy targets are price stability and full employment. The policy makers follow either cold-turkey or gradualist strategies. Policy expectations are adaptive or rational. The world economy consists of two, three or more regions.

Volume eight (2006a) further studies the interactions between monetary and fiscal policies in the euro area. It discusses the process of policy competition and the structure of policy cooperation. As to policy competition, the focus is on competition between the European central bank, the American central bank, the German government, and the French government. As to policy cooperation, the focus is on the same institutions. These are higher-dimensional issues. The policy targets are price stability and full employment. The policy makers follow cold-turkey or gradualist strategies. The policy decisions are taken sequentially or simultaneously. Monetary and fiscal policies have spillover effects. Special features of this book are numerical simulations of policy competition and numerical solutions to policy cooperation.

Volume nine (2006b) deals with the interactions between monetary and wage policies in the euro area. It examines the process of policy competition and the structure of policy cooperation. As to policy competition, the focus is on competition between the European central bank, the American central bank, the German labour union, and the French labour union. As to policy cooperation, the focus is on the same institutions. These are higher-dimensional issues. The policy targets are price stability and full employment. The policy makers follow cold-turkey or gradualist strategies. The policy decisions are taken sequentially or simultaneously. Monetary and wage policies have spillover effects. Special features of this book are numerical simulations of policy competition and numerical solutions to policy cooperation.

Volume ten (2007), unlike other books, provides readers with a practical yet sophisticated grasp of the macroeconomic principles necessary to understand a monetary union. By definition, a monetary union is a group of countries that share a common currency. The most important case in point is the euro area. Policy makers are the central bank, national governments, and national labour unions. Policy targets are price stability and full employment. Policy makers follow cold-turkey or gradualist strategies. Policy decisions are taken sequentially or simultaneously. The countries can differ in size or behaviour. Policy expectations are adaptive or rational. To illustrate all of this there are numerical simulations of monetary policy, fiscal policy, and wage policy.

Volume eleven (2008) studies the coexistence of inflation and unemployment in a monetary union. The focus is on how to reduce the associated loss. The primary target of the European central bank is low inflation in Europe. The primary target of the German government is low unemployment in Germany. And the primary target of the French government is low unemployment in France. The European central bank has a quadratic loss function. The same applies to the German government and the French government. The key questions are: To what extent can the sequential process of monetary and fiscal decisions reduce the loss caused by inflation and unemployment? Is monetary and fiscal cooperation superior to the sequential process of monetary and fiscal decisions?

Volume twelve (2009) deals with the strategic policy interactions in a monetary union. The leading protagonists are the European Central Bank and national governments. The target of the ECB is low inflation in Europe. The targets of a national government are low unemployment and a low structural deficit. There are demand shocks, supply shocks, and mixed shocks. There are country-specific shocks and common shocks. This book develops a series of basic, intermediate, and more advanced models. Here the focus is on the Nash equilibrium. The key questions are: Given a shock, can policy interactions reduce the existing loss? And to what extent can they do so? Another topical issue is policy cooperation. To illustrate all of this there are a lot of numerical examples.

Volume fourteen (2010) studies the strategic interactions between monetary and fiscal policies in a world economy. The world economy consists of two regions, say Europe and America. The policy makers are the central banks and the governments. The policy targets are low inflation, low unemployment, and low structural deficits. There are demand shocks, supply shocks, and mixed shocks. There are regional shocks and common shocks. This book develops a series of basic, intermediate, and more advanced models. Here the focus is on the Nash equilibrium. The key questions are: Given a shock, can policy interactions reduce the existing loss? And to what extent can they do so? Another topical issue is policy cooperation. To illustrate all of this there are a lot of numerical examples.

Further information about these books is given on the web-page:
http://carlberg.hsu-hh.de

References

ALESINA, A., BLANCHARD, O., GALI, J., GIAVAZZI, F., UHLIG, H., Defining a Macroeconomic Framework for the Euro Area, London 2001

ALESINA, A., GIAVAZZI, F., The Future of Europe: Reform or Decline, Cambridge 2006

ALLSOPP, C., The Coordination of Monetary, Fiscal and Labour Market Policies in the Euro Area, in: I. Begg, ed., Europe: Government and Money, London 2002

ALLSOPP, C., ARTIS, M., eds., EMU, Four Years On, in: Oxford Review of Economic Policy 19:1, 2003

ANDERSEN, T. M., Fiscal Stabilization Policy in a Monetary Union with Inflation Targeting, University of Aarhus 2002

ANGELONI, I., KASHYAP, A., MOJON, B., eds., Monetary Policy Transmission in the Euro Area, Cambridge 2003

ARESTIS, P., SAWYER, M., Reexamining Monetary and Fiscal Policy for the 21st Century, Cheltenham 2004

ARNOLD, L., Makroökonomik, Tübingen 2003

ARTIS, M., NIXSON, F., eds., The Economics of the European Union, Oxford 2001

BAIMBRIDGE, M., WHYMAN, P., eds., Economic and Monetary Union in Europe, Cheltenham 2003

BALDWIN, R., BERTOLA, G., SEABRIGHT, P., eds., EMU: Assessing the Impact of the Euro, Oxford 2003

BALL, L., Policy Rules for Open Economies, in: J. B. Taylor, ed., Monetary Policy Rules, Chicago 1999

BARRELL, R., WEALE, M., Monetary and Fiscal Coordination in the Euro Area, in: I. Begg, ed., Europe: Government and Money, London 2002

BEAN, C., Economic and Monetary Union in Europe, in: Journal of Economic Perspectives 6, 1992, 31 - 52

BEAN, C., Monetary Policy under EMU, in: Oxford Review of Economic Policy 14(3), 1998, 41 - 53

BEETSMA, R., et al., eds., Monetary Policy, Fiscal Policies and Labour Markets, Cambridge 2004

BEETSMA, R., DEBRUN, X., The Interaction between Monetary and Fiscal Policies in a Monetary Union: A Review of Recent Literature, in: R. Beetsma et al., eds., Monetary Policy, Cambridge 2004

BEETSMA, R., DEBRUN, X., KLAASSEN, F., Is Fiscal Policy Coordination in EMU Desirable?, in: Swedish Economic Policy Review 8, 2001, 57 - 98

BEGG, D., CANOVA, F., DE GRAUWE, P., FATAS, A., LANE, P., Surviving the Slowdown, London 2002

BEGG, I., ed., Europe: Government and Money: Running EMU: The Challenges of Policy Coordination, London 2002

BELKE, A., POLLEIT, T., Monetary Economics in Globalised Financial Markets, Berlin 2009

BERNANKE, B. S., WOODFORD, M., eds., The Inflation-Targeting Debate, Chicago 2005

BERTOLA, G., BOERI, T., EMU Labour Markets Two Years On, in: M. Buti, A. Sapir, eds., EMU and Economic Policy in Europe, Cheltenham 2002

BEYER, A., REICHLIN, L., eds., The Role of Money, Frankfurt 2008

BINI SMAGHI, L., GROS, D., Open Issues in European Central Banking, London 2000

BLANCHARD, O., Macroeconomics, Upper Saddle River 2009

BLINDER, A. S., Central Banking in Theory and Practice, Cambridge 1998

BOFINGER, P., Monetary Policy, Oxford 2001

BOYER, R., Coordination of Economic Policies in Europe, in: I. Begg, ed., Europe: Government and Money, London 2002

BRANSON, H. W., HENDERSON, D. W., GOLDSTEIN, M., eds., International Policy Coordination and Exchange Rate Fluctuations, Chicago 1990

BREUSS, F., Monetäre Außenwirtschaft und Europäische Integration, Frankfurt 2006

BREUSS, F., FINK, G., GRILLER, S., eds., Institutional, Legal and Economic Aspects of the EMU, Berlin 2003

BRUNILA, A., BUTI, M., FRANCO, D., eds., The Stability and Growth Pact, Houndmills 2001

BRYANT, R., The Coordination of National Stabilization Policies, in: A. Hughes Hallett et al., eds., Challenges for Economic Policy Coordination within European Monetary Union, Dordrecht 2001

BRYANT, R., International Coordination of National Stabilization Policies, Washington 1995

BRYSON, J. H., Macroeconomic Stabilization Through Monetary and Fiscal Policy Coordination: Implications for European Monetary Union, in: Open Economies Review 5, 1994, 307 - 326

BRYSON, J., JENSEN, H., VAN HOOSE, D., Rules, Discretion and International Monetary and Fiscal Policy Coordination, in: Open Economies Review 4, 1993, 117-132

BUITER, W. H., The Economic Case for Monetary Union in the European Union, in: Review of International Economics 5(4), 1997, 10 - 35

BUITER, W. H., GRAFE, C., Reforming EMU's Fiscal Policy Rules, in: M. Buti, ed., Monetary and Fiscal Policies in EMU, Cambridge 2003

BUITER, W. H., MARSTON, R. C., eds., International Economic Policy Coordination, Cambridge 1985

BURDA, M., European Labour Markets and the Euro: How Much Flexibility Do We Really Need?, in: Deutsche Bundesbank, ed., The Monetary Transmission Process, Hondmills 2001

BURDA, M., WYPLOSZ, C., Macroeconomics, Oxford 2005

BUTI, M., ed., Monetary and Fiscal Policies in EMU: Interactions and Coordination, Cambridge 2003

BUTI, M., FRANCO, D., Fiscal Policy in EMU, Cheltenham 2005

BUTI, M., ROEGER, W., INTVELD, J., Stabilising Output and Inflation in EMU: Policy Conflicts and Cooperation under the Stability Pact, European Commission 2001

BUTI, M., SAPIR, A., eds., Economic Policy in EMU, Oxford 1998

BUTI, M., SAPIR, A., eds., EMU and Economic Policy in Europe: The Challenge of the Early Years, Cheltenham 2002

BUTI, M., VON HAGEN, J., MARTINEZ-MONGAY, C., eds., The Behaviour of Fiscal Authorities, Houndmills 2002

CALMFORS, L., et al., EMU - A Swedish Perspective, Dordrecht 1997

CANOVA, F., PAPPA, E., Does it Cost to be Virtuous? The Macroeconomic Effects of Fiscal Constraints, in: NBER International Seminar on Macroeconomics 2004, Cambridge, Mass. 2006

CANZONERI, M. B., CUMBY, R. E., DIBA, B. T., How Do Monetary and Fiscal Policy Interact in the European Monetary Union, in: NBER International Seminar on Macroeconomics 2004, Cambridge, Mass. 2006

CANZONERI, M. B., CUMBY, R. E., DIBA, B., New Views on the Transatlantic Transmission of Fiscal Policy and Macroeconomic Policy

Coordination, in: M. Buti, ed., Monetary and Fiscal Policies in EMU, Cambridge 2003

CANZONERI, M. B., DIBA, B. T., The Stability and Growth Pact: A Delicate Balance or an Albatross?, in: A. Hughes Hallett et al., eds., Challenges for Economic Policy Coordination within European Monetary Union, Dordrecht 2001

CANZONERI, M. B., HENDERSON, D. W., Monetary Policy in Interdependent Economies, Cambridge 1991

CARLBERG, M., An Economic Analysis of Monetary Union, Berlin New York 2001

CARLBERG, M., Economic Policy in a Monetary Union, Berlin New York 2000

CARLBERG, M., Inflation and Unemployment in a Monetary Union, Berlin 2008

CARLBERG, M., Inflation in a Monetary Union, Berlin New York 2002

CARLBERG, M., International Economic Policy Coordination, Berlin New York 2005

CARLBERG, M., Macroeconomics of Monetary Union, Berlin New York 2007

CARLBERG, M., Monetary and Fiscal Policies in the Euro Area, Berlin New York 2006

CARLBERG, M., Monetary and Fiscal Strategies in the World Economy, Berlin 2010

CARLBERG, M., Monetary and Wage Policies in the Euro Area, Berlin New York 2006

CARLBERG, M., Policy Competition and Policy Cooperation in a Monetary Union, Berlin New York 2004

CARLBERG, M., Policy Coordination in a Monetary Union, Berlin New York 2003

CARLBERG, M., Strategic Policy Interactions in a Monetary Union, Berlin 2009

CARRARO, C., et al., eds., International Economic Policy Coordination, Oxford 1991

CAVALLARI, L., Inflationary Performance in a Monetary Union with Large Wage Setters, in: R. Beetsma et al., eds., Monetary Policy, Cambridge 2004

CAVALLARI, L., DI GIOACHINO, D., Macroeconomic Stabilization in the EMU: Rules versus Institutions, in: Review of Development Economics 9, 264-276, 2005

CHARI, V.V., KEHOE, P., On the Need for Fiscal Constraints in a Monetary Union, Working Paper no. 589, Federal Reserve Bank of Minneapolis 1998

CHOI, J. J., WRASE, J. M., eds., European Monetary Union and Capital Markets, Amsterdam 2001

CLAUSEN, V., Asymmetric Monetary Transmission in Europe, Berlin 2001

COLLIGNON, S., Monetary Stability in Europe, London 2002

COOPER, R. N., Economic Interdependence and Coordination of Economic Policies, in: R. W. Jones, P. B. Kenen, eds., Handbook of International Economics, Amsterdam 1985

COOPER, R., KEMPF, H., Designing Stabilization Policy in a Monetary Union, NBER Working Paper No. 7607, 2000

CUKIERMAN, A., Monetary Institutions, Monetary Union, and Unionised Labour Markets, in: R. Beetsma et al., eds., Monetary Policy, Cambridge 2004

DASEKING, C., Makroökonomische Interdependenzen in einer Wechselkursunion, Frankfurt 1994

DE BONIS, V., Stabilization Policy in an Exchange Rate Union, Heidelberg 1994

DEBRUN, X., Macroeconomic Policies in the European Monetary Union: Credibility, Coordination and Institutions, PhD Dissertation, University of Geneva 1999

DE GRAUWE, P., Economics of Monetary Union, Oxford 2005

DE HAAN, J., EIJFFINGER, S., WALLER, S., The European Central Bank: Credibility, Transparency, and Centralization, Cambridge 2005

DEMERTZIS, M., HUGHES HALLETT, A., VIEGI, N., Can the ECB be Truly Independent? Should It Be?, in: A. Hughes Hallett et al., eds., Challenges for Economic Policy Coordination within European Monetary Union, Dordrecht 2001

DEROOSE, S., LANGEDIJK, S., Economic Policy Coordination in EMU: Accomplishments and Challenges, in: M. Buti, A. Sapir, eds., EMU and Economic Policy in Europe, Cheltenham 2002

DEUTSCHE BUNDESBANK, ed., The Monetary Transmission Process: Recent Developments and Lessons for Europe, Houndmills 2001

DIXIT, A., Games of Monetary and Fiscal Interactions in the EMU, in: European Economic Review 45, 2001, 589-613

DIXIT, A., LAMBERTINI, L., Monetary-Fiscal Policy Interactions and Commitment versus Discretion in a Monetary Union, in: European Economic Review 45, 2001, 977-987

DORNBUSCH, R., FISCHER, S., STARTZ, R., Macroeconomics, New York 2008

DULLIEN, S., The Interaction of Monetary Policy and Wage Bargaining in the European Monetary Union, Houndmills 2004

DUWENDAG, D., KETTERER, K. H., KÖSTERS, W., POHL, R., SIMMERT, D. B., Geldtheorie und Geldpolitik in Europa, Berlin 1999

EICHENGREEN, B., European Monetary Unification, Cambridge 1997

EIJFFINGER, S., DE HAAN, J., European Monetary and Fiscal Policy, Oxford 2000

EUROPEAN CENTRAL BANK, Fiscal Policy Influences on Macroeconomic Stability and Prices, in: Monthly Bulletin, April 2004

EUROPEAN CENTRAL BANK, The Monetary Policy of the ECB, Frankfurt 2004

EUROPEAN CENTRAL BANK, The Relationship between Monetary Policy and Fiscal Policies in the Euro Area, in: Monthly Bulletin, February 2003

FATAS, A., MIHOV, I., Fiscal Policy and EMU, in: M. Buti, A. Sapir, eds., EMU and Economic Policy in Europe, Cheltenham 2002

FAVERO, C., et al., One Money, Many Countries, London 2000

FELDSTEIN, M., The European Central Bank and the Euro: The First Year, in: Journal of Policy Modeling 22, 2000, 345 – 354

FELDSTEIN, M., ed., International Economic Cooperation, Chicago 1988

FEUERSTEIN, S., Studien zur Wechselkursunion, Heidelberg 1992

FEUERSTEIN, S., SIEBKE, J., Wechselkursunion und Stabilitätspolitik, in: Zeitschrift für Wirtschafts- und Sozialwissenschaften 110, 1990, 359 – 379

FISCHER, S., International Macroeconomic Policy Coordination, in: M. Feldstein, ed., International Economic Cooperation, Chicago 1988

FISCHER, S., Roundtable on Lessons of European Monetary Integration for the International Monetary System, in: P. R. Masson et al., eds., EMU, Washington 1997

FLEMING, J. M., Domestic Financial Policies under Fixed and Floating Exchange Rates, in: IMF Staff Papers 9, 1962, 369 - 380

FRATIANNI, M., SALVATORE, D., VON HAGEN, J., eds., Macroeconomic Policy in Open Economies, Westport 1997

FRIEDMAN, B. M., HAHN, F. H., eds., Handbook of Monetary Economics, Amsterdam 1990

FUHRER, J., et al., eds., Understanding Inflation and the Implications for Monetary Policy, Cambridge 2009

GALI, J., Monetary Policy in the Early Years of EMU, in: M. Buti, A Sapir, eds., EMU and Economic Policy in Europe, Cheltenham 2002

GALI, J., Monetary Policy, Inflation, and the Business Cycle, Princeton 2008

GANDOLFO, G., International Finance and Open-Economy Macroeconomics, Berlin 2001

GASPAR, V., ISSING, O., TRISTANI, O., VESTIN, D., Imperfect Knowledge and Monetary Policy, Cambridge 2006

GHOSH, A., MASSON, P., Economic Cooperation in an Uncertain World, Cambridge 1994

GIOVANNINI, A., et al., The Monetary Future of Europe, London 1993

GROS, D., ed., Macroeconomic Policy under the Euro, Cheltenham 2004

HALL, S. G., HEILEMANN, U., PAULY, P., eds., Macroeconometric Models and European Monetary Union, Berlin 2004

HAMADA, K., The Political Economy of International Monetary Interdependence, Cambridge 1985

HAMADA, K., KAWAI, M., International Economic Policy Coordination: Theory and Policy Implications, in: M. U. Fratianni, D. Salvatore, J. von Hagen, eds. Macroeconomic Policy in Open Economies, Westport 1997

HANSEN, J. D., HEINRICH, H., NIELSEN, J. U., An Economic Analysis of the EC, London 1992

HANSEN, J. D., NIELSEN, J. U., An Economic Analysis of the EU, London 1997

HEFEKER, C., Lohnpolitik und Geldpolitik in Euroland, in: Vierteljahreshefte zur Wirtschaftsforschung, 71. Jahrgang, Heft 3, 2002

HEIJDRA, B. J., VAN DER PLOEG, F., Foundations of Modern Macroeconomics, Oxford 2002

HEISE, A., Theorie optimaler Lohnräume – Zur Tarifpolitik in der Europäischen Währungsunion, in: Vierteljahreshefte zur Wirtschaftsforschung, 71. Jahrgang, Heft 3, 2002

HUART, F., Spillover Effects of Fiscal Policy in EMU: A Misconception behind the Stability Pact, Discussion Paper, Lille 2002

HUGHES HALLET, A., HUTCHISON, M. M., JENSEN, S. H., eds., Fiscal Aspects of European Monetary Integration, Cambridge 1999

HUGHES HALLET, A., McADAM, P., The Stability Pact and the Interdependence of Monetary and Fiscal Policy Rules, in: A. Hughes Hallet et al., eds., Challenges for Economic Policy Coordination within European Monetary Union, Dordrecht 2001

HUGHES HALLET, A., MOOSLECHNER, P., SCHUERZ, M., eds., Challenges for Economic Policy Coordination within European Monetary Union, Dordrecht 2001

ILLING, G., Theorie der Geldpolitik, Berlin 1997

ISSING, O., On Macroeconomic Policy Coordination in EMU, in: Journal of Common Market Studies 40, 2002

ISSING, O., GASPAR, V., ANGELONI, I., TRISTANI, O., Monetary Policy in the Euro Area, Cambridge 2001

ITALIANER, A., The Euro and Internal Economic Policy Coordination, in: A. Hughes Hallett et al., eds., Challenges for Economic Policy Coordination within European Monetary Union, Dordrecht 2001

JACQUET, P., PISANI-FERRY, J., Economic Policy Coordination in the Euro Zone, Paris 2000

JARCHOW, H. J., Fiskalpolitik in einer Währungsunion, in: Finanzarchiv 50, 1993, 187 - 203

JARCHOW, H. J., RÜHMANN, P., Monetäre Außenwirtschaft, Göttingen 2003

KEHOE, P. J., Coordination of Fiscal Policies in a World Economy, in: Journal of Monetary Economics 19, 1987, 349-376

KENEN, P. B., Economic and Monetary Union in Europe, Cambridge 1995

KENEN, P. B., MEADE, E. E., Regional Monetary Integration, Cambridge 2008

KOPCKE, R. W., TOOTELL, G. M. B., TRIEST, R. K., eds., The Macroeconomics of Fiscal Policy, Cambridge 2006

KRUGMAN, P. R., OBSTFELD, M., International Economics, New York 2003

LAMBERTINI, L., ROVELLI, R., Independent or Coordinated? Monetary and Fiscal Policy in EMU, in: R. Beetsma et al., eds., Monetary Policy, Cambridge 2004

LANE, P.R., Monetary-Fiscal Interactions in an Uncertain World, in: M. Buti, ed., Monetary and Fiscal Policy in EMU, Cambridge 2003

LAWLER, P., Monetary Policy and Asymmetrical Fiscal Policy in a Jointly Floating Currency Area, in: Scottish Journal of Political Economy 41, 1994, 142 - 162

LEIDERMAN, L., SVENSSON, L., eds., Inflation Targeting, London 1995

LEVIN, J. H., On the Dynamic Effects of Monetary and Fiscal Policy in a Monetary Union, in: K. V. Maskus et al., eds., Quiet Pioneering, Michigan 1997

LEVIN, J. H., A Guide to the Euro, Boston 2002

LEVIN, J. H., A Model of Stabilization Policy in a Jointly Floating Currency Area, in: J. S. Bhandari, B. H. Putnam, eds., Economic Interdependence and Flexible Exchange Rates, Cambridge 1983

LEVINE, P., Fiscal Policy Coordination under EMU and the Choice of Monetary Instrument, in: Manchester School 61, Supplement, 1993, 1-12

LEVINE, P., BROCINER, A., Fiscal Policy Coordination and EMU, in: Journal of Economic Dynamics and Control 18, 1994, 699-729

MARK, N. C., International Macroeconomics and Finance, Oxford 2001

MASSON, P. R., KRUEGER, T.H., TURTELBOOM, B. G., eds., EMU and the International Monetary System, Washington 1997

McCALLUM, B. T., International Monetary Economics, Oxford 1995

McKIBBIN, W. J., Empirical Evidence on International Economic Policy Coordination, in: M. U. Fratianni, D. Salvatore, J. von Hagen, eds., Macroeconomic Policy in Open Economies, Westport 1997

MEADE, J., WEALE, M., Monetary Union and the Assignment Problem, in: Scandinavian Journal of Economics 97, 1995, 201-222

MICHAELIS, J., PFLÜGER, M., Euroland: Besser als befürchtet, aber schlechter als erhofft?, in: Vierteljahreshefte zur Wirtschaftsforschung, 71. Jahrgang, Heft 3, 2002

MOOSLECHNER, P., SCHUERZ, M., International Macroeconomic Policy Coordination: Any Lessons for EMU? A Selective Survey of the Literature, in: A. Hughes Hallett et al., eds., Challenges for Economic Policy Coordination within European Monetary Union, Dordrecht 2001

MOSER, T., SCHIPS, B., eds., EMU, Financial Markets and the World Economy, Dordrecht 2001

MOUTOS, T., SCARTH, W., Stabilization Policy within a Currency Area, in: Scottish Journal of Political Economy 35, 1988, 387 – 397

MULHEARN, C., VANE, H. R., The Euro, Cheltenham 2008

MUNDELL, R. A., International Economics, New York 1968

MUNDELL, R. A., CLESSE, A., eds., The Euro as a Stabilizer in the International Economic System, Dordrecht 2000

MUNDELL, R.A., ZAK, P. J., SCHAEFFER, D., eds., International Monetary Policy after the Euro, Cheltenham 2005

NECK, R., ed., The Macroeconomics of EMU, in: Open Economies Review 13:4, 2002

NECK, R., HABER, G., McKIBBIN, J., European Monetary and Fiscal Policies after the EU Enlargement, in: Empirica 31, 2004, 229 – 245

NECK, R., HOLZMANN, R., eds., European Monetary and Fiscal Policies: Myths and Facts, in: Empirica 29:3, 2002

NECK, R., RICHTER, C., MOOSLECHNER, P., Quantitative Economic Policy, Berlin 2008

NEUMANN, M. J. M., Internationale Wirtschaftspolitik: Koordination, Kooperation oder Wettbewerb?, in: J. Siebke, Hg., Monetäre Konfliktfelder der Weltwirtschaft, Berlin 1991

NEUMANN, M. J. M., Koordination der Makropolitik in Europa, in: B. Gahlen, H. Hesse, H. J. Ramser, Hg., Europäische Integrationsprobleme, Tübingen 1994

OBSTFELD, M., ROGOFF, K., Foundations of International Macroeconomics, Cambridge 1996

OECD, EMU: Facts, Challenges and Policies, Paris 1999

OECD, EMU: One Year On, Paris 2000

OHR, R., THEURL, T., Hg., Kompendium Europäische Wirtschaftspolitik, München 2000

ONORANTE, L., Interaction of Fiscal Policies in the Euro Area: How Much Pressure on the ECB?, in: R. Beetsma et al., eds., Monetary Policy, Cambridge 2004

PADOAN, P. C., Monetary Policy is not Enough: Pressures for Policy Change in EMU, in: I. Begg, ed., Europe: Government and Money, London 2002

PADOAN, P. C., ed., Monetary Union, Employment and Growth, Cheltenham 2001

PADOA-SCHIOPPA, T., The Euro and Its Central Bank, Cambridge 2004

PENTECOST, E. J., VAN POECK, A., eds., European Monetary Integration, Cheltenham 2001

PERSSON, T., TABELLINI, G., Political Economics, Cambridge 2000

PICHELMANN, K., Wage Discipline in EMU, in: M. Buti, A. Sapir, eds., EMU and Economic Policy in Europe, Cheltenham 2002

PISANI-FERRY, J., The EMU's Economic Policy Principles: Words and Facts, in: M. Buti, A. Sapir, eds., EMU and Economic Policy in Europe, Cheltenham 2002

PLASMANS, J., et al., Dynamic Modeling of Monetary and Fiscal Cooperation among Nations, Berlin 2005

POHL, R., GALLER, H. P., eds., Macroeconometric Modelling of the German Economy in the Framework of Euroland, Baden-Baden 2002

POSEN, A. S., ed., The Euro at Five: Ready for a Global Role? Washington 2005

POSEN, A. S., PISANI-FERRY, J., The Euro at Ten, Institute for International Economics, 2009

ROSE, K., SAUERNHEIMER, K., Theorie der Außenwirtschaft, München 2006

ROSE, K., SAUERNHEIMER, K., Zur Theorie eines Mischwechselkurssystems, in: M. Feldsieper, R. Groß, Hg., Wirtschaftspolitik in weltoffener Wirtschaft, Berlin 1983, 15 - 28

RÜBEL, G., Grundlagen der Monetären Außenwirtschaft, München 2009

SALVATORE, D., The Euro, the Dollar, and the International Monetary System, in: Journal of Policy Modeling 22, 2000, 407 – 415

SAPIR, A., et al., An Agenda for a Growing Europe, Oxford 2004

SARNO, L., TAYLOR, M., The Economics of Exchange Rates, Cambridge 2002

SAUERNHEIMER, K., Fiscal Policy in einer Wechselkursunion, in: Finanzarchiv 42, 1984, 143 - 157

SCHEIDE, J., Macroeconomic Policy Coordination in Europe, in: H. Siebert, ed., Macroeconomic Policies in the World Economy, Berlin 2004

SCHELKLE, W., Monetäre Integration, Heidelberg 2001

SEMMLER, W., GREINER, A., ZHANG, W., Monetary and Fiscal Policies in the Euro Area, Amsterdam 2005

SIDIROPOULOS, M., SPYROMITROS, E., Fiscal Policy in a Monetary Union under Alternative Labor Market Regimes, Discussion Paper, Strasbourg 2005

SIEBERT, H., Macroeconomic Policies in the World Economy, Berlin 2004

SINN, H. W., WIDGREN, M., KÖTHENBÜRGER, M., eds., European Monetary Integration, Cambridge 2004

SITZ, A., Währungsunion oder Wechselkursflexibilität, Frankfurt 2001

SMETS, J., DOMBRECHT, M., eds., How to Promote Economic Growth in the Euro Area, Cheltenham 2001

SPAHN, H. P., From Gold to Euro, Berlin 2001

SPAHN, H. P., Geldpolitik, München 2009

STABILISIERUNGSPOLITIK IN EUROLAND, in: Vierteljahreshefte zur Wirtschaftsforschung, 71. Jahrgang, Heft 3, 2002

STAHN, K., Reputation und Kooperation in einer Währungsunion, Frankfurt 2000

SUARDI, M., Monetary Policy Transmission in EMU, in: M. Buti, A. Sapir, eds., EMU and Economic Policy in Europe, Cheltenham 2002

SVENSSON, L. E. O., Monetary Policy Issues für the Eurosystem, in: Carnegie-Rochester Conference Series on Public Policy 51, 1999, 79 - 136

TAYLOR, J. B., ed., Monetary Policy Rules, Chicago 1999

TAYLOR, J. B., WOODFORD, M., eds., Handbook of Macroeconomics, Amsterdam 1999

TRUMAN, E. M., A Critical Review of Coordination Efforts in the Past, in: H. Siebert, ed., Macroeconomic Policies in the World Economy, Berlin 2004

UHLIG, H., One Money, but Many Fiscal Policies in Europe, in: M. Buti, ed., Monetary and Fiscal Policies in EMU, Cambridge 2003

VAN AARLE, B., GARRETSEN, H., HUART, F., Monetary and Fiscal Policy Rules in the EMU, Working Paper 2003

VAN AARLE, B., GARRETSEN, H., HUART, F., Transatlantic Monetary and Fiscal Policy Interaction, Working Paper 2003

VAN AARLE, B., WEYERSTRASS, K., eds., Economic Spillovers, Structural Reforms, and Policy Coordination in the Euro Area, Berlin 2008

VAN DER PLOEG, F., Macroeconomic Policy Coordination and Monetary Integration: A European Perspective, The Hague 1989

VIREN, M., Fiscal Policy, Automatic Stabilisers and Coordination, in: A. Brunila et al., eds., The Stability and Growth Pact, Houndmills 2001

VOLLMER, U., Geld- und Währungspolitik, München 2004

VON HAGEN, J., MUNDSCHENK, S., The Functioning of Economic Policy Coordination, in: M. Buti, A. Sapir, eds., EMU and Economic Policy in Europe, Cheltenham 2002

WALSH, C., Monetary Theory and Policy, Cambridge 2010

WELFENS, P. J. J., European Monetary Union and Exchange Rate Dynamics, Berlin 2000

WICKS, N., The Coordination of Economic Policies in the European Union, in I. Begg, ed., Europe: Government and Money, London 2002

WOHLTMANN, H. W., Transmission nationaler Wirtschaftspolitiken in einer Wechselkursunion, in: Jahrbücher für Nationalökonomie und Statistik 211, 1993, 73 – 89

WOHLTMANN, H. W., BULTHAUPT, F., KRÖMER, W., Wirtschaftspolitische Koordination in einer symmetrischen und asymmetrischen Wechselkursunion, in: K. Farmer, H. W. Wohltmann, Hg., Quantitative Wirtschaftspolitik, Münster 1998

WOODFORD, M., Interest and Prices, Princeton 2003

WYPLOSZ, C., ed., The Impact of EMU on Europe and the Developing Countries, Oxford 2001

Kolibri 360 GmbH
Ferdinand-Jühlke-Straße 7
99095 Erfurt, Deutschland
produktsicherheit@kolibri360.de